ALL THINGS
RECONSIDERED

ALL THINGS RECONSIDERED

My Birding Adventures

ROGER TORY PETERSON

Edited by Bill Thompson III

Houghton Mifflin Company

BOSTON NEW YORK 2006

For information about permission to reproduce selections from
this book, write to Permissions, Houghton Mifflin Company,
215 Park Avenue, New York, New York 10003.

Visit our Web site: www.houghtonmifflinbooks.com.

Library of Congress Cataloging-in-Publication Data

Peterson, Roger Tory.
   All things reconsidered: my birding adventures /
Roger Tory Peterson; edited by Bill Thompson III.
     p. cm.
Includes index.
ISBN-13: 978-0-618-75862-3
ISBN-10: 0-618-75862-3
1. Bird watching—Anecdotes. 2. Peterson, Roger Tory—
Travel. I. Thompson, Bill. II. Title.
   QL677.5P384 2006
   598.072'34—dc22   2006009769

Book design by Anne Chalmers
Typeface: Miller

All photographs and illustrations by Roger Tory Peterson unless otherwise
noted, with the exception of those on pages 98, 238, 306, and 313,
whose copyright holders are unknown.

Printed in the United States of America

DOC 10 9 8 7 6 5 4 3 2 1

CONTENTS

THE ROGER TORY PETERSON INSTITUTE

The legacy of America's great naturalist and creator of the Peterson Field Guide series, Roger Tory Peterson, is preserved through the programs and work of the Roger Tory Peterson Institute of Natural History (RTPI), located in his birthplace of Jamestown, New York. RTPI is a national nature education organization with a mission to continue the legacy of Roger Tory Peterson by promoting the teaching and study of nature and to thereby create knowledge of and appreciation and responsibility for the natural world. RTPI also preserves and exhibits Dr. Peterson's extraordinary collection of artwork, photography, and writing.

You can become a part of this worthy effort by joining RTPI. Simply call RTPI's membership department at 800-758-6841 ext. 226, fax 716-665-3794, or e-mail members@rtpi.org. Check out our award-winning Web site at www.enaturalist.org. You can link to all our programs and activities from there.

INTRODUCTION

IN THE MODERN ERA, by any measure, Roger Tory Peterson was a great man. His accomplishments greatly surpass those of his peers. A list of his accolades, awards, and honors would fill several pages of this book. His legendary field guide simplified bird identification so that everyone could understand and enjoy it. Today, millions of people around the world enjoy bird watching because of the simple, methodical identification methods Peterson put into print.

Roger Tory Peterson considered himself a teacher above all else, and his patience with his "pupils" is legendary. Today the Roger Tory Peterson Institute of Natural History carries on RTP's tradition of educating people about nature.

For me, Roger's reputation paled in comparison with what I learned about him the first time we met. It was at Hawk Mountain, in Kempton, Pennsylvania, in 1988, during that venerable sanctuary's sixtieth birthday celebration. He was the keynote speaker, and after his talk he took his traditional place at the book-signing table. A long line snaked around the presentation tent and out the door, into the night. My father and I waited patiently in line—not to get our field guides signed, but so that my dad, who had met Peterson and communicated with him many times over the years, could introduce me to him.

When our turn came, my dad said, "Roger, I'd like you to meet our son, Bill the third, an avid bird watcher who has just joined the staff of *Bird Watcher's Digest* as associate editor."

Roger sized me up, shook my hand, and said, "It's a pleasure to meet you. Come with me for a moment." We slipped out the tent flap behind his table, leaving a long line of befuddled audience seekers in our wake. "You've got young ears and I don't. Can you tell me what you think of the sounds these katydids are making? They sound quite different from our katydids in Connecticut."

I hardly knew what to think. I knew what a katydid sounded like, but I had never thought about regional differences in their calls. Obviously Roger Peterson had, and he was curious enough about it to seek a second, albeit uninformed, opinion.

Hearing another katydid, Roger exclaimed, "There, did you hear that one? Quite a bit thinner and higher than ours in Connecticut!" I nodded my assent and we stood for a few minutes more—the world's most accomplished field guide author and a twenty-six-year-old awestruck young man, listening to insect calls in the dark while hundreds of adoring fans waited a few dozen feet away.

"Well, we'd better get back inside before there's a riot. I've still got a lot of books to sign!" And with that we reentered the tent. To this day I remain impressed by Roger Peterson's insatiable curiosity about nature, his ability to sort out such minute differences in nature, and his kindness to a young bird watcher and editor just starting out. Those minutes alone with him are something I will always cherish.

A decade earlier, in 1978, my parents, Bill and Elsa Thompson, had started *Bird Watcher's Digest* in the living room of our Marietta, Ohio, home. It was the very definition of a family affair. We sent out a mass mailing of sample issues with an invitation to subscribe—six issues for seven dollars. My parents sent one of these samples to Roger Peterson and asked for his feedback.

Peterson replied with a lengthy letter, along with his check for a subscription. That letter's first sentence, "I was delighted to receive the copy of your first issue of the *Bird Watcher's Digest*," sent my parents jumping for joy. What followed were three pages of focused, article-by-article critique, which my parents and the magazine's editor, Mary Beacom Bowers, read and reread over the years.

Roger Tory Peterson wrote a regular column, "All Things Reconsidered," for *Bird Watcher's Digest* from 1984 until his death in the summer of 1996. This column covered a vast array of topics: some were stories of Peterson's birding adventures, others chronicled the lives of certain species or of his peers, and others charted the growth and changes in bird watching. Now, ten years after Peterson's death, it seems appropriate to revisit some of his work for the magazine.

I served as managing editor of *Bird Watcher's Digest* under editor Mary Beacom Bowers from 1988 until I assumed the editorship of the magazine, in 1995. Mary and I used to talk about Roger Peterson, and we never failed to marvel at his skills as a writer, which were nowhere near as well known as his skills as an artist, photographer, and lecturer. But Peterson was a writer of uncommon skill and depth. His writing style, like his speaking voice, was clear and gentle; he could tell a story (and he had many to tell) like almost no one else. Here was a man who could make a compelling argument about the beauty of the European starling or the incredible survival skills of the house sparrow with as much style and enthusiasm as if he were writing about the huge penguin colonies of Antarctica.

Reading this collection of Roger Tory Peterson's best columns from *Bird Watcher's Digest* will offer some insight into his perspective on the changes he saw in his lifetime. In preparing these columns for republication a decade later, we have changed some things to reflect today's reality—bird names, for example (the rufous-sided towhee is now the eastern towhee), and the names of organizations and publications. But many other things we have left in their original form, as a sort of time capsule for the reader to open up and examine.

The date at the end of each column is the issue of the magazine in which the column appeared. Not every column was written as an original piece for the magazine, however. Hard at work revising his field guides—working even on the day he died—Peterson managed to write his column for twelve years, throughout his seventies and early eighties. For some columns, he chose to revise and update material he had written years earlier. Works such as *Birds Over America* and *Wild America,* published in the 1940s and 1950s, were fertile sources that Peterson revisited in order to expose new audiences to his unique and insightful perspective on our natural world. This was one of the reasons we named the column (and subsequently, this book) "All Things Reconsidered."

The status of many of the birds Peterson wrote about has changed, including the California condor (now breeding in the wild in Arizona and California), the peregrine falcon (now breeding throughout its original range in North America, as well as in cities, where it was never previously found), the cattle egret (common in appropriate habitat continent-wide, but not here in 1952!), and, of course, the ivory-billed woodpecker, which was reported by several observers in 2004 and later, in the bayous of Arkansas, but the status of which remains uncertain.

Poring over Peterson's writing for his *Bird Watcher's Digest* columns, and the associated correspondence, I was reminded of his creative talents. Good writing stands on its own and is timeless. Peterson's work still exceeds so much of what passes for good writing today. I feel lucky to have known him, to have worked with him, and to be able to share his work with you here, in this book.

—Bill Thompson III
May 2006

ALL THINGS
RECONSIDERED

Audubon's "mystery bird," the carbonated warbler. (Carbonated Warbler
[*Dendroica carbonata*], 1825, by John James Audubon, accession number
1863.17.60 in the collection of The New-York Historical Society)

On Audubon and Those Confusing Warblers

SEVERAL OF MY FRIENDS have taken me to task for giving two of the color plates in my eastern field guide the title "Confusing Fall Warblers." They are *not* confusing, they insist. Perhaps not to them, but the little greeny-brown jobs remain confusing to 95 percent of the bird watching crowd—or at least to those who do not consider themselves "hard-core."

Even Audubon was confused. Of the thirty-eight species of wood warblers found normally in eastern North America he eventually knew all but one. In attempting to sort them out, he was relatively late on the scene. Early on, Linnaeus, the creator of the *Systema Naturae,* and his successor, Johann Georg Gmelin, as well as a number of other workers, had already named and described twenty-five species of North American warblers. That was before Alexander Wilson published his *American Ornithology,* wherein he described another ten. By the time Audubon came on the scene, twenty years later, he was able to add only two new ones: Swainson's warbler and the now nearly extinct Bachman's warbler, both furtive southerners first discovered by his friend the Reverend Bachman of Charleston. After Audubon, only one species, Kirtland's warbler, a rarity restricted to the pine barrens of Michigan, remained to be described.

But Audubon tried hard; he named and illustrated ten or eleven species that did not exist—variants or obscure plumages of already well-known species.

Many birders have found that the sumptuous showcase of Audubon's prints published by Abbeville Press—*The Baby Elephant*

Folio—was beyond their pocketbooks. But if they did purchase the book, they may have looked only at the pictures, ignoring the text prepared after considerable research by my wife, Ginny, and me. Inasmuch as the tome weighs eighteen pounds, it is not exactly a field guide or bedtime reading. For the benefit of a wider audience, I have pulled things together and adapted from the book the following capsule accounts of the eleven "species" of warblers that led Audubon astray:

"CHILDREN'S WARBLER" *(Yellow Warbler)*
When Audubon painted two little yellowish birds at Oakley Plantation in Louisiana, he tentatively inscribed his drawing "Louisiana Warbler," *Sylvia ludoviciana*. Later, feeling quite certain that they represented something new, he crossed out the scientific name and inked in *Sylvia childreni*, naming it "children's warbler" in honor of the secretary of the Royal Society, John George Children, who managed his affairs in London. He had drawn not a new species but a female and immature yellow warbler. Obviously he became aware of this at a later date, because it was omitted in his octavo *Birds of America*.

It is understandable that Audubon, having virtually no books, should be confused by obscure plumages of certain warblers. Any modern field guide would have informed him that with the exception of the unmistakable female redstart, the yellow warbler is the only warbler with yellow (not white) spots in its tail. Had he known this simple fact, he would have been spared two major errors in the original Elephant Folio.

"RATHBONE'S WARBLER" *(Yellow Warbler)*
This is another instance in which Audubon mistook two juvenile yellow warblers for something new. He wrote:

> Kind reader, you are now presented with a new and beautiful little species of Warbler, which I have honored with the name of a family that must ever be dear to me. . . . I trust that future naturalists, regardful of the feelings which have guided me in naming this

species, will continue to [give] it the name of Rathbone's Wood-Warbler. I met with the species . . . only once. They were actively engaged in searching for food amongst the blossoms and leaves of the *bignonia.*

Audubon's good intentions toward the Rathbones went for naught. He did not state where he collected these young yellow warblers, but his original pastel was inscribed July 1, 1808, at the "Falls of the Ohio." Later, in 1825, it was used as a basis for the color plate that was inscribed with the same date as the pastel. Curiously, he defines the bird's range in his *Birds of America* as "Mississippi—only one pair seen."

"PINE SWAMP WARBLER" *(Black-throated Blue Warbler)*
When Audubon painted these birds in the Great Pine Swamp of Pennsylvania on August 11, 1829, he took Alexander Wilson as his authority, as did his contemporary, [Thomas] Nuttall, in his own manual. Audubon wrote that this bird "delights in the dark humid parts of thick underwood, by the sides of small streams." Several years later, in his octavo edition, he corrected this error, putting the blame on Wilson:

> The birds represented in Plate 48 of my large edition as *Sylvia sphagnosa,* are the young of the Black-throated Blue Warbler, the female of which resembles them so much that I looked upon it as a species distinct from the male. I have no doubt that this error originated with Wilson who has been followed by all our writers. Now, however, the *Sylvia* or *Sylvicola sphagnosa* of Bonaparte which he altered from Wilson's *S. pusilla,* must be erased from our fauna.

We must remember that Wilson, Audubon, and their contemporaries were at the very frontiers of ornithology and that such misconceptions were inevitable. In presenting the new plate in the miniaturized version, Audubon combined the figure of the upper bird, a female, with that of the male, which in the original plate was shown alone on a spray of columbine.

"BLUE-GREEN WARBLER" (*Cerulean Warbler*)

When Audubon painted this bird in Louisiana, in August 1821, he again believed he had found something new. He named it the "blue-green warbler," *Sylvia rara*. Later he realized that it was simply a female or possibly a young male cerulean warbler. In his octavo *Birds of America*, published several years later, he combined his original color plate of the cerulean warbler with this one. He dropped out the lower bird of the earlier version; it apparently had been copied by Havell the engraver from a drawing by Wilson.

Knowledge of birds was growing rapidly at that time, and Audubon's own revisions were extensive. His critics pointed out certain errors and discrepancies in the text of his *Ornithological Biography*, and thus he was able to make corrections when he published the smaller octavo version.

"HEMLOCK WARBLER" (*Blackburnian Warbler*)

Here again Audubon was misled by Wilson into cataloging a female warbler as a distinct species. He wrote:

> It is to the persevering industry of Wilson that we are indebted for the discovery of this bird. He has briefly described the male [actually the female] of which he had obtained but a single specimen. Never having met with it until I visited the Great Pine Forest where that ornithologist found it, I followed his track in my rambles there, and had not spent a week among the gigantic hemlocks which ornament that interesting part of our country before I procured upwards of twenty specimens.

Audubon never did correct this mistake in his octavo edition, which was prepared several years later, even though he correctly added a female to his original plate of the male Blackburnian. Of this supposed "species" he wrote:

> The tallest of the hemlock pines are the favorite haunts of this species. It appears first among the highest branches early in May, breeds there, and departs in the beginning of September. Like the blue yellow-back warbler [parula warbler] its station is ever

amidst the thickest foliage of the trees, and with as much agility as its diminutive relative it seeks its food by ascending from one branch to another, examining most carefully the underparts of each leaf as it proceeds.

"AUTUMNAL WARBLER" (Bay-breasted Warbler)

In 1829, while investigating the Great Pine Swamp near Mauch Chunk, Pennsylvania, where he collected so many Blackburnians, Audubon painted two plain-looking warblers that were unfamiliar to him. They were obviously young bay-breasted warblers, and inasmuch as it was late August, we might assume they were early fall migrants because bay-breasteds have never been known to nest that far south. Audubon bestowed the new name *Sylvia autumnalis,* but later, when he reworked his text in the octavo edition, he must have had second thoughts. There was no mention of this "species," nor was the plate included. It became simply one of those "confusing fall warblers," which to this day are the bane of the average birder.

"VIGOR'S WARBLER" (Pine Warbler)

One day in May 1812, Audubon discovered a small yellow-breasted bird fluttering in the tall grass on a little island in Perkiomen Creek on his farm, Mill Grove, near Valley Forge, Pennsylvania. It perched on the bladelike leaves of the spiderwort on which he drew its portrait. Believing it was something new, he called the diminutive bird "Vigor's Warbler" after Nicholas Vigor, an English naturalist. Actually it was an immature pine warbler, a species that had already been described by Wilson and that Audubon came to know well, particularly during his years in Louisiana. But this individual, away from its usual haunts in the pines, threw him off. It seemed different, and this is quite understandable; pine warblers can vary a lot, with few marks that are distinctive other than the strong wing bars. In his octavo *Birds of America,* rewritten later, Audubon made no mention of this "species." He was pioneering, and although birds new to science were still being described, most Americans were so busy pushing other frontiers that they had little time for ornithology. Today birders are legion. The binocular has replaced the gun, and field guides have made identification quick and accurate.

"Roscoe's Yellowthroat" (Common Yellowthroat)

When Audubon made the drawing of this bird in 1821, his inscription at the bottom of the plate identified it as "Louisiana Yellow-throat." Under the impression that it was new, he changed the name to "Roscoe's Yellow-throat," in honor of William Roscoe, an English historian. But later, when he published his octavo *Birds of America,* he vetoed the idea. Recomposing the plate of the "Maryland Yellow-throat," he added this figure, which he then presumed to be an immature male of the common species.

Audubon described still another yellowthroat from a California specimen obtained from Mr. Townsend, naming it "Delafield's Ground Warbler," in honor of Colonel Delafield, president of the Lyceum of Natural History in New York. He said that it so much resembled the "Maryland Yellow-throat," that one might easily confuse the two species. Years later it was designated as a mere subspecies by the checklist committee of the American Ornithologists' Union.

"Selby's Flycatcher" (Hooded Warbler)

When Audubon was at the plantation of James Pirrie in Louisiana during the summer of 1821, he painted still another rather nondescript warbler, which he thought was new. The notes on his original drawing indicate that he first called it "Louisiana Flycatcher," *Muscicapa ludoviciana.* Later he renamed it "Selby's Flycatcher" in honor of a British ornithologist, Prideaux John Selby. Actually it was an immature hooded warbler. Scarcely a month later he drew the hooded warblers that appear on plate 190 in his Elephant Folio. Somehow he did not make the connection between this young bird and the adults he drew subsequently. Hooded warblers are common in the wooded countryside of the southern states, and Audubon undoubtedly knew them well, but females and especially immature birds are variable.

Determining the exact identity of some of Audubon's birds, especially immatures, has demanded a degree of detective work and intuition on the part of later scholars. In fact, several of his birds have never been satisfactorily identified to this day.

Wilson, often called the "Father of American ornithology," had the jump on Audubon by about twenty years; therefore he was the first to describe and name ten species of warblers that were new to science. But there was equivocation at that time as to whether some of theses little birds were warblers or flycatchers. And there were certain other warblers, such as the ovenbird and Louisiana waterthrush, that were regarded as thrushes. Audubon lumped them with the robin and the wood thrush in the genus *Turdus*. As for the two waterthrushes, Louisiana and northern, he knew them both and figured them correctly in his Elephant Folio, then had a change of mind and lumped them as one in his revised octavo edition, inventing a new name—"Aquatic Wood Wagtail." This, of course, muddied the waters for a while, but eventually other scholars changed things back. However, the inappropriate name "waterthrush" remains.

"BONAPARTE'S FLYCATCHER" *(Canada Warbler)*

When Audubon first drew this little bird, poised on the fruiting branch of a magnolia, he inscribed it as a "Cypress Swamp Flycatcher," then changed it to "Bonaparte's Flycatcher," in honor of Prince Charles-Lucien Bonaparte. Later, when he published his octavo *Birds of America*, he again changed the name to "Bonaparte's Flycatching Warbler." In due time it was confirmed that it was a warbler, not a flycatcher, and not a new species as he had thought, but actually a young female Canada warbler, a species that he was to paint again eight years later under the name "Canada Flycatcher."

There is an evolution in names, and although some stick, no matter how inappropriate, others change. Many birds portrayed by Audubon are known by names that are quite different today. Usage has dictated some; others have been modified as their relationships were clarified.

If the author of every new bird book decided to change names to suit himself, chaos would result. Hence the scientific organization known as the American Ornithologists' Union (AOU) has set up a checklist committee to pass on questions of nomenclature. The scientific names they decide on become official. As for English names, the checklist committee of the American Birding Association (ABA) has helped to standardize those we use today.

In his great folio, Audubon painted forty species of North American warblers, including three western varieties sent to him by Mr. Townsend. This does not include the dozen invalid forms he so optimistically described and named. Of the forty, only one—Swainson's warbler—still carries the same scientific name he gave it—*Limnothlypis swainsonii*. But even that species carried a different common name—"Brown-headed Worm-eating Warbler." As for the vernacular or English names of the forty warblers, twenty-five go by approximately the same names today, whereas fifteen do not. So it would seem evident that common names have been more stable than scientific nomenclature.

"CARBONATED WARBLER" *(A mystery)*

This is one of Audubon's mystery birds, a very convincing drawing of a bird that had never been seen and described before, nor has it been since. He wrote:

> I shot the two little birds here represented, near the village of Henderson, in the State of Kentucky, in May 1811. They were both busily engaged in searching for insects along the branches and amongst the leaves of a Dogwood Tree. . . . On examination they were found to be both males. I am of the opinion that they were each young birds of the preceding year, and not in full plumage, as they had no part of their dress seemingly complete, excepting the head. Not having met with any other individuals of this species I am at this moment unable to say anything more about them. They were drawn like almost all the other birds which I have represented, immediately after being killed.

Audubon's portrayal of this puzzler does not seem contrived. His "Carbonated Warbler," deep yellow with a black cap, streaked breast, and strong wing bars looks quite logical, but quite unlike any known species. One could easily dismiss such a bird as being a mutant or an aberrant individual; but the anomaly is that there were two. We would not expect to find two identical mutants at the same time. There is a remote possibility that it was a species already close to extinction. Inasmuch as the Kirtland's warbler, unknown in Audubon's day, numbers scarcely more than four hundred individuals in its restricted range in the Michigan pine barrens, and the Bachman's warbler of the southern swamps is sometimes not recorded for several years in succession, it is possible that this bird, the "Carbonated Warbler," actually did exist, and that it was a species at the end of the line.

—JANUARY/FEBRUARY 1984

WHAT ARE YOU REALLY?

ARE YOU A BIRD WATCHER, an ornithologist, an ornithophile, an aviphile, a bird lover, bird fancier, bird bander, birder, bird spotter, lister, ticker, twitcher—or what? As for myself, I am primarily a bird artist and a bird photographer, a visual person obsessed by birds. I watch them, and they undoubtedly watch me; their eyes are better than mine.

I favor the term *bird watcher* for general use because it is inclusive. It describes almost everyone who looks at birds or studies them—at nearly every level, from the watcher at the window who simply feeds birds all the way to elitists like the fellows of the American Ornithologists' Union (AOU) and even Nobel laureates such as Konrad Lorenz and Nikko Tinbergen, who have won distinction for their behavioral work on birds.

Let us consider some of the alternative names.

ORNITHOLOGIST

It is risky to call yourself an artist if you merely dabble with watercolors or oils as a weekend hobby. It is equally presumptuous to call yourself an ornithologist just because you identify birds, take notes, or make lists. Ornithology implies a high level of expertise of a scientific nature. Most professional ornithologists these days have degrees, either a doctorate or at least a master's. A very few nonprofessionals who devote their time year after year to some specialized problem of avian research might be included in this rarefied category.

A generalization that might be made is that the average person who watches birds is interested in what the bird *is*, while the or-

Peterson with birders, bird watchers, listers, tickers, and twitchers.
(Virginia M. Peterson)

nithologist is more involved with what it *does.* The laboratory ornithologist, a special breed, might not be satisfied with the external
appearance of birds—he probably couldn't separate a juvenile bay-
breasted warbler from a blackpoll anyway, unless he has it in the
hand. He dissects birds and probably knows more about their insides
than he does about living, free-flying birds. Most fellows of the AOU,
and many of the elective members as well, look with disdain on the
field identification buffs. They contend that anyone who watches
birds seriously should have a problem to work on. This rather lordly
attitude was why the American Birding Association (ABA) came into
being—as an antidote of sorts, to promote birding as a game or a
sport. This splinter group aspired to form an elite of its own that
would set themselves apart from the hoi polloi—the hundreds of
thousands, indeed millions, who call themselves bird watchers.

Back in the early years of this century, around 1920, when I was
cutting my teeth, so to speak, on the Junior Audubon leaflets, people

who watched birds fell into two basic categories—ornithologists, who usually shot birds, and bird lovers, who didn't. Frank Chapman, in his *Color Key to North American Birds*, published in 1903, pointed up the dichotomy when he wrote: "From the scientific point of view there is but one satisfactory way to identify a bird. A specimen of it should be in hand." Then, aware of an increasing dilemma, he wrote, "[But] we cannot place a gun in the hands of these thousands of bird lovers we are yearly developing." He used the term *bird lover* freely in his writing. If we insist on speaking of dog lovers and horse lovers, *bird lover* would be a logical usage. But dogs and horses are pets, almost like members of the family; wild birds are not. Loving involves reciprocation, or at least the hope of reciprocation, and birds do not reciprocate in an amorous or affectionate way. They couldn't care less about us, even though we feed them and call them "our feathered friends."

If someone is so naïve as to call me a "bird fancier" I quickly correct him. He may be on his third martini at a social gathering and may simply want to get in on the conversation, which seems to be about birds. "I don't keep birds," I tell him, "I prefer my birds wild." The proper word, of course, is *aviculturist*.

Usually the avicultural crowd and the ornithologists do not mix, but there are a few notable exceptions. Sir Peter Scott and John Henry Dick are artists with their own aviaries, mostly of waterfowl, which they use as models for their canvases. Dillon Ripley of the Smithsonian and John Delacour also maintain waterfowl collections that have been essential to their behavioral research.

Birder

Bill Oddie, the popular British television personality and perceptive birder, in his *Little Black Bird Book* asks, "What is wrong with 'bird watcher'? I honestly don't know. There may be something like a million people in this country [England] who would confidently claim to be bird watchers, and that's too many to constitute an elite. So— the correct word is 'birder.' This implies a fair degree of conviction and expertise."

Guy Mountfort, Phil Hollom, and I dedicated our *Field Guide to the Birds of Britain and Europe* to "Our Long-Suffering Wives." This was followed by a quote from Shakespeare's *Merry Wives of Windsor*: "She laments, sir. . . . Her husband goes a-birding."

It has always been assumed that in those times "birding" must have meant wildfowling or bird shooting. Not so, insists my Swedish friend Sven Wahlberg, a self-styled Shakespeare scholar. It really meant that the husband had gone to a brothel or was chasing the gals. Good reason for a wife to lament! Other Shakespeare scholars may dispute this interpretation, so I'll leave it right there.

The term *birding* did not surface in the ornithological literature until 1896, when Florence Merriam, one of the founding mothers of the Audubon movement, wrote a book entitled *A-Birding on a Bronco*. I haven't seen the book for years and cannot remember whether she just watched birds (I presume she did) or shot them, as did most bird observers in those days. Her contemporary John Burroughs, the popular nature essayist, counseled the serious bird student: "Don't ogle it through a glass, shoot it!"

Curiously, the term *birding* slipped from our vocabulary after Florence Merriam used it in the title of her book. Did she coin it? To my knowledge, the meaning of the word *birder* as we use it today never surfaced in any standard dictionary until Webster published its *New Collegiate Dictionary* in 1977, wherein 22,000 new words and meanings were introduced. On page 112 we find: "BIRDER (1) a catcher or hunter of birds, esp. for the market. (2) one that birds." Referring to the verb BIRD, I find "to observe or identify wild birds in their natural environment." So far, so good. Then turning to BIRD WATCHER, I read: "birder." They are interchangeable.

Throwing up my hands, I concede that even Webster cannot keep up with the subtleties of our ever evolving ornitholanguage.

When I am asked by the media, as I often am, how many birders there are, I am forced to be equivocal. "Do you mean birders or bird watchers?" I ask. It depends on your definition. *Bird watchers* may include anyone who feeds birds. Practically everyone up and down our road at Old Lyme, Connecticut, puts out sunflower seeds or suet.

A survey in 1980 by the U.S. Fish and Wildlife Service estimated that well over *half a billion* dollars are spent yearly in the United States for birdseed.

And do we include sportsmen? Several million, mostly men, shoot ducks, quail, and pheasants. They certainly watch birds (through the gunsight rather than the binocular), but their focus is on relatively few species.

If we are to include these peripheral categories, we could contend that there are between 20 and 40 million bird watchers in the United States. A few years ago the Bureau of Outdoor Recreation came up with a figure of 11 million. But who really knows? More recently Robert Arbib, editor of *American Birds,* arrived at a far more conservative estimate of the number of *birders.* His rationale was that one is really not a birder unless he or she occasionally goes out looking for birds beyond the confines of the backyard. The birder owns a binocular, field guide, and scope. Arbib discounts "companionate" birders, go-alongs who are out there only because they want to be with their spouses or children. Although millions of people own field guides and other bird books, Arbib puts the maximum number of bona fide birders countrywide at 150,000.

Only a small fraction of these would be called hard-core, but the number is growing fast and will continue to increase as advanced or specialized bird guides see the light of day. What a contrast to the old days, when my first *Field Guide to the Birds* was published, in 1934. It came close to being turned down by Houghton Mifflin because one of the editors—a birder at that—thought there were not enough people who would buy a book costing $2.75, the price necessary to cover the printing of the four color plates!

LISTER OR TICKER

Birders make lists of the birds they see; if they don't, they should. Thus the conscientious birder might also be called a "lister" or a "ticker." A tick is a checkmark on the checklist.

There are all kinds of lists. Dearest to the hearts of most birders is the life list, which includes those birds ticked off anywhere in the world during one's lifetime. My own life list is still under 4,000. Who holds the world record at this time? A short while back it was Stuart Keith, who had reached 5,450; but according to the 1983 *Guinness Book of Records,* Norman Chesterfield of Wheatley, Ontario, is now ahead with 5,556. However, it is rumored that Stuart Stokes of Australia claims 6,125; but to my knowledge this has not been documented.

Then there is the North American list. There are about 840 species on the ABA Checklist, including the many accidentals. Like Dick Davenport of the Doonesbury cartoons, I still do not have Bachman's warbler, and I am still just short of qualifying for the 700 Club (I'm at 696). If I include those birds *on* the ABA list that I have seen *outside* the ABA area—birds seen in the West Indies, Mexico, Japan, or on the high seas, et cetera—I am closer to 800; but that would be against the rules of the game. Apparently the only way to break 700 is to go at least twice to Attu. I will have to go again. Benton Basham, by going all out in 1983, was the first birder to pass the 700 mark in one year—711 to be exact—and thus to become the superstar. And by so doing, he brought his life list for North America to 750, equaling that of the reigning champ, Paul Sykes.

For those who do not have the funds or the stamina to join Larry Balch at Attu, there is the state list or, if you are really provincial, the county list. When I was a teenager, I saw my first black-crowned night-heron on the banks of Silver Creek just over the line in Cattaraugus County, New York. I ran over the bridge and chased the bird across the creek into my home county, Chautauqua.

There are also backyard lists, January 1 lists, "Big Day" lists, and Christmas count lists. The variations are endless. When I was a young man, one of my lists was birds heard on the soundtracks of movies. I had a very special list for the wren-tit, a common bird around the studios of Hollywood—a bird with an unmistakable voice. The range of this species is almost entirely within the state of California, but my researchers in movie theaters over the years extended its range to Wyoming (in the Wallace Beery movie *Wyoming*), Kentucky (*National Velvet*), Lake Champlain (*Northwest Passage*), and even Austria (*The Waltz King*).

Another kind of list would be birds photographed. It was the late Allan Cruickshank's goal to photograph every North American bird. It has also been Don Bleitz's dream and that of several other bird photographers I know. On my recent trip to Attu, I was more interested in documenting such rarities as rufous-necked stints and other Asian shorebirds on film than in ticking them off on my checklist. I had seen most of them anyway—in Asia, Africa, or elsewhere—but had never photographed them. Photography is my therapy, so my most exhilarating hours on Attu were spent with ace photographers Ken Fink and Allan Nelson.

Bird banders, at least those who use mist nets to snare the migrants, are listers too; but they are more akin to the bird-in-hand ornithologists of the old days. When confronted with a technical identification problem, they usually do not refer to their field guides but use a different set of criteria—wing formulas, et cetera, by which they separate one difficult flycatcher from another.

A "ticker" is a shade different from a lister. I have known tickers who merely follow other birders around and scarcely look at the bird when they are spotted but wait for their leader to call them off. I remember particularly a friend from Brooklyn who often followed our group around the Ramble in Central Park, building up his list without the benefit of a binocular.

TWITCHER

When I first heard the term *twitcher*, I assumed it meant the same as ticker, but not so. This was invented by the bird watching fraternity in Britain. We do not use it on this side of the ocean, and I hope we never will because it has a slightly demeaning connotation. I had always thought it was synonymous with *ticker*. So I asked my friend John Parslow, coauthor of one of the competing British field guides, about the origin of the word. He replied that, as a matter of fact, he was one of the very first twitchers. About twenty years ago he and a friend, who tore about the roads of England on their bikes running up lists, learned of a rare warbler that had been reported on the coast. They dropped everything, jumped on their bikes, and pedaled like mad for a couple of hours, stopping only to have lunch by the road-side. The weather was foul, and as they wolfed down their sand-wiches they were shaking, partly from the cold and partly from their impatience to get going lest this rare tick slip through their hands. Another young chap who joined them commented, "You're a couple of twitchers." And that, according to Parslow, is how the word entered the birders' lexicon.

Other birders may dispute this origin, but by definition a twitcher is a birder who races around the country frantically collecting rare birds for his list. To quote Bill Oddie again, "What distinguishes the *real* twitcher is his degree of emotional involvement. . . . If this kind of birder gets to hear of a bird that has been sighted that would be a tick for him he is so wracked with nervous anticipation (that he might see it) or trepidation (that he might miss it) that he literally twitches with the excitement of it all." He adds, perhaps with tongue in cheek, "I have seen certain twitchers twitch, shake, and even throw up under stress."

I suppose that those birders that Larry Balch entices to join him on Attu to endure three weeks of hardship in an attempt to boost their North American life lists past the 700 mark could properly be called "twitchers." However, they eschew the term and prefer to be known as "hard-core." Certainly Joe Taylor qualified as a bona fide twitcher when, hearing of a rare Mexican hummingbird at someone's feeder in Texas, he flew down there, ticked it off, and returned to Rochester the same day.

The "Rare Bird Alerts"—telephone numbers that you can dial to learn the latest hot news—cater primarily to the twitching crowd. And a crowd it is. *Thousands* poured into Newburyport to see New England's first Ross's gull, and last summer thousands flocked to Nantucket off the coast of Massachusetts to ogle North America's first western reef-heron from West Africa. The local cabdrivers did a land-office business and even pointed out the heron before they turned off the ignition. I might comment that twitchers seldom discover their own rarities; they zero in on reports that have reached them through the grapevine.

Gestalt and Jizz

These are snob terms, sometimes used by the elite when they describe their observations. They are part of their gamesmanship, I suspect. *Gestalt,* according to my Webster's, is a word derived from the German, meaning "a structure, configuration or pattern of physical or biological phenomena so integrated as to constitute a functional unit." In simpler words, a bird's gestalt is its general look or character. But my dictionary does not even mention the word *jizz,* a vulgar invention that apparently means the same thing. I have concluded that it is a slangy contraction of *gestalt. Jizz* is widely used by hard-core birders in Britain but has not caught on there except among a few avant-garde types who subscribe to *British Birds.* When one of these fellows speaks of the jizz of a confusing fall warbler or an even more confusing juvenile sandpiper or immature gull, he implies that he instinctively knows the subtle differences in character but cannot really explain them to you.

In Peter Harrison's new book *Seabirds* he writes: "Jizz is not created by any particular feature of plumage, nor by behavioral traits, or even by shape, though much does depend on shape. Jizz is rather a combination of ill-defined elements which allows a bird to be defined as 'elegant,' 'powerful,' 'impressive,' etc. Despite its abstract connotations jizz can enable a bird to be recognized instantly."

Rather like recognizing a friend or a neighbor at a distance. But what about strangers?

Then there are the buzzwords that the hard-core lads bestow on the birds they are looking at through their scopes. I remember some of the Griscomisms that were dropped by Ludlow Griscom, the Guru of Cambridge, years ago when we birded the Cape and the mouth of the Merrimac. For example, something ordinary was "just a weed bird." Today's version would be "a ho-hum bird." At the other extreme, a continental first such as that western reef-heron might be called "a cosmic mind-boggler." I am sure that the British have their own variations of these terms.

The thrust or function of the various bird journals is quite clear. *The Auk, The Wilson Bulletin,* and *The Condor,* with their computerized charts and graphs, are designed mainly for scholars and professionals. These, the true ornithologists who espouse science rather than the chase, probably do not number more than a few thousand.

The *Journal of Field Ornithology,* formerly called *Bird Banding,* is strictly for the bander, and by its very nature there is a lot of good ornithological fare of a technical nature.

Birding, the publication of the American Birding Association, is designed specifically for the birders, those men and women who make a sport or a game of ticking off birds on their checklists. Ornithogolfing. "The list is the thing." No hard-core birder would be without this little magazine, nor without the next one.

American Birds focuses on the bird rather than the birder. It is the only publication that monitors bird populations on a continental scale. This is most important, because if we are to regard birds as a litmus of the environment, we must take note of their increases and declines so as to take remedial action if we can.

In addition, there are scores of mini-magazines and newsletters of a regional or local nature that are worth reading.

Bird Watcher's Digest is well named, I think, because it covers the whole spectrum, from watching birds at the feeding tray to more sophisticated birding. And because it picks up items that have immediacy and are not likely to find their way into the technical literature, even many of the academics subscribe and find pleasure in its pages. After all, bird watching can take many forms, and *it is fun*!

—MARCH/APRIL 1984

A LETTER TO LARS JONSSON
(After the 1984 Birdathon)

(Lars Jonsson, at the age of thirty, has become Sweden's best-known bird artist. He may be one of the world's best, in my opinion. A tall, well-made young man, six foot six or thereabouts, he has Scandinavian good looks combined with the height of a basketball star. I first met him in Sweden and later visited his home and studio on the Baltic island of Gotland. Lars is best known for a five-volume series of lavishly illustrated guides to European birds that he has written and illustrated. First published in Swedish they have been translated into English. —R.T.P.)

Dear Lars:

I must explain why I spoke only a dozen words to you when we ran into each other in the woods at High Island in Texas. You had come all the way from Sweden to see spring migration in North America, and I had flown down from Connecticut. When we met so unexpectedly on the path, far from our respective homes, you smiled, we shook hands, and my only words were "I can't stop . . . this isn't normal birding . . . we're trying for a record." You nodded, as though you understood, and I hurried down the path to escape the several warbler watchers who advanced toward me, field guides in hand. Our leader, Victor Emanuel, acting like a basic training drill sergeant, turned them away saying, "Not now . . . we've got to keep moving."

It was the National Audubon Society's annual "Birdathon," a fund-raising contest in which sponsors pledge anything from five cents to a dollar or more for each bird we list within the twenty-four-hour period of a single day. In 1982, in Texas, with the same group of top birders, we had broken the all-time continental record with a total of 235 species. The following year, 1983, I teamed up with some of the superstar birders in California, and we ended with a tie—235. So on this day, April 23, 1984, the Texas contingent was out for blood. But when we met you, Lars, in midafternoon, we had a severe handicap, which I will explain later.

I flew down to McAllen, on the Rio Grande, a day early, so that I could put in twelve hours of sleep before our midnight to midnight endurance test. During our 11:00 P.M. to midnight snack at an all-night pancake house, we were joined by four people from the press: the celebrity George Plimpton, *Time* magazine's John Leo, an ace photographer from the *New York Times*, and Nancy Schute, a freelancer from Washington. We had avoided television coverage because on-camera interviews would inevitably steal time from our listing. Besides myself and Victor Emanuel, who planned the whole thing, our party of birders included John Rowlett and his sister Rosanne, who have the best eyes and ears in Texas, and Ted Parker of Louisiana, who can match them eye for eye and ear for ear, and who holds the world's record for a big day—330 species in the Manu of Peru.

As we finished our midnight coffee, Victor laid down the rules to the press: no questioning or interviews while we were in the field; they were okay only when we were traveling together in the van. They agreed to behave; and they did. As we walked to our van just after midnight, our first bird was a dickcissel overhead in the night sky, its flat, buzzy "raspberry" note just discernable above the ambient noise of the truck traffic.

Our first nocturnal stop was at the nearby Santa Ana Tract, one of the last refugia for certain Mexican species on the lower Rio Grande. The gate was locked, so, having gained permission, we parked the van and walked silently single-file along the dirt roads and trails, stopping and straining our ears. We also made use of our tape recorders to stimulate the night birds. A gaggle of gallinules and a lone least bittern were vocal among the reed beds, but we probably would have missed the least grebe had we not played our tape. It an-

Peterson (far right)*, with Jonsson* (far left). (Virginia M. Peterson)

swered immediately with a loud, chattering trill to the excellent recording on the new field guide cassette that we brought with us.

We were seldom out of hearing of the *pur-we'eeer* of pauraques on the road, but the owls were slow to respond. Finally we caught the tremolo of a screech-owl and then another. We had almost given up on the elf owl, a rarity that we would not get elsewhere, but when we were about to retrace our steps to the car, two birds called back and forth with their unowl-like, puppylike notes.

As we proceeded upriver into the more arid country, we picked up most of the other night birds—poorwills, lesser nighthawks, barn owls, great horned owls, and finally, near the Girl Scout camp, a pair of ferruginous owls, the rarest of the lot. We had missed that one on the 1982 Birdathon. But the most memorable moments were just before dawn, while we were listening to the sonorous hooting of no less than four great horned owls. A pack of coyotes, at least a dozen, started yipping and then rose to a frenzied crescendo of song. It was the most remarkable coyote chorus I had ever heard. After several minutes of this eerie music, they suddenly lapsed into silence, leaving the still air to the owls.

We were just below Falcon Dam when day broke among the mesquite groves that lined the river. One bird after another—green jays, brown jays, chachalacas, ladder-backed and golden-fronted woodpeckers, olive sparrows—greeted the rising sun. Black-hooded (Audubon's) orioles sounded exactly like small boys learning to whistle.

Although we finally ticked off all three kingfishers—green, ringed, and belted—on the fast-flowing river below the dam, we made sure they were on our side. Any bird on the Mexican side does not count according to the rules. This seems ridiculous to me, because the river is scarcely a hundred yards wide, and yet later we were allowed to count the frigatebird that we spotted at the limit of vision—at least a mile out in the Gulf. Birds do not recognize geographic boundaries, and therefore it seems to me that the birder, not the bird, should conform to geographic rules.

A most extraordinary thing happened as we were walking along a sandy track through the mesquite. Ted Parker exclaimed, "Black-tailed gnatcatcher! I hadn't expected it here!" Rosanne played her tape of the bird, and it answered. A moment later, coming through the mesquite on the other side of the fence was Jerry Maisel of California, with his own tape recorder! After acknowledging the rest of us, he spotted George Plimpton and called out "Long time no see." I presume he was on a big day of his own, so without too many words between us we went our respective ways. We did, however, pick up a bona fide black-tailed gnatcatcher half an hour later in the proper environment.

By 9:15 A.M., when the two planes met us on the small airfield at Falcon Dam, we were five birds ahead of our 1982 tally. But it was still a bit too early in the day for migrating raptors such as Swainson's hawks to be riding the thermals. However, we did manage to spot two or three Swainson's shortly after we took off on our two-hour flight northward. John Rowlett's incredibly sharp eyes picked up a wild turkey in the open oak woods below and also a soaring white-tailed hawk, which we all checked on. We were now seven ahead of our 1982 list and in high spirits—all except Ted Parker, who groped for a plastic tote bag that served him well before he dozed off in a queasy coma.

When we reached the small, makeshift airstrip of limestone on the Bolivar Peninsula, we noticed that the press plane that had preceded us had not yet landed. We could see a large white van that awaited us and a small figure standing beside it. It was Rhea Coppening of Audubon's Texas office. She waved to us. We noticed that our other plane was now flying away in the distance, gaining altitude and circling back. Both planes made several passes over the airstrip, which seemed in poor repair and a bit too short for our Cessnas.

We needed at least fifteen hundred feet of runway. After conferring on the intercom, the pilots scouted for a paved road free from utility poles, but we could find none that did not have at least one or two cars on it. I began to feel uneasy about the whole thing and had visions of the news in *Time* magazine under "Milestones": "DIED, George Plimpton, 57, in a plane crash while birding with veteran reporter John Leo." Of course our plane with its five passengers and pilot could escape this fate because we would see what happened to the others.

Victor and the pilots finally decided that a landing was not feasible and made the decision to head for the airport at Galveston. I knew then that our bid for the record was going down the drain.

At Galveston, we hired a large helicopter, which, after a fifteen-minute flight, landed all of us on the beach at Bolivar within walking distance of masses of shorebirds, terns, herons, ibis, and other goodies. But we had lost an hour and thirty-five minutes of precious time. I calculated from past experience that each four or five minutes lost would mean the loss of a species; thus we had lost a minimum of eighteen birds. We were wiped out. Had it not been for this stroke of bad luck, we would have ended the day with not less than 241 species, possibly with as many as 246, and most likely with about 243.

And that, Lars, was why we were in such a desperate hurry at

High Island and why we spent so little time there. Obviously there was not nearly the heavy fallout of warblers and other migrants that we had witnessed in 1982. Mrs. Johnson's place down the road, usually packed with migrants, was lean pickings because most of the oleander hedges had been killed by last winter's freeze. Even so, we could have added at least a dozen more species at High Island had we been able to stay longer. Time was against us.

Striking inland to the pine forests, which normally would have given us twenty more species typical of east Texas, we had the impression that because of the lateness of the season several of the breeding warblers were not yet on territory. Two or three days later might have made the difference. We even missed the Acadian flycatcher, which Rosanne tried to call up with her tape, a tape so good that I thought I was hearing the real thing. But so beautiful was the setting sun on Lake Charlotte that I lay down on its shelly shore to rest and drink in the beauty of it all.

We ended our day with a nocturnal foray by marsh buggy at Anahuac, where we added four more, including a yellow rail. Blinded by our spotlights, the bird was caught by hand, then released.

Our final total was 223, 12 short of our previous record and 20 short of our potential goal.

The California team easily eclipsed us several days later with 243. They now hold the record.

On the first of May, Victor and the Rowletts teamed up with Jim Tucker and Jim Vardaman to try to bring things back to Texas. Ted Parker and I could not go. They fell short with a very respectable 238.

There is always next year.

Next time our paths cross, Lars, I hope we can just look at birds in a leisurely manner, sketch them, and enjoy them as artists should.

Sincerely,
Roger

—JULY/AUGUST 1984

RETURN TO
THE PRIBILOFS

THIRTY-ONE YEARS have now passed since my British colleague James Fisher and I made our epic tour around the perimeter of the North American continent, which we narrated in *Wild America*. For a few short weeks our book made the bestseller list. The climax of our hundred-day odyssey during the spring and early summer of 1953 came when we flew to the Pribilofs, that cluster of foggy islands far out in the Bering Sea off the west coast of Alaska.

Both James and I had read and reread Rudyard Kipling's "The White Seal" in *The Jungle Book,* and we also knew that famous old Smithsonian report *The Seal Islands of Alaska,* written back in the 1870s by an agent of the U.S. Treasury, Henry W. Elliott. It was Elliott's report, with its topographical detail and place, seal, bird, and man names, and the numerous watercolor drawings by Elliott himself, that inspired Kipling's classic tale. To James, who had read everything he could find about the seal islands, these days at the terminus of our North American journey were the fulfillment of a lifelong dream.

On the day we left Anchorage in our DC-3, the morning papers had predicted Olympian fireworks. Spurr, the eleven-thousand-foot volcanic peak at the head of the Aleutian Range, had been spitting smoke and ashes for the last day or two. An eruption seemed imminent. It would be well timed if it came on this day, the Fourth of July (it did not erupt until several days later). Bob Reeve, owner of the airline, had instructed our pilot to show us an Alaskan brown bear; and sure enough, from the water's edge a brown form retreated along one of the well-worn bear trails that led inland across the moors. Our plane banked and circled low while all twenty passengers pressed their noses against the windows. At Cold Bay, where the Aleutian chain of islands starts, our plane made its last fuel stop before striking out across the Bering Sea, across 250 miles of water to the Pribilofs, the islands of the seals.

Usually fog blankets the Pribilofs, and the pilots who make this run for the Reeve Aleutian Airways must slip under the overcast at low elevation to land the plane on the field at St. Paul. But on that visit with James Fisher and two friends who joined us, Finnur Gudmundsson of Iceland and Bill Cottrell, the sun was shining as we neared our destination. As we came in, we could see the swarms of seals on their hauling beaches and the neat white houses of the town of St. Paul. After our plane taxied to a stop, we stepped out into a garden of bloom such as we had never seen before—anywhere. Millions of yellow poppies lifted their faces toward the sun, and fields of tall blue lupines stretched to the horizon.

There had been ten successive days of sun, a thing almost unheard of in the Pribilofs. "This much sun is not good for people," complained the resident Aleuts. They pointed out with alarm that the last time they had that much sun was in 1919, when influenza struck them down. We, of course, desired the sun for our photography, and all records were broken when fair weather prevailed for another two weeks. How could we be so lucky! Other film crews had spent weeks in the fog without ever seeing blue sky. While James shot stills, I used my 16-millimeter Bell + Howell movie camera.

At no great distance from the village, every nook, every ledge, along miles of rock wall was occupied by murres, puffins, auklets, kittiwakes, and fulmars. The murres stood erect, facing the rocks, their dark backs to the sea. Each attended its big, greenish pyriform egg. As we approached, the birds faced about, presenting their white waistcoats. I tried to count them as they stood shoulder to shoulder on a hundred yards of cliff, and using this sample estimated a minimum of 1 million murres on the ledges of St. Paul. This estimate I later found to be much too high. Large sections of the island have no suitable cliffs; 300,000 was closer to the mark.

Tufted puffins, even more bizarre than the puffins of the Atlantic, stood in pairs just below the lip of the cliff edges. While I peered through the range finder of my Bell + Howell, they would turn their huge orange beaks from side to side as they tried to make sense out of the apparatus peeking at them through the tall grass. Others flew by against the wind, their golden locks flowing over their shoulders. We had expected the other puffin of the Pribilofs, the horned puffin, to be quite like the familiar species of the Atlantic. But it laid its egg far back in the rocky crevices, so that nothing but a blasting charge could

Tufted puffins can be found year-round offshore along much of the Pacific Coast.

dislodge it, whereas the tufted puffin usually nested in the turf in the orthodox Atlantic puffin manner.

Besides the two species of murres and the two puffins, there were three other members of the auk family. Sitting by themselves in pairs or small groups were smaller white-breasted birds with stubby, upturned red bills. These were the paroquet auklets, or *baillie brushkies* as the Aleuts called them. They nested deep in the cliff crevices, from which we heard their high, musical trills.

Horned puffins lay their eggs in well-protected rock crevices.

There were foxes about, scouting sure-footed the accessible ledges near the cliff top for eggs, and when we heard odd, honking, yapping sounds under the ledges, we thought we were hearing foxes. The sounds proved to be coming from crested auklets: slaty birds with smiling, orange beaks and forward-curling head plumes. *Canooskie*—"little captain"—is the Aleut name for this queer, noisy little auk. Smallest of all were the least auklets—*choochkies*. No larger than a starling without a tail, they perched and chirped in busy little bands on the piles of beach drift and boulders above high-tide mark.

As for the land birds, the moors were musical with snow buntings, Lapland longspurs, and rosy finches. Occasionally we would hear the thin tinkling of a winter wren in the rocky spree.

Aside from a few holdovers, such as molting harlequin ducks and Steller's eiders, nesting rock sandpipers, and a few lingering shorebirds, we saw little else, although on later trips I was to see a pair of snowy owls and a McKay's bunting that might have been nesting. There is always the possibility of a stray from Asia, but we saw none; the chances are better earlier in the season.

On July 15, three days after James said good-bye to us and boarded his plane for the long flight home to England, Clarence Olson, the di-

Least auklets are known as choochkies in the Pribilofs.

rector of the Pribilof sealing operation, announced that the *Penguin*, the Fish and Wildlife Service launch, would make a run for Walrus Island, the smallest of the four Pribilofs, to count the sea lion herd. A bull northern or Steller's sea lion is three times the weight of a bull fur seal but not as aggressive. No one had been out to Walrus for about four years. Usually thick fog and heavy surf prevent landing, but on that day conditions were ideal. An hour's run took the *Penguin* to the lee side of the low, rather flat island, where we dropped anchor and scrambled into a large dory. A welcoming committee of sea lions swam out to greet us, pacing the boat as they leaped about like porpoises to look us over. In our walk around the island, where walrus once lived, we estimated about four thousand sea lions and their pups.

Top billing in the great show on Walrus Island at that time went to the murres. As we advanced, a solid mass of birds, acres of them, receded reluctantly and then closed in again after we had passed, each jostling with its neighbors for a few square inches of space. The air above was a blizzard of buzzing birds, bewildering, countless. Although thick-billed murres (formerly known as Arctic or Brunnich's murres) were dominant in 1940, when Ira Gabrielson made his survey, we found the colony in 1953 to be almost entirely common murres. Our first guess was about 2 million birds, but after making a few sample density counts and taking the detailed ship charts of the island, plotting the occupied acreage, and using simple mathematics, we arrived at a figure of about 1 million. It was one of the largest murre colonies in the world.

But a great change has taken place in the last thirty years. The sea lions had evacuated the northern tip of St. Paul and moved to Walrus Island, which is now one heaving mass of these great blubbery mammals. The murres were dispossessed. There is no longer room for them except on a small offshore stack known as Murre Rock, where about two hundred pairs still compete for space.

➤

Before my recent return to these islands, in 1983 and 1984, I made one interim visit, a very short one at the time of the 1968 meetings of the American Ornithologists' Union in Alaska. Our scheduled field trip was too early in the season for the great show of wildflowers. By contrast, in 1953, Bill Cottrell identified about 100 of the 170 species known to grow there. But this time even the lupines were still in bud. Many of the seabirds were just arriving, and although the bull fur seals were establishing their beachheads with furious territorial battles, the females had not yet come in from the sea. My advice to anyone who hopes to get the most from a visit to the Pribilofs is: Do not go before July 1—unless you are one of those hard-core listers hoping for Asian accidentals. Then late May would be best.

I recall little about that brief visit except Stuart Keith's disastrous encounter with a fur seal. Stuart assured us that the way to react to a challenging bull was to hold your ground. "Turn him away," he said. A charging bull called his bluff, and, instead of running like mad, Stuart, with British face-saving aplomb, simply turned on his heel and *walked* away. Result: thirty stitches—fifteen in his calf and fifteen in his trousers!

Reeve Aleutian Airways still takes tourists to St. Paul two or three times a week. The main difference is that the planes are larger (Lockheed Super Electras), and the hostesses are prettier. But until last year the neighboring island of St. George was accessible only by ship or boat. James Fisher, Finnur Gudmundsson, Bill Cottrell, and I got there in the U.S. Fish and Wildlife Service launch, the *Penguin,* which made the crossing every two weeks.

But by unplanned coincidence in 1983, I was on the very first tourist flight to St. George, a Lindblad tour with Peter Alden as my coleader. We were flown out from St. Paul in a small plane that could take only half of our group at a time. The Australian pilot who had been flying the mail to St. George for the last several years landed us on the little airstrip that the Aleuts had laid down on the red volcanic soil. Near the end of the runway, among a group of resting glaucous-winged gulls, was a smaller bird. Putting our scopes on it, we identified an adult Franklin's gull, far out of its range. It was one of the few records for Alaska.

St. George had changed very little in thirty years. The little Russian Orthodox church that guards the town looked just the same, and so did most of the frame houses, but the old unoccupied rooming house where we had spread our sleeping bags and where the fox had sneaked in and tried to make off with Bill Cottrell's shoes was now spruced up, open for business. An upstairs dining room served very good meals.

St. George has only 20 percent of the Pribilof fur seals, and because the harvest had become uneconomical, it was no longer carried out. Today the only hope of survival for the local Aleuts, other than governmental handouts, is commercial fishing and tourism. Inasmuch as we were the first birders ever—aside from occasional biologists—we were given a warm welcome.

Although St. George has a minority of the seals, it has 80 percent of the birds. This is because of the far greater height of the cliffs, which rise sheer to a thousand feet or more at Staraya Artil. Approaching this avian metropolis by boat, James Fisher and I were staggered by the traffic pouring out to sea from the big cliff; perhaps as many as a million birds were in sight at one time. In 1983, scanning things from the cliff top, Peter Alden and I had no comparable impression. There were fewer birds.

On my initial visit to the Pribilofs, in 1953, I shot only 16-millimeter movies, from which I made my film *Wild America,* shown for several years on the Audubon Screen Tour circuit. I had always wanted to go back and make proper transparencies of the birds on 35-millimeter Kodachrome. In 1983, saddled as I was with a tour group, it was difficult to get what I wanted, so I returned in June 1984 with my wife, Ginny.

The town manager of St. Paul, whom we met in Anchorage, put us in the hands of a biologist, Bill Rodstrom, who greeted us when the plane landed at St. Paul. We were given the VIP treatment and were free to go where we chose without the restraints imposed by a busload of tourists.

After we checked in at the hotel, one of the two bus drivers, an enthusiastic young lady who was just getting into birding, told us that Kenn Kaufman's group (which had just left on the plane) had identified a rufous turtle-dove about two miles north of town. If accepted, it would be the first North American record for this Asian species. But there were lingering doubts. Kenn's high-powered Questar showed the tips of the outer primary feathers on one wing to be worn. Was the bird an escape from a Japanese fishing boat?

Later that day, we located the bird on a beach where a flock of glaucous-winged gulls were having a convention. The dove was very shy. By the appearance of its rump and tail, I judged it to be the highly migratory Siberian race rather than the Japanese subspecies. There was no doubt about its identity; it was in excellent plumage, showing the striking checkerboard pattern of black and rufous on the wings. In spite of its shyness, Ginny with her 400-millimeter lens and I with my 600 managed to get off several shots. One or two were quite good. Later examination of these transparencies showed at least one outer primary of the left wing to be cleanly broken off an inch from the tip. The other visible primaries did not seem to be worn.

So the mystery remains. If we entertain doubts about this bird, a logical candidate as an off-course stray, we must question the records of some of the West Indian doves that have been reported from the

Florida Keys. The Cuban residents of Key West keep plenty of cage birds, as I well know, having once accompanied a federal investigator there.

The rufous turtle-dove was seen in the same area by later tour groups. It was obviously finding plenty of flies and other goodies among the rotting kelp.

At the time of our visit last June, controversy was raging between the Aleuts and the Humane Society of the United States and Friends of Animals. Even though the annual harvest of young bull fur seals was to be reduced to about 22,000 in 1984, a last-ditch effort to stop the harvest entirely was launched by a coalition of the humane organizations. The Aleuts countered that they, the Aleuts, were the "endangered species," arguing that "there are only a few thousand Aleuts in the world, and some of us have no other way to make a living. . . . Give us another two or three years," they pleaded, "until we can develop our fishing facilities."

An enlarged harbor, designed to handle an Aleut fishing fleet, was being blasted near the town of St. Paul. Our young biologist friend Bill Rodstrom was there to monitor the blasting, in order to see whether there was a disrupting effect on the birds that occupied the nearby cliffs. By his latest reports, there was little or none. Fledging success near the town was about the same (low) as that on the cliffs elsewhere on the island.

As part of a dowry for the Aleuts' self-development, the bird cliffs had been bought by the U.S. government for a reported $7 million. And yet, one morning, we saw a small group of men from the village returning from the cliffs near Zapadni after an egging expedition, a tradition that had been going on for a century or more. If the government now owns the bird cliffs, I wondered, will the Aleuts still have subsistence rights to continue shooting the birds and taking their eggs?

The seal harvest of 1984 ended on August 3 with 22,078 seals killed. A harvest is planned for 1985, but there is doubt about a viable market for the furs. The treaty, I am told, is being renegotiated. If the

United States reneges on the treaty and gives up the seal harvest as a drain on the taxpayers' pocketbook, some say that Japan may then be free to begin pelagic sealing in conjunction with its regular fishing program. This would be disastrous, and what might have seemed to be good intentions on the part of the humane groups could prove counterproductive. The fur seal could be reduced to the endangered level again. On land it would receive some reprieve under the Marine Mammal Protection Act, but what about the sea? The next several years will tell.

James Fisher had been particularly fascinated by the fur seals and, because of his research, perhaps the best chapter in *Wild America* (including a detailed appendix) is about these animals. At that time, the total population of fur seals, including those on St. George forty miles from St. Paul, was at least 1.7 million. But it had not always

The population of northern fur seals declined by about half between the 1950s and the 1980s.

been as large. Although the herds had been well managed during the early Russian occupation, the seals declined drastically after the United States purchased Alaska and its satellite islands. By the first decade of this century, neglect of the herds and particularly the sealing at sea, mostly by the Japanese, had reduced the herds to fewer than 125,000 animals. The fur seal was threatened with speedy extermination.

In 1911, the envoys of Canada, Russia, Japan, and the United States gathered in Washington to sign a treaty that outlawed pelagic sealing. To exploit and at the same time to preserve and build up the herds, only young, unmated bulls of a certain age and size were to be harvested. According to agreement, 15 percent of the skins went to Canada and to Japan. In similar fashion, Russia managed its own colonies on the Commander Islands.

Inasmuch as only one mature bull is essential to service a harem of forty cows, the sacrifice of the young, idle bulls was deemed to make little difference to the stability of the population. Obviously, sealing at sea was far more disastrous. It was nondiscriminating as to age or sex, and every cow taken at sea meant not only its own death but also that of the pup ashore and next year's unborn pup, already conceived.

Because of the management strategy, the herds in the Pribilofs built up to maximum strength by the 1950s. But now, thirty years later, they are down by more than a third to well under 1 million—perhaps as low as 870,000—for reasons that are not entirely clear. Almost certainly it is not because of the harvest. Hookworm has killed as many as 100,000 pups some years. The number that are snared incidentally at sea by the burgeoning commercial fisheries is perhaps the most decimating factor.

➤

But what has all this to do with birds? One cannot talk about the Pribilofs without bringing in the fur seals. The survival problems of seals and seabirds are similar; both depend on fish. The deepwater gill nets of the commercial fishing fleets not only ensnare many seals but also drown untold numbers of seabirds. It has been estimated that gill nets of the Japanese North Pacific salmon fishery alone ensnare and drown 150,000 to 200,000 marine birds—mainly diving birds, such as murres and puffins—each year. A U.S. State Department environmental impact statement estimates that, overall, the Japanese kill about 1 million seabirds annually in their efficient purse seine nets and trawler gill nets. The murres and some of the other cliff nesters lay but a single egg and have a low reproductive potential. They cannot sustain this continued drain.

It was once estimated that about 2.5 million birds nested on the cliff faces of St. George. There are certainly not that many now. On my 1983 visit, I noted particularly the great reduction of red-legged kittiwakes on that island.

In a recent letter, Bill Rodstrom informed me that this year was the poorest yet for nesting success on St. Paul. Fewer than 10 percent of the black-legged and red-legged kittiwake nests still had live young at the end of the season. Red-faced cormorants also had a dismal year. Murres did somewhat better, although there were more dead chicks than he had seen in the past. Is overfishing affecting this food supply?

Add to these woes the constant threat of spills in these oil-exploited seas and the future looks bleak. We may never again see the numbers of birds that crowded the cliffs when Fisher and I made our 1953 visit.

—November/December 1984

"BWANA NDEGE"—
RETURN TO KENYA

As we left the dining room in one of Nairobi's excellent restaurants, the African headwaiter addressed me as "Bwana Ndege"— Swahili for "Mr. Bird."

It was our first night in Kenya, and we had planned a month's safari, mostly in tents, not in the lodges favored by so many tourists. There were four of us: my wife, Ginny; her daughter, Mimi; and Mimi's husband, Wes Henry. Wes was an old Africa hand, having spent three years in East Africa, mostly in Amboseli, while working for his doctorate. His thesis evaluated the impact of tourism on the ecosystem of the game parks. We visited his old camp hidden in a patch of forest, where elephants, giraffes, and impalas had been his intimates. Snowcapped Kilimanjaro loomed against the sky to the south.

I had first seen East Africa in 1957 and have returned half a dozen times since. Although I am depressed by some of the changes I have witnessed, especially the deforestation in the highlands and the degradation of the land in the arid north, I find Amboseli, on the border of Tanzania, much better for wild grazing animals and some other wildlife than it was twenty or thirty years ago.

A German woman who was filming with a 16-millimeter Bolex disagreed with me. "Better for people," she said, "but not for the animals. Too many tour buses." She had been spoiled by an earlier visit to the Mara, an extension of the Serengeti, where wildlife photographers in their own vehicles could avoid the crowd. I told her how the Masai herdsmen, with their great herds of cattle, had once crowded out the wildebeests, zebras, and antelope in Amboseli, but when the park was established, the contest over the precious source of water was resolved. Water was pumped out of the park for the Masai, providing plenty of this life-sustaining necessity for their cattle. The wild herds of ungulates in Amboseli then increased. However, I agreed with the lady that perhaps there really *were* too many tourists; and local governments would like more lodges built to accommodate tourist needs.

Amboseli is not as attractive as it was when I first knew it. The groves of fever trees and acacias are a shambles. At first I thought this was the result of elephant damage. Elephants had obviously pushed down many of the trees; others, untouched, were dead or dying. Wes explained that this was because of a rise in the water table in recent years; seepage was forcing salts toward the surface, killing the trees, which died from the top downward. The thinning of the groves has meant less habitat for vervet monkeys, baboons, impalas, forest

The black rhinoceros—one of the "big six" many people visit Africa to see. It's staring at a wagtail.

birds, and raptors but more grassy grazing grounds for wildebeests, zebras, gazelles, and buffalo.

Many of the people who flock to the parks and reserves are biologically illiterate and are interested only in "the big six"—the lion, elephant, rhino, buffalo, leopard, and cheetah—especially the lion. A pride of lions, once discovered, is almost invariably ringed by a half dozen vehicles, most of which, according to Wes Henry's researches, click shutters or simply look for no more than four or five minutes before moving on. Often when I have stopped in my own Land Rover to watch or photograph a bird, another vehicle has pulled up. "Where is it?" the driver would ask breathlessly. "On top of that bush," I would reply, "a red-capped lark." I suspect that when he drove off he probably muttered, "Another of those damned bird watchers!"

However, bird watching is becoming increasingly popular among the tourists who come to East Africa, especially at favored spots such as Lake Baringo, six hours' drive north of Nairobi, where binocular addicts make up a fair proportion of the clientele. It was Terry Stevenson, who usually leads the early morning bird walks at the Lake Baringo Club, and his team that broke the African record last year by spotting 308 species during a midnight-to-midnight birdathon. They claimed the world record, unaware that Ted Parker of Louisiana State University had attained a total of 331 in Peru a year earlier. Now the Kenyans are talking about a competitive "International Birdathon." So please take note, Pete Dunne. Pete has already launched his own "World Series of Birding" in New Jersey. It is now in its second year. It is evident that the birding game has reached tournament status globally.

＞

Kenya, not a large country, boasts more than its fair share of Africa's birds, nearly 1,300 species. Compare this with the North American list of approximately 850 (including accidentals) that have been recorded north of Mexico. More than 500 species have been found in the environs of Nairobi alone.

The several days in Amboseli at the beginning of our safari were nostalgic for Wes, a return to the locale where he had experienced some of the greatest days of his life. From then on we were in the skilled hands of Bob Lowis—"Bobbie"—who over the years has taken a surprising number of my high-powered birding friends on tented safaris. Even in earlier days when big game hunting was still legal in Kenya, Lowis never led shooting safaris, and—most important—he knows his birds.

The drive from Nairobi, where Lowis took over, north to Nanyuki is a dreary journey, and whereas only a few years ago we would have seen at least a few wild animals, today mile upon mile of new farms have fenced them out. Kenya's birthrate is one of the highest in the world, averaging six children per family, and I shudder to think of the pressures on the land in another twenty or thirty years, when each of those six has six. Kenya is aware of this problem. However, the Aberdares, still clothed extensively in forest, have been set aside as a refuge for wildlife, and we hope this range of mountains will continue to be preserved. Turacos, deep green with bright red wings, intoned their harsh notes in the moss-hung trees near our camp, and scores of other birds challenged our identification skills. My favorite song in the Aberdares is the wheeling roundelay of Hunter's cisticola, a little brown job that compensates for its undistinguished appearance by delivering an unforgettable song.

Samburu, a half day's drive to the northwest, at the edge of the desert country, was drier than I had ever seen it; the muddy river that harbored so many hippos and crocodiles was now a river of sand. While we were having lunch along its parched banks, a great murmuration of concern among the superb starlings and white-browed sparrow weavers told us that something was amiss. Investigating the dithering birds, Bob almost stepped on a deadly puff adder that proceeded to disgorge a small bird it had eaten.

The Rift Valley lakes are always alive with birds, and on our way south to the Mara we broke our journey with a three-day stay at Lake Naivasha. The introduced coypu, a muskratlike animal from South America, had completely eliminated the floating gardens of lavender water lilies that I filmed fifteen years ago when I acted as cameraman

A superb starling, more colorful than a European starling.

for the Canadian Broadcasting Company, but the fishing eagles, yellow-billed storks, and pelicans were as numerous as ever. On the lawn at the Lake Hotel an ugly marabou stork brazenly stole tidbits from the tables while we were having tea, and sacred ibis and hadadas wandered about unconcernedly only a few feet away.

We missed our friend Alan Root by only a day; he had gone to the Serengeti for a new filming project, but his housekeeper allowed us to follow his pet aardvark around the grounds as it rooted up the earth for termites. Later we saw one of these strange "ant bears" in the headlights of our car.

While at Naivasha we took our meals and slept at "Elsamere," the home of the late Joy Adamson of *Born Free* fame. It is now a shrine to her memory. A pair of red-winged starlings had a nestful of young under the eaves, and the troop of handsome colobus monkeys that Joy had befriended over a period of years came down from the fever trees at noon to be fed. The last time I had had the privilege of staying in her home, Joy and her husband apparently were not on speaking terms. George was sleeping in a pup tent in the compound with his pet lion, Boy, the same lion he was forced to shoot later after it had attacked and killed one of his men. It is still not certain who killed Joy near her own camp in the Samburu area two or three years ago. Initially it was reported that she had been ambushed by a lion; later a servant was implicated, but he was acquitted.

➤

The climax of our safari was to be the Mara, close to the Tanzania border, which we reached by way of a rough road over the southwestern highlands. En route we stopped at the camp where Isak Dinesen's (Karen Blixen's) *Out of Africa* had just been filmed, but its star Robert

Redford had already gone. A party of Masai were still awaiting delivery of a couple of captive lions for the final scene.

After dropping down the escarpment, we were on the vast plain, green again after recent rains. It was disconcerting, however, to pass group after group of Kenyan soldiers in their foxholes; they were on training maneuvers. All through that first night, from our camp just inside the reserve, we could hear distant rifle fire and the tattoo of machine guns as they practiced their war games. Rockets and flares lit up the sky while sheet lightning played along the horizon.

Whereas the tourist in the posh lodges is protected from the realities of life in the raw, we had a taste of the real thing in our own hidden retreat in the acacia grove. We could hear hyenas and lions not far away as we tried to sleep. One evening a long procession of elephants presented an unforgettable picture against a bloodred sunset, and after we had gone to bed they all came by our camp, but caused us no harm. Later, in the wee hours of the morning, Ginny and I were rudely awakened by a leopard sounding off with its coughing

An elephant in the African bush.

roar literally inches from my head, with only the heavy canvas of the tent between us. This leopard was our nightly visitor in camp and actually chewed up the boot of one of our staff. It could probably have ripped open our zippered tents with ease but was unfamiliar with "packaged meat."

Our only unpleasant incident took place after a lone Masai wandered through our camp one afternoon ostensibly looking for a lost cow. That evening while we were around the campfire, Bob's tent was slashed with a knife, and a blanket and his trousers and wallet were gone. This was the only night our askari was not on guard; he was sick.

➤

Birding was better than I had known it previously in the Mara. Besides the usual secretary birds, ground hornbills, various eagles, and a pond full of woolly-necked storks, I saw my first black stork, a rare migrant from eastern Europe.

At the carcass of a zebra, presumably killed by a lion, five species of vultures and a couple of marabou storks competed with two spotted hyenas for the goodies. When the hyenas had finished, the scavenging vultures, mostly white-backed and Ruppell's griffons, clambered over one another in a pile, like a seething mass of gigantic maggots. Although repulsive when feeding, these undertakers of the plains are majestic when riding the thermals above.

We came upon two colonies of Jackson's widowbirds bobbing up and down like yo-yos as they danced to lure the sparrowlike females to their grassy bowers. But our prize find was a martial eagle that had struck down a migrating European white stork. It refused to leave its hard-won prey, even when we were close enough to take full-frame shots.

I am not an obsessed lister; but bird photography is my therapy, and I would rather shoot a roll of film on some relatively common species than add a new bird to my life list. Well, almost. It depends on the species—"trash bird" versus rarity.

Because Noble Proctor had given us such glowing reports of Lake Baringo, where he took a group last January, Wes and I chartered a twin-engine plane to fly us up there for a couple of days, leaving our spouses in the Mara, with instructions to Bob Lowis to protect them from the lions and the leopards. Actually, while we were away, Ginny and Mimi tried tracking the leopard, hoping to photograph it. They got only its eye-shine at night as it circled their campfire. Lowis pronounced it "bold and elusive."

The Baringo Club, operated by Block Hotels, is one of the best places in Kenya for bird photography. While you are having lunch in the attractive restaurant you can have Jackson's hornbills, fan-tailed ravens, doves, superb starlings, white-browed sparrow weavers, and chestnut sparrows sharing the feeder hardly more than an arm's length away. In the date palms outside, bristle-crowned starlings and white-bellied go-away birds gorge themselves on the ripening fruit. The well-tended flower gardens are alive with sunbirds, bee-eaters, and shrikes.

A boat ride through the marshes that flank the lake brought us close to Goliath herons, spoonbills, squacco herons, black-headed herons, and a number of other long-legged waders. Except for the fishing eagles, the big island in the center of the lake was not quite as productive ornithologically as the mainland, but at the island camp vitelline masked weavers sat on our teacups, and a flock of helmeted guinea fowl allowed point-blank photography.

While Wes and I were enjoying all this with Mark Ross, the young ornithologist on duty at Baringo, we heard singing and chanting in the nearby woods. Heading down to investigate, we found a tribal dance going on in a clearing—not one contrived for tourists but the real thing, complete with spears, painted bodies, and ocher hair. These were the Njemps, a hybrid tribe somewhat akin to the Samburu and the Masai. They were in high spirits because storm clouds were blackening the sky; the rains had finally come. They were celebrating the end of the long drought.

Returning to rejoin our wives in Nairobi for the flight home, we instructed our driver to take a detour down the west side of Lake

A group of Masai herdsmen.

Nakuru. This remarkable saline lake is now a national park, and I am pleased with the part I played in its inception. My first visit, in 1957, came shortly after the Mau Mau uprising had ended and before *Uhuru*, when British rule ended and sovereignty was returned to the peoples of Kenya.

Leaving the Stag's Head Hotel in the attractive modern town of Nakuru, Bayard Read and I had piloted our Land Rover southward, dropping over a gentle hill into a belt of fever trees, tall yellow acacias harboring a great variety of intriguing songbirds—emerald cuckoos, robinchats, tinkerbirds, and scores of others that we were at a loss to name. On the other side of the woodland stretched a broad plain of long yellow grass where a pair of secretary birds stalked with mincing gait and several ground hornbills, large as turkeys, shambled awkwardly. Beyond lay the lake, its thirty-square-mile expanse literally covered with flamingos, mostly lesser flamingos, but with a few pods of greaters. Leslie Brown of Nairobi had estimated no fewer than 1,000,000 birds and, more likely, 1,250,000. As far as I was concerned there might have been 2,000,000 or more. But I trusted his careful calculations.

Leslie Brown, John Karmali, and two or three other Kenyans urged me to tell the world about it, so on my return I devoted my column, "Bird's-Eye View," in *Audubon* magazine to Nakuru. I wrote, "This past August, in Africa, I witnessed the most staggering bird spectacle in my thirty-eight years of bird watching. I once saw a million seabirds pour from a single sea cliff in the Bering Sea. . . . I have landed among a blizzard of sooty terns in the Dry Tortugas and amidst the milling gannets of Bonaventure and the Bass, but none of these fabulous concentrations can compare with the flamingos of Lake Nakuru." (The article misspelled Nakuru six times; the editor interpreted my handwritten manuscript as Nakurn.) In conclusion I added, "I wonder if the residents of the favored town of Nakuru realize what a gem is theirs? Do they realize that it is not only a local showplace, but almost unique in the world, a magnet for visitors from distant lands?"

My article was picked up by the Nakuru press, and influential people took notice. As a result the lake was declared an inviolate sanctuary, except for several thousand acres near the north end, a concession to a few local duck hunters. It was then only another step to national park status. Lake Nakuru soon boasted more visitors than any other tourist attraction in Kenya with the exception of Nairobi Park.

The spectacle of the flamingos almost blinds one to the hosts of other waders and waterfowl that feed along the margins or dot the placid surface of Lake Nakuru. Flocks of sacred ibis, white with black wing edgings, fly over the shallows; spoonbills swing their ladles in the tepid soup. There are herons of several sorts, blacksmith plovers and stilts by the score, as well as greenshanks, wood sandpipers, ruffs, and other Palearctic waders on their winter sojourn. Ducks dot the water—redbills, yellow-billed ducks, cape wigeon, and knobbills, as well as Egyptian and spur-winged geese.

Several years after my initial visit, a salt-tolerant fish—one of the tilapia—was introduced into Lake Nakuru, and now there are hundreds of cormorants and hundreds, if not thousands, of white pelicans and pink-backed pelicans. These newcomers do not seem to have affected the flamingos; they do not compete for the same food. Indeed, blue-green algae, the staple of the lesser flamingo, is inexhaustible. The birds sift it from the saline water, pass it through their digestive tracts, fertilize the lake, and the algae reproduces itself within a twenty-four-hour period.

The main change that I noticed was that, because of the drought, the water level had dropped drastically, forcing me to walk far over the mudflats to reach the flamingos. My biggest surprise was to find that the few waterbuck had increased to thousands (there are no lions in the neighborhood to keep them down), and we even saw a single buffalo, a new addition to the local mammalian fauna. In the distance we saw several Rothschild's giraffes, a rare form of the common giraffe. There is now talk about releasing a dozen rhinos, perhaps more. This should keep the birders in their cars! So far we have been allowed to wander freely on foot, a privilege not granted in most other parks. The narrow belt of acacias and fever trees around the lake that constituted the original park has been expanded to three times its width, and Nakuru is no longer just a bird lake.

Birding in the brushy plains, scrublands, riverine woodlands, montane forests, and lakes of East Africa is as exciting as any in the world. Many species are large, showy, and rather tame, and because of the semiopen terrain are relatively easy to photograph. During our stay of less than one month, I exposed exactly one hundred rolls of film, and Ginny shot fifty, making a combined total for us of more than five thousand transparencies of birds and mammals, as well as a few butterflies and flowers.

—JULY/AUGUST 1985

RUFFS AND REEVES

THESE DAYS I am at my desk or drawing board ten hours a day, seven days a week, working on the western *Field Guide to the Birds*. To be quite honest, I'd rather be out somewhere, just watching birds.

Ornithological journals and new books, still unread, accumulate on a nearby worktable. From time to time, for a breather, I may pick up the latest issue of *American Birds* to see what I've been missing at some of the birding hot spots.

American Birds is the only magazine that monitors bird populations on a continental scale—telling us of their ups and downs, their increases and declines. It also informs us of the rarities that make birding such a popular sport. However, there are a number of state or regional publications that do much the same thing for their own local bailiwicks. One of my favorites is *Records of New Jersey Birds*, published four times a year by the New Jersey Audubon Society.

I was thumbing through the field notes in the autumn issue when I read about the ruffs that were causing such a stir at Pedricktown in the lower Delaware Valley. These spectacular sandpipers from overseas have been appearing year after year at Pedricktown, consorting with the more modestly endowed North American shorebirds that are en route to the Arctic. In spring 1985 at least twelve different individuals were spotted by excited ruff watchers during March and April. There were nine males in breeding dress and three females, which traditionally are called "reeves."

I had never seen a ruff on our side of the Atlantic until my friend Noble Proctor showed me one here in Connecticut several years ago.

But I already knew the bird well on its home ground. I had seen it in passage in England and had even found a nest in Sweden, but it was in Holland, at DeBeer, that I was witness to the fantastic courtship ballet for which this sandpiper is famous.

DeBeer was one of the many fine bird refuges in the Netherlands. It was located right across the river mouth from the Hook of Holland, where the ferry docks after its night passage from Harwich, England. I am not sure whether this sanctuary still exists, because even at that time, thirty years ago, the pressures of commerce and the development of tidewater facilities threatened this choice bit of wetland.

My Dutch friends Tekke and Kist, who translated the European field guide into Dutch, and Professor Van Oordt, piloted me in my rented Austin to this low-lying coastal island where so many of the rare waders of western Europe found haven. In a broad depression, hemmed in by coastal dunes, was an extensive fen where the birds nested, unmolested by grazing cattle or by people—except for the occasional bird watcher who carried a special permit. As we crossed the water meadows, the mewing cries of lapwings came to our ears from every side, and the pure notes of redshanks indicated that they were nesting there too (we later found a nest).

Threading a tortuous path across the broad fen was a sluggish stream, narrow enough in places to hop across. It was on the banks of this little creek—if it could properly be called a creek—that the ruffs had established their arena, a flat, worn place on the muddy bank, where they cavorted and gyrated every day during the latter part of April and early May. Here, ruffs had probably danced and fought their mocks battles for years, for these dancing places are traditional. Some dancing grounds in Holland are known to have been used for more than a century.

After setting up my portable green burlap blind, I watched the performers at a distance of only a few yards. There were eight males, each one different in color pattern except for two white-ruffed birds that were about as similar in appearance as it is possible for two ruffs to be (no two ruffs are exactly alike). Another bird had a white ruff

The ruff (female ruffs are called reeves) is a rare visitor from Eurasia along the Atlantic Seaboard.

crossed by narrow black bars; one had a rufous ruff and rufous ear tufts, another a rufous ruff and black ears; there was also a black-ruffed bird with cream-colored ears and another blackish bird with white flecks on its ruff.

The flamboyant jousters stayed together as a group. Periodically they would fly off together and would usually return together. It was at the moment of return that I witnessed the greatest activity—much jumping up and down, wing waving, crouching, pirouetting, and posturing. They opposed each other like bantam cocks, with hackles spread to the fullest. The females, smaller by a third, were as nondescript as the males were resplendent. Whenever a reeve walked across the dancing ground as though she couldn't care less, every male was triggered into a frenzy of activity. If she paused to preen or feed close to one of the cocks, he would crouch low and remain motionless as if in gallant submission. During two days in the blind, I exposed several hundred feet of color film. I reported my adventure in my column "Bird's-Eye View" in *Audubon* magazine, and later I showed the best of my 16-millimeter footage to Audubon screen tour audiences in my film *Wild Europe*.

I have wondered: From which direction do our vagrant ruffs in North America come? Do they hop the North Atlantic as a few stray lapwings have done, or do they come by way of the narrow gap of the Bering Strait, which separates Alaska from Siberia? I suspect that they reach us via the latter route, because ruffs have definitely bred on the North Slope of Alaska, and they have also been seen courting at Gambell.

On any day in late April or May, the number of ruffs dancing and jousting on the fens and tundras that extend across the vast expanses of Siberia and northern Europe must run into the millions. In winter small contingents can be found anywhere from western Europe to India, but by far the greatest numbers spend the winter in Africa, where concentrations of nearly a million have been recorded at a single roost in the Senegal Delta and even greater numbers in Mali and in the Sokoto region of Nigeria. Indeed, tropical Africa swarms with ruffs except in the forested regions. Inevitably during their massive movements from one hemisphere to another, a few become lost and turn up far from home.

Until recent years, practically every ruff recorded in the United States was spotted in the fall, after most of the males had shed their jousting uniforms. At that season they look much like the drab females—in other words, like large pectoral sandpipers. Don Roberson, in his scholarly book, *Rare Birds of the West Coast*, lists fifty-two records for California prior to 1980, all of them in the fall or winter, none in breeding plumage. And yet in the eastern states, where the ruff is occurring with increasing frequency, we are beginning to see more and more brightly plumaged males, especially at favored spots such as Lake Onondaga in upstate New York and Pedricktown on the inside flank of New Jersey. At least three of the 1985 Pedricktown birds were repeats. Their photos were on file, confirming that they had returned to this favored bit of marshy meadow each spring for the last three or four years.

Surely they must be breeding somewhere on our continent, but where?

—JANUARY/FEBRUARY 1986

VULTURE VIGILS
ON FIVE CONTINENTS

JUST THE OTHER DAY a letter came to my desk with a bizarre proposal. The writer, when visiting Panama, had observed black vultures eating goose droppings. Everyone there knew that the *zopilotes* ate goose droppings; the vultures were the sanitation crew around the barnyard. Why not, he suggested, introduce the black vulture into the United States to clean up the mess on golf courses and in city parks where feral Canada geese were becoming such a nuisance?

I had to tell the man that the black vulture was already a resident of the United States, living as far north as southeastern Pennsylvania and southern Ohio, and still extending its range. It will be nesting in New Jersey before long, I am sure. One even spent the winter at a turkey vulture roost here in Connecticut. It was an interesting idea, anyway, but whether our resident black vultures will ever develop a culinary taste for Canada goose droppings remains to be seen.

Thinking back about vultures, I can only guess at how many days, even weeks, out of my life I have spent watching and photographing these ghoulish scavengers, so beautiful in the air, so unbeautiful when eyeball to eyeball.

Not far from the Taj Mahal in India I once sat beside a dejected Hindu herdsman while a swarm of vultures devoured his favorite ox, recently deceased.

In Ethiopia, during the dicey time when Haile Selassie's reign was drawing to a close, I used my 400-millimeter lens on lammergeiers (or bearded vultures) at a village garbage dump. Later, in the highlands, I baited these magnificent long-winged bone crackers with a

White-backed vultures feed on a zebra carcass.

dead goat while I sat behind my camera and tripod in the doorway of a tribesman's hut.

On another occasion, trying for griffon vultures in Spain, Guy Mountfort and I waited an entire day in two expertly concealed blinds. We placed the body of a deer in an open place at the foot of a gnarled dead cork oak. It was a perfect setting—one that Gustave Doré, the nineteenth-century illustrator, would have chosen for vultures. But not even a kite came to investigate. The Spanish horsemen and *guardas* who had helped us construct the hides seemed disappointed in the Inglés and the eccentric Americano when we returned to the *coto* at sundown and reported our lack of success.

Four years later, near the same spot in the Marismas, I tried a dead cow, and although one Egyptian vulture came to investigate during my absence, I drew a blank on the griffons. Yet Guy Mountfort, setting up his blind near the completely stripped and sun-dried backbone of a fallow deer, within twenty minutes focused his lens on nine vultures of three species—griffon, Egyptian, and the rare cinereous or "black" vulture.

My own experience with various vultures has shown them to be very capricious. Are they naturally wary—do they see the photographer through the holes in the blind? Or does the carrion have to be at precisely the right state of decomposition? Or, if vultures have recently fed, are they no longer interested in bait?

Once, at Bear Mountain in New York State, I hauled a deer that had collided with a car to an open slope, put up my burlap blind, and camouflaged it with wild grape vines, hoping to get close-ups of turkey vultures. For two long days I stewed in my own sweat while the carcass, thirty feet away, ripened and flies swarmed. The vultures, at a discreet distance, sat hunched in a tall, dead hemlock, like undertakers waiting to officiate at a burial. Had they detected my presence? On the third day, discouraged, I dismantled my blind. Less than three hours later a friend chanced by; as he approached, a cloud of vultures flew up. All that remained of the deer were a few scattered bones.

➤

In Africa my luck has varied. In western Uganda, before the days of Idi Amin and under the armed protection of a corporal of the game guards (in case of lions), I built a blind in a thornbush. The goat I purchased at the butcher shop in a nearby town soon brought in a host of white-backed vultures, several hoodeds, a white-headed vulture, a marabou stork, two white-necked ravens, and a black kite. Another goat on an equally promising hillslope in southern Kenya lured no takers up to the second day. I was surprised that not even a hyena had touched it during the night. I have had my best luck at lion kills in the Mara of Kenya and on the Serengeti Plain of Tanzania, where the big herds support large numbers of vultures.

There is a peck order of sorts among the African vultures. If bait is put out, the first ones to come in are often the hooded vultures, smaller than the others and less able to stand up for their rights. They may sample the goodies, and, once the coast seems clear, the white-backed vultures and Ruppell's griffons swarm in to tear the carcass apart. The white-headed vulture, more of a loner, comes later, and finally, when the bait is reduced almost to a skeleton, the powerful lappet-faced vulture arrives to crack the bones and feast on the marrow.

However, if lions have made the kill, hyenas usually have a go at it before the vultures have a chance. Then the hooded may be the *last* in the sequence, looking for any small tidbits left over.

It is appalling to watch scores of vultures, mostly white-backed, with a scattering of Ruppell's griffons, literally climbing two or three deep over one anothers' backs like a swarm of gigantic maggots. As my friend Al Maley comments: "A vulture has no culture. . . . Its food habits are simply offal!"

Our largest North American vulture, the California condor, is much in the news these days. It is now down to six in the wild (one breeding pair) plus the ten captives at the San Diego Zoo and eleven at Los Angeles, where it is hoped they will reproduce. The surviving birds flying high over the Sespe range can see Los Angeles from their station in the sky, at least on days when smog does not blot out the sprawling

White-backed vultures range throughout sub-Saharan Africa. Vultures often hold their wings extended while perched to help regulate their body temperature.

city, which lies only thirty or forty miles away. These six birds are now being trapped and brought in, with the National Audubon Society opposing this move by the fish and game department.

I remember my first visit to the condor country, fifty years ago. It was in 1936, when I stepped to the station platform in Los Angeles with scarcely more than six hours between trains. Five Junior Audubon members from the Eagle Rock High School, learning I was in town, took me to Sespe Canyon. My guides were four boys and a pretty blond girl, who looked like a teenage Marilyn Monroe. (In retrospect, could she have been Marilyn Monroe? Did she go to Eagle Rock High School?) These five well-informed kids showed me my first condors—tiny specks in the blue—and hurried me back to the station with only minutes to spare.

Four years later I saw condors to better advantage by abandoning the canyon floor and climbing to the ridges where the great birds glide on deflected air currents. As they floated past, with primary tips spread like fingers, they seemed prehistoric birds and, in a sense, they were, if we accept the opinion of one biologist who believes they are a "senile species far past its prime."

My old friend, dear Alexander Sprunt, less lucky than I on his first condor quest, was discovered by a group of bird watchers, I was told, lying beside the road at Sespe, trying to look like a cadaver. But the wily cathartids were not so easily duped.

In those days there was a population of about sixty birds that remained rather stable for at least another decade. In June 1953, James Fisher, the British ornithologist, and I drove through California on our one-hundred-day, thirty-thousand-mile tour around the continent. Sydney Peyton, a local orange grower and condor expert, offered to take us to see the condors, and the outing proved to be a high point of our transcontinental odyssey.

Leaving the citrus groves behind, we piloted the car into the foothills. The Sespe ridge is not high, but it is rugged, and quite soon we were hairpinning and spur-cutting up a road that quickly became a track. Every now and then Peyton got out to unlock a gate. After about an hour of skillful maneuvering, with Peyton's son at the wheel,

Today there are approximately two hundred California condors in the wild.

we reached the summit ridge. Below us, and around us, was chaparral. Mountain quail intoned a fruity *wook?*, and wren-tits sang their accelerated trill. James Fisher ticked off these new birds for his world life list, and they were soon to be followed by the lazuli bunting and Lawrence's goldfinch.

"But we aren't after dickey birds," I reminded him. "I'm worried about the cloud cover. Even if we could see, it's bad soaring weather for raptors."

On a rocky overlook we sat down to wait. Later James wrote in *Wild America*:

Peyton produced from a paper bag the most wonderful oranges. The cloud flowed around the deep, broad canyon below us; then suddenly it lifted like a curtain. Quickly we put down our big oranges and swept the amphitheater of rocks with our field glasses. A dark semicircular cave on a flat sandstone face held our attention.

"That's the cave in Hopper Canyon," said Peyton, "one of the best places—a roosting place." And as he spoke two specks floated across the rock wall, half circled, slid out of sight, but not before we had got a quick focus on them with telescopes.

"So small," I said. "Can they be?"

"Oh yes, they're condors," said Peyton. "How far away do you think that cave is?"

"Mile, or so?"

"Four. Seven miles by trail. But the birds don't like the weather. I hope they'll soar, but I'm very much afraid they won't."

We looked for the sun. Would it break through the cloud veil enough to warm the canyon basins? Certainly the cloud was lifting, breaking. We waited, scanned the great wall in Hopper Canyon, and ate more oranges from Peyton's inexhaustible bag. We finally had to give up. Regretfully we turned to the car.

"Why the hurry?" said Peyton, quietly, from behind his binoculars. We followed the slant of them, to a speck in the sky. The speck was a California condor, and it was coming our way.

It came right over. I could not estimate its height, but we had a perfect view. It was like a bomber, its flat-winged posture quite unlike the glider-dihedral of the turkey vulture. It was huge, black, pale-headed, and as it came over, the big white bands forward on its underwing showed it to be an adult. For five minutes we watched its monstrous ten-foot span, its primaries spread like fingers. It made a couple of slow flaps, as if it had all the time in the world, caught a new thermal, and soared away to the southeast until it became a tiny speck and disappeared.

"Tally most incredibly ho!" James said as he ticked it off on his checklist. It had been well worth seeing . . . worth traveling ten thousand miles to see.

At the time that James Fisher and I visited the condor country, a last-ditch attempt was being promoted by a faction of conservationists who believed that when a bird is so desperately down, any straw—even artificial propagation—is worth grasping. Belle Benchley, director of the San Diego Zoo (who introduced James to koalas), had demonstrated that she could successfully hand raise Andean condors. By removing and incubator-hatching the first egg, a second fertile egg could be procured in a short time. Then, by removing the half-grown young, a double breeding could be induced the following year. This resulted in four hand-reared young in the period in which it would take wild birds to raise a single youngster. In the belief that this could be duplicated with California condors, a permit was issued by the California Fish and Game Commission, over the protests of an opposing faction of conservationists. Two birds were to be trapped alive. Although Lew Walker of the Arizona-Sonora Desert Museum tried for several months to accomplish his mission of trapping the birds (outside the reservation), he failed because they would not step into the noose (they rest on their tarsi). The permit ran out; nearly thirty years were lost before biologists revived the project.

How long will it be, we wonder, before the California condor joins the La Brea condor, the Grinnell eagle, the La Brea stork, the La Brea owl, and the California turkey? In the slow flow of time, many more species have lost their grip on existence than grace the globe today. The California condor has seen a lot of history; it was here long before man became man. Today the last six wild birds still patrol the sky, while above, at a height of thirty-thousand feet, jet planes from California's mushrooming airfields trace their ribbons of frozen vapor through the blue.

⤙

Though the California condor may be seeing its last days (we hope not), its even biggest relative to the south, the Andean condor, survives in some numbers, especially in the more southern reaches of the Andes. In Chile I have seen as many as eighteen in a day's drive.

Thirty years ago, during my flamingo expeditions to western Bolivia and northern Chile, I looked for this largest of all soaring birds, and in nearly a month of fieldwork in the high cordillera, I observed but one. On the coast, however, I saw several in an afternoon's walk along the sea cliffs, so I decided that rather than attempt to photograph these elusive giants in the mountains, I would try for them by the sea (apparently they are absent from the two-hundred-mile-wide belt of dead desert between the Andes and the coast—there is nothing there to eat).

The coastal city of Antofagasta, Chile, lies in a rainless region, devoid of vegetation, even grass, so my companion, Luis Peña of Santiago, and I soon discovered that vulture bait—animals such as goats—was nonexistent. However, there were burros. How they managed to survive was a question. Several near the municipal refuse dump were feeding on garbage and paper. Inquiries at the dump disclosed no dead burrows, but the horribly filthy man who lived in an igloo of garbage said he could perhaps find us a dead dog or two. When we returned later that day, he delivered three mongrels, recently deceased. Two were red, one was gray. Other pariah dogs circled about us, sniffing at their departed comrades in an embarrassed sort of way.

We gave "the king of the garbage dump," as Peña called him, a couple packs of cigarettes for his trouble. Gingerly lifting the three canines by their tails, we placed them in the back of our Dodge Power Wagon for the thirty-mile haul to the coastal promontory where we knew condors would pass. The sun was setting in a splash of color over the Pacific when we arrived at our encampment, and we decided it best to bury the dogs in a shallow trench to foil the night-foraging foxes. We dug the pit thirty feet from the truck and at least fifty feet from my sleeping bag, but apparently every flea harbored by these three dogs found me before morning, and for some days later I was still scratching the miserable bites they inflicted on my exposed arms.

Picking a site for the blind was done carefully—we found an open spot with a photogenic cluster of rocks on which the condors might sit, and another pile of rocks on a slope a hundred feet away, where we constructed a natural blind. There were many loose granite rocks at our disposal, and these we stacked into a circular wall, enclosing the top with a piece of canvas weighted at the edges by sand and stone. Just before we put the finishing touches on this small fortress, three turkey vultures soared lazily past, and then, heading directly for us, sailed a condor, a juvenile. It passed over at less than one hundred feet, circled back to investigate us more carefully, then moved on. This was bad. We had not yet put out the dogs, but we had not wanted the birds to see us at work.

It was late in the morning before I got into the blind, where I stayed until my companion relieved me at 6:00 P.M. The turkey vultures had arrived within twenty minutes, but they were cautious and sat all afternoon at a distance of a hundred yards. Once in a while, a vulture soared over the now fetid dogs, and its dark shadow crossed the canvas that separated me from the sun. But no condors. The wind by now had freshened, while the air in my crowded quarters was not so fresh. The breeze blew directly up the slope from the carcasses to my stuffy hideout.

Through the numerous chinks in my rocky cell, I could see the ocean to my right. Once I caught a sight of a great flock of guanay cormorants, a long black river of birds, an endless ribbon beating low over the waves. I wondered whether vultures have such keen eyes that they could see me through the small holes of my blind. Spreading my focusing cloths and my dark jacket against the walls to eliminate this hazard, I plugged them in place with small stones.

I was willing to spend three days if necessary to get my pictures—
and three days I stayed. On the second morning the turkey vultures
came within six feet of the bait, and I got several portraits—but I
could have accomplished as much in New Jersey. It was not until the
morning of the third day that a vulture touched the carrion. Three
birds were so bold as to start to feed, and immediately vultures
poured in from all directions. From my peephole I counted fifty on
the sand. Then, as suddenly as this activity had built up, it subsided.
A wave of fear seemed to come over the mob. Withdrawing to a distance of fifty yards or more, they just sat and waited. It must have
been about this time that the two condors flew over. I did not see
them, but Luis Peña reported that they circled overhead two or three
times, then continued down the coast.

A fourth day might have produced results, but I had to return to
catch my plane. I don't really know whether more days would have
turned the trick. I recalled that John Pemberton, many years ago, put
out thirty carcasses before he succeeded in getting photographs of
California condors.

If I ever try for Andean condors again, it will be at Paracas, south
of Lima on the coast of Peru, where they soar along the cliffs searching for dead sea lions and other stranded marine fare.

—MARCH/APRIL 1986

RETURN TO
THE SERENGETI

TANZANIA, larger than Britain, Ireland, France, the Netherlands, and Denmark combined, is less often visited by intrepid birders than its smaller East African neighbor, Kenya. It is especially famous for the vast herds of wildebeests and other ungulates that migrate seasonally through the Serengeti Plain.

Because access from Nairobi had become more difficult in recent years, I had not been in Tanzania for twenty years, not since 1966, when I joined John Livingston and a film crew from the Canadian Broadcasting Corporation as a cameraman and consultant.

This last February I had my chance to go again because my wife, Ginny, thought I should have a respite from my labors on the western field guide. I needed no urging, even though I knew it would delay progress on the book by yet another three weeks or more. But I go stir-crazy if I am at my desk and drawing board for more than three or four months at a stretch.

Wes Henry, my stepson-in-law, and my old friend John Wana-maker were the leaders of our group, the members of which were mostly alumni of Principia College. I had just purchased a 600-millimeter Nikon ED-IF lens, and the Minolta people had loaned me their sensational new self-focusing 9000 to try out, but when I learned that the fifteen people—ten men and five women—were to travel together in a single big yellow tour bus, I knew that it would be all but impossible to photograph birds. If even one of the fifteen moved while I was focusing the 600-millimeter lens, I'd get a fuzzy picture. So I opted for a separate Land Rover with a roof hatch, where I could stabilize my long lens on a cloth bag filled with rice.

This vehicle I shared with my friend Seymour Levin—"Sey"—who, like me, had brought enough equipment to stock a small camera shop.

During this first week of February, the big herds of wildebeests, somewhere between 1.2 and 1.8 million strong and increasing, were in the southern Serengeti. The females, exceedingly pregnant, were on the eve of dropping their calves, held back only by the reluctance of the clouds to release the life-giving rains.

To reach Ndutu, the lodge within a half hour's drive of the herds, we took the long, tortuous route past Lake Natron, a desolate soda lake where the bulk of the East African flamingos congregate to breed. Although at least 4 million lesser flamingos feed on the blue-green algae in the foul alkaline lakes of the Great Rift Valley, their nesting stronghold was a mystery until 1954, when the late Leslie Brown,

Masai boys with cattle in the Serengeti.

scouting by air, found their secret colony far out on the soda flats of Lake Natron. The local Masai never ventured out on the treacherous mud. They could not see the nesting colony, upward of a million birds, because it was invisible in the distance, lost in the shimmering mirage. However, the young birds, when quite grown but lacking the pink plumage of their parents, would suddenly appear after a long trek in the open pools at the edge of the soda flats. Because the Masai had never seen a nest, they believed the young emerged fully feathered from the mud, a phoenixlike phenomenon.

➤

Lake Natron, lying in an alkaline sink of the Great Rift, is about forty-five miles long and twenty miles across. It looks rather like a moonscape, or a scene out of Hell, with four or five pools of open water surrounded by miles of crystalline soda that appears a coconut-icing pink from a distance. Mirages shimmer in the stupefying heat.

We could see a few flocks of flamingos that had come to drink at the seepage of springs around the edges. Forewarned, we had taken with us flasks of water to prevent serious dehydration. I recalled Leslie Brown's horrifying description of his ordeal when he tried to reach the colony on foot. A foolhardy thing to do, but how was he to know? Starting out from camp at the foot of Mount Gelai (9,653 feet), he had walked a little way out onto the white soda that lined the shore; it was hard and firm—an aircraft could have landed on it. It stretched away, glittering in the sun with blinding whiteness. With the reflected heat striking him in the face, he walked out over the hard soda until it began to give way to pink, slushy water. Although he had gum boots, he tried a pair of mud boards, but because of the viscous mess he found them too difficult to use. He discarded them.

The soda crust was overlaid by a thin layer of pink, stinking water, already hot from the sun and scumming with dead locusts that had flown into it. He began to crack through the crust, which grew thinner as the water deepened, and each of his footsteps was marked by a foul-smelling black patch. He crossed the slushy water to a soda flat that looked firmer. It was not flat and hard as was that near shore but had formed polygonal plates with raised edges rather like giant water lily leaves. They had weak spots where he broke through to the mud beneath.

—✦—

Panting and gasping with the effort, he floundered on and on until he cracked through with both feet. Crawling out on hands and knees, he reeled with fatigue. His gum boots were full of chunks of crystalline soda that were cutting his feet. It was hopeless. Far more exhausted than he knew, he had to retrace the same ground in the hottest hours of the day, and without any spare water. When, after an agonizing struggle, he regained the hard soda, he sat down, took off his gum boots, and had a look at his feet. They gave him an unpleasant shock. They were covered with enormous, bright red blood blisters, which, exposed to the air, slowly turned brown, then black.

A seven-mile walk over the lava rubble brought him back to camp, where he lay down in a cool stream rushing down the mountainside. He sucked in the fresh water by the gallon while little fish nibbled at his blisters. But he didn't care.

The ordeal was not yet over. Next morning, with intense burning pain in his feet, which had turned septic, he faced a forty-five-mile drive to Magadi along a rough and twisted track. At Magadi he languished for ten days in the hospital of the soda company, with his feet in bandages. They did not have to be cut off as he had feared, but in the end he had to have skin grafts.

—✦—

I thought of this when we arrived at our campsite on the lower slope of Mount Gelai, the very same spot, I suspect, where Leslie Brown had pitched his tent. There was a rushing stream nearby where the Masai watered their cattle and where baboons came to drink. To reach this idyllic spot, where we put up our own tents, we had to negotiate the roughest track imaginable, first up a rocky streambed, then over a tussock-covered hill where an unskilled turn of the wheel would have sent our vehicle toppling down the slope.

Next morning, while the other members of our party went upstream to a beautiful waterfall, we took the Land Rover down to the lake. A few flamingos were close inshore, drinking fresh water from the spring, while wildebeests and zebras grazed nearby. We drove out on the soda flats until the dark tracks of our vehicle warned us to turn back. I tried the 600-millimeter lens with its 1.4X extender on the nearest flamingos and got some fairly good shots. On our return I had a chance at some white-fronted bee-eaters.

That afternoon, all of us went to a Masai village, where I photographed a gang of more than a hundred donkeys, each with its attendant cattle egret. We had another go at the flamingos and then started homeward, to be met by a blinding dust storm, the worst I had ever experienced. Driven by winds of fifty to sixty miles per hour, it hit us like a brown wall. When we reached camp just as darkness fell, we found that most of our tents had been blown flat (mine hadn't!). Soon it was pelting rain. Despite the wind and rain, the tents were put up again, only to be flattened at 11:00 P.M. by another tornadolike blast funneling down the canyon.

So this was Africa? The neophytes in our party who had never been to Africa before were dismayed by the long, very long, rough rides through arid scrub and by the dust and the heat. They had had to put up their own tents and, so far, had seen few animals. It was not at all like the posh lodges and game viewing their friends had told them about. I had warned them beforehand that Natron would be the pits, sort of a hellhole, but reassured them that things would get better and better and better until we reached Ngorongoro Crater, the nearest thing to Eden on this earth.

As we drove south through the open plains and acacia groves, antelope, zebras, giraffes, and wildebeests became more frequent. White storks, hundreds of them, were on passage from South Africa to Europe and Asia. Abdim storks, black with white bellies, were even more numerous; some stalked the plains, others milled high overhead on the thermals. They were on their way to their seldom visited nesting grounds in the Sudan.

At Ndutu Lodge, overlooking a half-dry lake bed where lions lounged and zebras came to drink, I ran into a number of old friends—it was like a gathering of the clan; yet I can walk through the supermarket at home without meeting a soul that I know!

Even the most single-minded birder cannot ignore the mammals—the dik-diks (small antelope), impalas, gerenuk and Tommies (both gazelles), Grant's gazelles, hartebeests, hyenas, jackals, bat-eared foxes, and even serval cats. Swarming across the open plain were countless wildebeests. These big-bearded gnu surrounded our vehicle—hundreds of thousands of them, from horizon to horizon.

Far out on the plain, we came upon Hidden Valley and a small lake where the herds slaked their thirst and where red-billed ducks, yellow-billed ducks, hottentot teal, Egyptian geese, and other web-footed fowl dabbled about. Elegant crowned cranes stripped the sedges of their seeds. But, I wondered, why so many terns? There were no fish in this transient lake. The terns were gull-billed, and I soon discovered what they were eating—dung beetles, huge scarabs that rolled their balls of dung over the ground wherever we looked, and with so many wildebeests there was plenty of dung with which to play their rolling games and in which to lay their eggs.

➤

The plains en route to Seronera, to the north, were relatively empty. The migrations would be under way after the big rains in April. I had not visited Seronera since the modern lodge was built. Recent travelers had said things were run-down, but I thought the lodge was splendid, imaginatively designed around a rocky kopje (small hill). It must have cost millions, and the swallows, swifts, and rock hyraxes had made it their happy home. The problem was to keep baboons out of the rooms.

What a far cry from my first visit to Seronera, nearly thirty years ago, when I went there alone with my driver. I thought I was the only nonnative other than the district commissioner within five hundred square miles until I ran into Bruce Wright, a Canadian who was studying lion predation. I slept alone in a thatched hut with lions roaring and hyenas howling right outside. I didn't know whether I should sleep in the bed or under it.

On one of our early morning drives, we came upon a martial eagle, the most powerful of Africa's raptors, that had taken a dik-dik and had carried it into a large acacia. Although the bird was tame enough, poor light precluded photography.

On our way to the hippo pool west of Seronera, we suddenly jammed on our brakes. There in front of us was a green mamba (a deadly snake) that was confronting a chameleon of the same emerald shade of green, but the battle was a standoff. The lizard was obviously too large for the snake to swallow.

Ngorongoro Crater, where we spent three memorable days, was the high point of our safari. More than one hundred square miles in area, it is the year-round refuge of perhaps 25,000 herd animals. The beleaguered rhinos are slowly increasing in number. There are now about twenty. We saw five, one with a baby.

Our camp for three nights was on the floor of the crater, close to a fever tree forest teeming with elephants. My tent was under the umbrella of an immense strangler fig, and I thought of the accident last year in which one of these ancient parasitic trees, no longer supported at its core by its host tree (long since decayed), collapsed without warning. It wiped out several tents, killing one young woman and gravely injuring several other people.

Our driver, Pius, who had served twelve years in the Tanzanian army, became quite adept at spotting and maneuvering close to birds for my lens, even the little brown jobs. He knew that I had enough blacksmith plovers, crowned plovers, and laughing doves. I wanted rosy long-claws, rufous-winged larks, Fisher's sparrow-larks, antchats, and the various wheatears and pipits.

With a population of more than one hundred lions in the crater, kills are frequent. They are usually made at night, as Bill Gunn and I discovered when we were filming for CBC (we followed lions about with the floodlights of our car). By dawn the lions, hyenas, and jackals have usually had their fill, but the vultures do not arrive until it is warm enough to ride the thermals from their roosts, often in canyons many miles away. White-backed vultures and Ruppell's griffon vultures are the most numerous. When everything is reduced to a few scraps of skin and bones, the Nubian or lappet-eared vulture, biggest of all, arrives to break the bones and extract the marrow. When a wildebeest or a zebra is killed by a lion, seven or eight other species of mammals and birds may feed on it, and all flows back to the ancient soils of Africa.

✦

Stopping briefly at Olduvai, a desolate gully where Mary Leakey had discovered the million-year-old fossilized bones of *Zinjanthropus,* the early hominid, we found that the marble plaque commemorating the discovery had been shattered by a Masai warrior who struck it with his spear.

A new lodge that did not exist when I made my earlier trips was Gibbs' Farm, a delightful English-style luncheon stop with a garden full of birds. A cement-lined pool planted with water lilies and cattails was alive with grosbeak weavers building their intricate globular nests among the reeds. Sunbirds of two sorts probed the red-hot pokers. A white-eyed slaty flycatcher hopped to the ground near me to investigate a large wolf spider, which raised its forelegs in defense. The flycatcher backed off.

✦

Lake Manyara is where the lions climb trees; at least they used to. We saw no tree-climbing lions this time, nor any leopards. (Had they been poached?) But the birds were as good as ever, especially along the riverbank near the hippo pools, where cars are allowed to leave the road. Water dikkops or stone curlews eyed us from the river's edge. Common sandpipers, ruffs, and yellow wagtails from Eurasia stalked for flies on the backs of the hippos. Large flocks of fulvous and white-faced whistling ducks and Egyptian geese lent animation to the scene.

When we returned to the pool after lunch, hundreds of white pelicans and pink-backed pelicans had gathered. I had once filmed a Dalmatian pelican there, the first record for East Africa. As we watched the show, a dust storm like the one we experienced at Natron blew in across the flats, quickly enveloping us and the birds in a brown pall. The pelicans, yellow-billed storks, and marabous huddled shoulder to shoulder, heading into the wind and rain. When the wind changed direction they shifted in unison, always facing the gale. By contrast, a nearby herd of wildebeests presented their rumps to the wind.

➤

If bird listing is your thing, Kenya is preferable to Tanzania. But for the big herd animals and dramatic landscape, go to Tanzania. A compromise would be the Mara on the Kenya border, where Lars Lindblad has recently established a luxury camp for his Intrepids clientele.

We were told that since the film *Out of Africa* reached the theaters, tourism in East Africa has increased by 30 percent. Certainly for well-heeled birders, or for those who have simply saved their pennies, there is no better place to build up a world list.

—MAY/JUNE 1986

Marabou storks occur from Senegal to Sudan and the Transvaal.

FLORIDA'S
HOT SPOTS

GEORGE HARRISON once asked me to name my favorite places for birding in North America, the best spots. I paused a moment and said, "There are so many good places."

"Well, let's say the top ten or twelve," he replied.

I quickly named eleven, then added a place I had not yet seen but would soon visit—the Big Bend of the Platte River in Nebraska, rendezvous of the migrating cranes.

George and his wife, Kit, set out the following year in their Oldsmobile station wagon with all their camera gear to travel to these strategic places, which have been magnets not only to me but also to innumerable other birders. Over the next few months they covered 32,693 miles getting to and from these places, 25,935 by car and 6,768 on commercial airlines. The end result was their book published ten years ago, *Roger Tory Peterson's Dozen Birding Hotspots*.

If I were to name a dozen hot spots on our continent for bird photography, rather than binocular birding, I would have to think a bit. The fish wharfs at Monterey, California, would certainly be high on the list. There among the shops, ship chandleries, and boat slips, I have photographed as many as twenty species of birds at frame-filling proximity in a single day—loons, grebes, scoters, cormorants, pelicans, and gulls, as well as marbled godwits, turnstones, and other shorebirds on the adjacent beaches.

On the eastern side of the continent, I would rate the Ding Darling Wildlife Refuge on Sanibel Island on the southwest coast of Florida as tops. There I can make the five-mile drive along the dyke that winds through the mangroves, shooting birds from the car by simply rolling down the window partway so as to steady my 400-millimeter lens.

The Intrepids, a travel club of which I once acted as president, had a board meeting last April at Captiva, just across the bridge from Sanibel. We all stayed at 'Tween Waters Inn, Lloyd Wright's haven for fishermen and bird watchers, where fish crows come to the balconies for a handout, chuck-will's-widows call at night, pileated woodpeckers fly between the palm trees, and brown pelicans vie with a big orange tabby cat for fish when the boats come in. A very tame egret that has been around for four years is also on hand when the fish are gutted at the dock, and a little blue heron will actually take shrimp from the hand.

Each posh home on this barrier island and along the Sanibel waterfront has its own herons or white ibis that seem to regard the well-kept lawns as their own bailiwicks. Willets and sanderlings mix with the bathers on the outer beach, and ospreys nest on platforms that have been put up on poles for their convenience. But the adjacent Ding Darling Refuge is the star attraction.

That refuge was named after the famed political cartoonist and conservationist from Iowa who designed the first federal duck stamp in 1934 (the same year my first field guide came out). In 1936 he conceived and launched the National Wildlife Federation and in 1938 designed its first stamp sheet—sixteen game birds and mammals handled in a manner reminiscent of his cartoons. The following year I painted fifteen songbirds for the sheet of eighty subjects and have been involved in one way or another with the stamp program ever since.

The afternoon is not the time to see the refuge at its best. In fact my wife, Virginia, and I found the place almost deserted when we made the tour in midafternoon shortly after our arrival. The sun was in our eyes, photography was impossible, and all we saw was a single egret and a couple of anhingas. I had never seen so little at the Ding Darling. And yet, when I went out at 6:30 the next morning, just as the rising sun was clearing the trees, I had never found it better. Egrets,

A little blue heron at Ding Darling National Wildlife Refuge.

tricolored herons, little blues, and great blues stalked the mangrove-lined ditch beside the road, and I exposed roll after roll of Kodachrome. When I reached the first open body of water, a feeding frenzy was going on—at least a hundred egrets and herons interspersed with spoonbills and a few white ibis were gobbling up a run of tiny fish. Anhingas spread their wings in the morning sun, while cormorants swam and dived in the shallows. On a sandbar just offshore, at least two hundred willets, dunlins, knots, and dowitchers crowded together while black skimmers knifed the water nearby.

Each morning the tableau was repeated, and I wondered whether the members of the television crew from British Broadcasting who planned to film the Ding Darling were aware of the timing of this early morning show. They were scheduled to go on the air live at five o'clock on Saturday afternoon as part of a worldwide "Bird Watch."

My old school pal Lorimer Moe, who now has his own bit of Eden on Sanibel, suggested that we go to Corkscrew Swamp, the sanctuary owned and operated by the National Audubon Society for the benefit of the wood storks that nest in the ancient stands of cypress. I had memories of Corkscrew as it was more than thirty years ago, when John Baker acquired the primeval tract for the Audubon and ordered the long boardwalk to be built so that people could see the nesting storks as well as the herons, ibis, pileated woodpeckers, and barred owls that frequented the swamp.

In those days, before the AOU Check-list Committee changed the name, we called the wood stork the "wood ibis." Some years they nested by the thousands, depending on water levels, but recently their numbers have dropped drastically, and some seasons they have not been able to bring off their young. This year only a few birds, perhaps two hundred, were attempting to nest at the time of our visit. We were told that because of water levels the storks would have trouble getting enough food for their ravenous young. Aside from the few wood storks that flew overhead, we saw little else. Perhaps it was too late in the day.

Having remembered the way Corkscrew was in the old days, I was saddened, for this was a reflection of much of the rest of South Florida and particularly of Everglades Park, farther south, quite in contrast to the Ding Darling and the mangrove coast, where there seemed to be plenty of birds.

I planned to visit Everglades Park; I hadn't seen it for some years. Ginny didn't want me to make the five-hour drive by myself, so she put me in the hands of George Weymouth, an expert tour leader who guides groups around Sanibel and elsewhere in Florida to supplement his income as a wildlife artist and bird carver. He would drive and also help me haul my tripods and heavy camera bags.

As we were speeding along the highway that slices across the state just north of the park, I was surprised to see a big yellow sign that read "Panther Crossing—Five Miles." I took a photograph of it for my slide collection of signs—"Moose Crossing," "Alligator Crossing," "Slow down for Koalas and Children," et cetera. George told me that so many panthers or cougars—at least twenty of them—had been killed crossing the old road that the highway had been widened and broad verges were opened up so that a panther or deer could see what was coming and not be killed as it leaped blindly across just as a car bore down on it. Some estimates place the present population of panthers at no more than thirty. If this is so, highway kills must have been the decisive factor, exceeding reproductive replacement.

➤

As George Weymouth and I left Homestead and drove through the groves of slash pine that led into the park, we noticed that the crows that fed so fearlessly along the grassy edges were all American crows—every one of them—whereas at Sanibel and Captiva every last crow was a fish crow, with its distinctive *ca* or *ca-ha*, not the honest-to-goodness *caw* of its larger relative. For the first time in my life I was able to take frame-filling shots of ordinary American crows, every feather shining. Cattle egrets, recent invaders of Florida, also stalked the grassy verges, looking for insects, and with the crows made dramatic studies in black and white.

Anhinga Trail, a long boardwalk into the marsh, has always been the best place for close-ups of anhingas and purple gallinules. I photographed them there when the boardwalk was first built, forty years ago, and since then thousands of tourists have exposed countless rolls of film of these obliging birds. The pair or two of purple gallinules that are always on hand must be the most photographed birds in all of Florida. But where were the ibis, wood storks, and herons?

We did see spoonbills and egrets as they came to roost in the trees on the far side of one of the other ponds farther down the line, looking like so many pink and white Christmas tree ornaments. But the glades were not anything like they were nearly fifty years ago, when I drove down the old dirt road before the park was created.

John Baker of National Audubon had a lot to do with the establishment of the park in 1947, because it was evident that this watery wilderness had already been reduced by more than half. It has been estimated that in the 1930s 2.5 million long-legged wading birds visited the Everglades each spring, as compared with 250,000 today, a

90 percent decline. However, we can take comfort in the knowledge that roseate spoonbills and reddish egrets have increased elsewhere in Florida and in Texas and that several of the egrets and herons as well as the glossy ibis have pushed their breeding ranges north as far as New England. White ibis and wood storks seem to have had the greatest declines.

In 1937 it seemed as though every white ibis in Florida had gathered in the "jams" on the St. Johns River north of Lake Washington. The birds were well protected that year by the Audubon wardens and by the weather. Seven of the eighteen miles of road that we traversed from Lake Washington to Turtle Mound, where we kept the boat, had been flooded by torrential rains, and fish swam down the road in front of the car! When we reached the square mile of willows and buttonbush where the birds congregated, we could stand in our flat-bottomed boat and look into the nests. Long, gooselike strings of white birds twisted down out of the blue sky in snaky streamers. The late Alexander Sprunt calculated there were 500,000 birds; but others, more cautious, put the figure at 200,000. The following year the site was abandoned. Ibis shift with the varying water levels, especially in the state of Florida.

The Everglades is a vast "river of grass" with an average water depth of only eighteen inches. It springs from the broad overflowing sump of Lake Okeechobee and crawls for a hundred miles down an imperceptible slope at the rate of a tenth of a mile a day until it reaches the saline waters of Florida Bay.

Since the beginning of the century, developers have been draining the Everglades, turning the rich muck south of Lake Okeechobee into farms and diverting water to be used by growing Miami. To control the yearly cycle of water flow, there were all sorts of management projects, resulting in fourteen hundred miles of dikes, levees, ditches, and canals. A great highway, Alligator Alley, cutting midway across the glades, blocked much of the natural flow into the park, which then was nourished erratically mainly by rainfall.

But all this may change. The Army Corps of Engineers, recognizing past mistakes, is planning to correct things. The straitjacketed

Kissimmee River will be forced back into its old oxbows. Alligator Alley will have more bridges and culverts to allow the seasonal water flow into the glades, and twenty-three well-placed undercrossings will reduce the roadkills of wildlife.

— ✦ —

Paradoxically, when George Weymouth and I returned late in the afternoon to the marina at Flamingo, we had some of the best photography of the day. A "great white" heron, the white morph of the great blue, strode around as though it owned the place. Was it the same one that frequented the wharves fifteen or twenty years ago? I doubt it. Although it looked superficially like a great egret, its pale flesh-colored legs identified it. White ibis probed the lawns near the parking lot. Several black vultures came in when the fish were being gutted, allowing us an eyeball to eyeball approach. Turkey vultures, less trusting, sailed lazily overhead.

At Flamingo, as at 'Tween Waters and many another place in Florida, the seriocomic brown pelicans had literally become bums, finding it easier to demand a handout than to fish for themselves. How different was the public attitude toward pelicans in John James Audubon's day. He wrote, "I procured specimens at different places but nowhere so many as at Key West. There you would see them flying within pistol shot of the wharfs, the boys frequently trying to knock them down with stones."

Audubon noted that the numbers of pelicans had been considerably reduced, "so much indeed that . . . where twenty or thirty years ago [the birds were] quite abundant very few individuals are now seen." He found the pelicans "year after year retreating from the vicinity of man," and he feared they would be "hunted beyond the range of civilization" and the student of nature would be obliged to sail to Tierra del Fuego to see them.

Today when a pelican appears on a Florida dock, people throw fish, not stones. At Venice, Florida, I saw a pelican walk into a fish store and stand expectantly before the counter!

We can thank Theodore Roosevelt for saving the pelican when its numbers were at low ebb, by creating the first federal refuge, on the

Brown pelicans wait to be fed a fishy lunch. (Virginia M. Peterson)

east coast of Florida. The three-acre Pelican Island was followed by fifty-six more wildlife refuges during Roosevelt's tenure as president. Now there are more than four hundred, embracing millions of acres.

On our way home from the park by way of Fort Myers, George and I stopped at the salt lagoon that separates the sea from the high-rise condominiums where the beautiful people loll under their beach umbrellas. If there is a better place to photograph shorebirds at close range, I do not know if it. I suppose it is because of the beach strollers and sunbathers that the birds have become so tolerant of people like me with cameras. Resting my camera lens on a monopod instead of my unwieldy tripod, I clicked off shots of black-bellied plovers (still in winter plumage), turnstones, knots, western sandpipers, whimbrels, godwits, piping plovers, Wilson's plovers, and even a clapper rail that ventured out of the mangroves. Best of all was a very tame reddish egret that danced for me in its crazy manner. One could spend a whole day there, working one side of the lagoon, then the other.

When I unloaded my gear at 'Tween Waters and put twenty more rolls of exposed film into the refrigerator, Ginny informed me that during my absence things had gotten even better at the Ding Darling. A remarkably tame red-shouldered hawk had posed for her at a distance of less than fifteen feet, a yellow-crowned night-heron went about its business of building a nest close to the road, and the pelicans at the Captiva marina put on a great show as usual.

But I was content with my luck. I had also put on a tan and felt normal again. Now back to the drawing board!

—July/August 1986

Tricolored herons breed inland and along the coast of southern Florida.

THE MAINE
STORY

THAT DAY this past summer when I stepped from the car and stood on the hillside opposite the Audubon Camp in Maine I could not fight back the tears. There were too many memories. Across the tidal inlet was Hog Island, with its weathered buildings, looking much as they did fifty years ago—the old ship chandlery known as the Queen Mary with its boat dock, the headquarters buildings, and, surrounded by spruce trees, the "fish house," where we had slide lectures and classes.

This was to be the fiftieth anniversary celebration of the camp; it was to have been a joyous occasion, but we had just learned that Carl Buchheister had died that very morning. Carl, who launched the camp as its first director, had wanted so desperately to be there; it was the spot on this earth that he and his wife, Harriet, loved the most. But his failing body would not allow him to leave his wheelchair and life support system in North Carolina. There was only one way for him to join us. He could at least be with us in spirit.

Indeed, of the many guests who gathered, I was the only one who had been there the day the camp opened, way back in 1936, except for one camper, Juliet Richardson (now Juliet French), who was the first one to step off the train when the campers arrived.

Actually, I first laid eyes on Hog Island several years before that, when I was scarcely out of my teens. At that time I was acting as nature counselor at a boys' camp—Chewonki—at nearby Wiscasset. On one of my days off I was invited by a local resident, Mrs. Sortwell, to sail among the islands in her yacht and point out the birds. I clearly remember that after we had cruised past the ship chandlery on Hog

Island I spotted an osprey's nest. There have always been ospreys on Hog Island, usually three pairs that build their bulky nests in the tops of the largest conifers. They seem to have survived the DDT syndrome and are again raising normal broods.

It was in the fall of 1934, the year my first field guide was published, that John Baker took the helm of the faltering Audubon Society. I joined the staff on November 1, the very day Baker assumed the presidency. One of my first assignments was to do something about the Junior Audubon Clubs that had sparked my own interest in birds fifteen years earlier.

But John, a man who believed that education at the grassroots level was the key to future conservation activism, felt that just enrolling kids, giving them little membership buttons and leaflets with pictures to color, was not enough. He instructed me to prepare materials for the teachers. However, this would only partially do the trick, he reasoned. Wouldn't it be more effective to get to the teachers and youth leaders more directly? They would become the pupils, and we would be the teachers; thus the camp idea was conceived. The camp in Muscongus Bay in Maine was the first of several in various parts of the country.

In early June 1935, the year before the camp opened, I was sent to Maine to scout Hog Island as well as the woods, lakes, and fields on the nearby mainland and also to investigate the many islands in Muscongus Bay where some of the seabirds nested. A professional photographer from *Life*, Charlie Jacobs, accompanied me with his battery of still cameras, while I used an antique Bell + Howell, with which I took movies on inflammable 35-millimeter black-and-white stock. That was before the advent of convenient 16-millimeter cameras and Kodachrome.

The ospreys were easy enough to film, but not so the single pair of bald eagles that had their huge nest on Allen Island across the bay. After setting up my blind and covering it with spruce boughs, I hid for four hours before one of the parents dropped in with a large fish to feed the two half-grown young.

Although there was a small colony of great blue herons a half mile from camp on Hog Island and a larger one on the other side of Muscongus Bay, both rookeries were in situations that were almost impossible for satisfactory filming. I had been told of a small heronry on an island near Boothbay Harbor where the nests were fairly low. Selecting a smooth rock on which to put my blind, I then tried to get an intrusive sapling out of the way. I intended to bend it over as I would a birch and tie it down. But this was no birch. When I shinnied up and leaned backward, it did not bend but snapped off with a loud crack. Down I went, flat on my shoulders on the granite. For the next several days I was in great pain whenever I tried to get into or out of bed. That ended my wildlife photography in Maine for that season.

On the day camp opened in 1936, I was there again with my Bell + Howell. Baker asked me to film the arrival of the first campers at the railroad station. Juliet, already mentioned, came down the steps, where she shook hands with Baker and Buchheister. I documented it all—I thought. Later I discovered there was no film in the camera!

That first season at camp I was the bird instructor; Allan Cruickshank was my assistant. In succeeding years Allan took over my job. He had his own sense of humor and was very adept with the one-liners—rather like Bob Hope. Although we were very competitive, I could never top him.

When that first boatload of campers, mostly women, had been ferried across from the mainland, Allan and I met them at the dock. We introduced ourselves, then Allan said, "Ladies, if you behave and do your work well, Roger Peterson might take you on an owl walk." This was typical Cruickshank banter; but one young woman from Boston took Allan at his word. Just before the two-week session ended, she came to me and said, "What about that owl walk? I've done all my classwork and my fieldwork; I've done it well, I think." Obviously she was serious about the owls, so I thought a moment and said, "I'll meet you after lights out, and we'll see what luck we have."

That night, meeting outside the dorm, we started down the path that wound around the perimeter of the island through the spruce and balsam forest, and it *was* an owl walk, just that. I hooted like a barred owl on my cupped hands, but no answer. I intoned like a great horned. We listened. The owls didn't give a hoot.

Unbeknownst to us, a young woman from the Bronx and a friend were curious about what we were up to. They sneaked out of the dorm and tried to follow us. One of them stumbled in the dark and fell into the new well that was being dug. Having sprained her ankle, she couldn't get out. It was precisely at that time that John Baker arrived from New York to see how things were going. Carl Buchheister was leading him along the path to the cabin where he was to spend the night when they heard sounds of distress from the well. They fished out the young lady and were carrying her to the infirmary just as we were returning from our unsuccessful owl walk! I have often wondered whether that was why John Baker assigned me to other duties in the New York office the following summer.

The program at the Maine camp reflected the philosophy of Carl Buchheister. I had first met him when he was a Latin teacher at the Lawrence School of Long Island. He had formed a bird club at this prestigious girls' academy, and I was invited to speak. That was before Baker asked Carl, a very kind and dedicated man, to join the Audubon staff. Carl shared my own views and those of Baker, who felt that classroom biology and natural science were oriented too much in the Germanic tradition of the scalpel and the microscope. Young people and their teachers might know about the muscles in a frog's leg yet remain ignorant about the living animal, its habits, or even its name. The camp was designed to correct this, to take teachers outdoors and give them valid field experience.

Later, when Carl succeeded John Baker as president of the National Audubon Society and his duties consumed all of his time, the camp program was put successively in the hands of Bartram Cadbury, Duryea Morton, Stephen Kress, and an impressive number of instructors and docents. Even some of the boys who worked in the kitchen went on to distinguished careers in natural history and conservation.

When Joe Cadbury, Bart's brother, was the ornithology instructor on the island, he censused the nesting warblers and other birds year after year. There is talk that this project should be picked up again. In these days of acid rain, spruce budworm outbreaks, and destruction of the tropical rain forest, we might expect some of the birds to reflect these ecological ailments.

Since its inception, something like twelve thousand students have shared the delights and insights of the Maine camp. During our brief get-together to mark the fiftieth anniversary, Carl Buchheister was never out of our minds, but we kept things upbeat, as he would have wished.

On the day of the big celebration, it took three boats to hold us all as we sailed into the bay on a nostalgic voyage. Joe Johanson, the head boatman and manager, guided our little fleet among the islands, while Bart Cadbury, Dur Morton, Steve Kress, Phil Schaeffer, and I commanded the microphones, calling out birds whenever they were spotted. Before docking on a lovely spruce-covered island for our picnic lunch, we sailed past Eastern Egg Rock, where the puffins are now breeding. I thought of my first landing there with Allan Cruickshank shortly after we opened camp in 1936. Although Allan was a health buff who should have lived to be a hundred, he unfortunately did not reach his seventieth birthday. The summer after his death a few old friends gathered on the rock to dedicate it to his memory as a wildlife sanctuary, and I gave the eulogy. Allan was the most colorful of all the camp instructors and is missed by all who had the fortune to be in his classes. Whenever a new bird for the camp list was sighted on a boat trip into the bay, he would stand on his head on the fo'c'sle, until finally his wife, Helen, made him stop the practice.

During these days of ecological enlightenment, when we are bombarded with so much doom and gloom, it gives us a lift of spirit when we see a turnaround. Today, most of the birds of Maine's littoral are faring better than they did before the Audubon camp was opened in '34, and *far* better than they did at the turn of the century, when these same birds were at their nadir.

Nesting cormorants had been completely eliminated from New England waters by fishermen, who regarded them as competitors, suitable only for bait or for target practice. Just when survivors from the Maritime Provinces began to nest again south of the border is a vague guess, but in 1931, when Bob Allen of the Audubon Society made a survey cruise down east on the Maine coast, he discovered several newly established colonies, including a small group of eight nests on Old Hump Ledge in Muscongus Bay, a site that was to be monitored religiously over the years by the Audubon campers. In 1936 Allan Cruickshank and I found that the Old Hump colony had expanded to 150 pairs. Ten years later Cruickshank estimated that no fewer than 2,100 pairs nested in Muscongus Bay. Since then, double-crested cormorants have established colonies along almost the entire length of the New England coast, as far south and west as Long Island Sound in Connecticut, where the first ones took up residence within the past year or two.

➤

The studies by H. L. Mendall a few years back indicated that Maine's cormorants fed mostly on fish of no commercial importance—cunner, sculpin, and gunnel. Obviously they do not compete economically, yet a few fishermen who claim that some birds get into their weirs want them destroyed.

It is ironic that herring gulls, beautiful as they are, are now considered "trash" birds because they are so abundant and have such omnivorous habits. By 1900 the species had become *endangered,* on its way out because of egging and the unrelenting slaughter by the millinery trade. The National Association of Audubon Societies gave warden protection to the last viable colonies on the Maine coast just in the nick of time, and the state legislature backed things up with legal protection.

In addition to the omnipresent herring gulls, there are now plenty of the great black-backed gulls. They have had a major buildup since the early 1930s, when the first ones began to repopulate the Maine coast. More wary and less resilient than the herring gulls, the blackbacks had been forced by persecution eastward to New Brunswick by

Double-crested cormorants have enjoyed a population explosion since the 1970s.

1870, and thereafter none nested in the United States for more than fifty years.

On our earlier boat trips we sometimes saw a few eiders, but it was not until 1949 that they nested again in Muscongus Bay. Because of legal protection they were no longer egged by fishermen farther east, and their numbers were building up. Now, on our fiftieth anniversary cruise throughout the islands, we saw eiders around every rocky shoal. Some females were shepherding well-grown broods of young, while the molting males formed flocks of their own.

An exciting spin-off of the Audubon presence in Maine has been the rehabilitation of the puffin. This was inspired by the imagination of Stephen Kress, who is currently director of the camp. These chubby, penguinlike birds with great triangular red bills, which give them a clownlike aspect, were all but exterminated a century ago by fishermen who trapped and shot them. Only two small colonies survived in Maine. (As a footnote, Audubon stated 150 years ago that although many puffins still bred in the islands at the mouth of the Bay of Fundy, perhaps there was not one bird "for a hundred that bred there twenty years ago." Obviously, their decline was precipitous.)

Puffins had nested on the Egg Rocks prior to 1880, before sheep grazing and shooting eliminated them. Steve Kress conceived the idea of bringing them back by flying in young birds from Newfoundland and nursemaiding them by hand until they fledged and could take to the sea. This project was launched in 1973, but inasmuch as a young puffin takes several years to reach the breeding stage, it was not until 1981 that the first five pairs returned to raise young of their own—the first parents in a hundred years. This past season nineteen pairs raised young.

In 2005 there were nearly three hundred breeding pairs of Atlantic puffins on Egg Rock.

Puffins, like penguins, seek company, and the more friends around, the more social interaction. Steve Kress, always innovative, conceived the idea of carving and painting wooden decoys, which he placed on strategic boulders so as to lure any seafaring puffin that winged past.

Each summer dedicated young docents camped out on Eastern Egg Rock and fed the babies, which at first look like balls of lint retrieved from the vacuum cleaner. Over the last fourteen years, up to and including this summer, 1,017 young puffins have been fledged on Eastern Egg Rock, and another 347 have been fledged on Seal Island, a new transplant site. All these birds have been flown in from the large colony on Great Island in Newfoundland. The pilot who has flown the birds from Newfoundland the past three years and donated the use of his plane and fuel is Dr. William Brennan. Dr. Tony Diamond, a Canadian biologist, was employed this year by the Audubon as a consultant to conduct experiments with the young transplanted puffins, so as to learn more about the effects of food stress on chick growth. This is of real concern because seabird foods have been overfished in many areas.

The much publicized success with the puffins is not the only groundbreaking work that has been going on at Eastern Egg Rock. Terns of three species—common, arctic, and roseate—are now nesting again by the hundreds, lured in by hand-painted decoys, much as the puffins have been. In addition, laughing gulls, long absent, have returned, but the resident blackbacks are being kept in check because of the pressures they would otherwise exert on the puffins and terns. Even Leach's storm-petrels, which fly in from the sea to their burrows at night, have been lured in by using tape recordings. It is evident that the art of attracting birds has now gone far beyond the garden, the feeding tray, the birdhouse, and the birdbath. Another dimension is being explored.

—November/December 1986

The Peregrine Story

THE DISPASSIONATE brown eyes of the peregrine, more than those of any other bird, have been witness to man's struggle for civilization, from the squalid tents on the steppes of Asia thousands of years ago to the marble halls of European kings in the seventeenth century.

Two thousand years before the Christian era, in Asia, falconry—"the oldest sport on earth"—provided a means to an end. It meant meat on the table, a method of getting game beyond the range of the swiftest arrow. In the dark heart of Asia, a hunting eagle was worth from three to ten horses. There the birds were flown even at wolves.

Marco Polo reported that the Great Khan of Cathay journeyed once a year to the eastern part of his kingdom, riding on a pavilion borne on the backs of four elephants. Ten thousand falconers and their hawks went along, and twelve gyrfalcons attended by twelve officers rode with the khan in his pavilion. Men on horseback gave the signal when cranes or other birds appeared overhead. Then the curtains of the pavilion were drawn while the khan, in sensuous splendor, watched the sport from his couch.

The Ottoman sultan Bayazid had seven thousand hawks, and Frederick II Hohenstaufen built whole castles for his birds. The kings of the East exchanged their birds with the kings of the West until even the Vikings knew of falconry.

Queens, czars, even popes flew their birds. A knight was as proud of the falcon on his wrist as of the sword at his side. Bishops carried their birds to the church and down the aisle, releasing them as they approached the altar. Hawking was the pastime of an idle gentry, a

The peregrine falcon was removed from the endangered and threatened species list in 1999. This is a captive falconer's bird.

pastime that was bound to decline with the social upheavals of the seventeenth century.

The peregrine, alone of all the sharp-winged falcon tribe to span the globe, is found on all the continents except Antarctica, and on many of the larger islands. Alexander Wilson, the pioneer of American ornithology, did not like the name peregrine (traveler) because he believed the bird to be nonmigratory. He called it the "great-footed hawk," and so did Audubon, but later "duck hawk" became the name in common usage. In recent years we have gone back to the original name, the one that has always been used in England.

The most efficient flying machine, the best-designed bird, the fiercest and fastest bird—all these superlatives have been claimed for the peregrine. It may well be the swiftest bird, but its ordinary cruising speed is not much greater than that of the pigeons it catches. It is in the "stoop," the plunge when it partially closes its wings and pumps in for the kill, that the peregrine attains the rocketlike speed for which it is famous.

I still remember the Sunday afternoon nearly sixty years ago when Joseph Hickey showed me my first peregrine aerie on the Palisades of the Hudson River. We scanned the dark cliffs with our glasses for the patch of white that splashed the nesting ledge. On a stub to one side perched the bird, its black mustaches and big yellow feet showing plainly. Many times during those pre-DDT years I watched the peregrines on the Palisades—so beautifully cut, like giant swallows.

In those days we always spoke of "the Palisades duck hawk." I had no idea there were half a dozen aeries between the Fort Lee Ferry and West Point. The oologists knew them all, but they kept their secret. The falconers knew, too, but they had long had an understanding among themselves not to molest the Hudson River birds.

It was one of the high points of my birding career to be taken in the early 1940s to fourteen aeries in a weekend, the farthest not more than one hundred miles from New York City. I even went overside to examine some of the eggs. It took a great dose of nerve to back off the edge of a three-hundred-foot cliff with nothing but pitons and a half-inch rope for support. The river looked so very far down.

Formerly a few peregrines nested in ancient wind-topped trees along the Mississippi. In 1941 I saw such an aerie in northern Louisiana, one hundred miles south of any other known nest in eastern North America. The man who directed me to it was nearly blind. He had dimly made out the silhouette of a sharp-winged bird circling about a tall cypress stub and protesting. He wondered if it could be a Carolina parakeet but added that "it sounded just like the duck hawks we have here in winter." A week later, Dr. Walter Spofford showed me another aerie in a wind-topped cypress in Tennessee.

In both Europe and Asia, peregrines long nested on cathedrals, temples, and old castles. It was predictably only a matter of time before they would take up residence in New World cities. In winter, some birds hunted pigeons from the skyscrapers of Boston, Albany, Philadelphia, and Washington, while New York City's canyons harbored a dozen or more. Among the favorite command posts for winter peregrines in New York fifty years ago, when I lived there, were the Clason Point gas tank, the George Washington Bridge, the Riverside Church, the New York Hospital, Hearns Department Store in Greenwich Village, and the Lincoln and Chrysler buildings. The Riverside Church bird fell into disfavor with the rectory because it used the ledge outside his office to dismember the local pigeons.

The main disadvantage of most modern buildings from the peregrine's point of view is that they tend toward simple lines, devoid of gingerbread and suitable niches. When a pair tried unsuccessfully to nest on the Sun-Life Building in Montreal, an eighteen-by-eighteen-inch tray—filled with gravel—was put out so that the eggs would not roll from the ledge. With this help, the birds brought up two young in 1940 and continued to nest there each year until 1952.

Joseph Hickey wrote that "about four hundred nesting sites of the peregrine had been reported east of the Rocky Mountains up to the close of 1940, although several times this number were believed to exist." Most of the latter would be far to the north. Richard Bond placed the breeding population of western North America at 750 pairs. By all estimates the peregrine was a rarity, numbering in the low thousands, with, I guessed at the time, no more than five thousand individuals on the continent.

The rather small brotherhood of falconers was not a threat to the birds. Many hawk-shooting sportsmen had been converted by the beauty of a well-trained peregrine on the wrist of a falconer. Some falconers gave lectures about the birds of prey and took a protective interest in nearby aeries, even though they took no birds for training.

In all the long history of falconry, nothing is more bizarre than the short-lived episode that took place at Fort Monmouth, New Jersey, at the outbreak of World War II. Government questionnaires were sent out by the hundreds asking for live hawks, preferably peregrines. They were to be trained to intercept enemy pigeons. The idea had possibilities, but it soon got out of hand. Birds were also to be trained to dive at airborne troops, slitting their parachutes with knives attached to their breasts.

Soon the unit involved had three birds, a redtail, a kestrel, and one peregrine. My friend Louis Halle, who once kept a pet hawk, was assigned the care of the birds, and an unhappy man he was. Some of his friends who did not fully understand the anatomy of an army, and how helpless a man can be there, seemed to blame him for the whole idea, even though he had only the rank of private at the time. Falconers and ornithologists everywhere protested. They regarded the plan not only as unworkable but, if developed on a large scale, as a threat to the existence of the peregrine. Under pressure, the Pentagon stopped the program.

A grim feud of long standing aligned another group of peregrine addicts against the falconers. They were the oologists. The rarer the bird, the keener the collector was to acquire its eggs. Peregrines were such a challenge that some oologists specialized in their eggs. One collector in Philadelphia had a cabinet full, drawer upon drawer, which represented years when the aeries along the Susquehanna and elsewhere in eastern Pennsylvania fledged scarcely a single young bird. A Boston oologist was reputed to have 180 sets—more than seven hundred eggs. Common were sixty, eighty, and one hundred sets.

The oologist claimed he caused less damage than the falconer, because when he took the eggs the bird laid again. This they sometimes did, after three weeks or so—a smaller clutch—but the eggers were on hand to get those, too. Forty years ago I was shown a cliff in California where a collector pitched his tent before the eggs were laid, so he would be there first. He told me that he took the eggs at this aerie each year for twenty-nine years, "but now, due to the pressure of civilization, this site is no longer occupied."

Egg collecting seems to have died out completely in the United States. How different one hundred years ago, when thirty men climbed one cliff on the same day for a single set of eggs!

Meanwhile, the falconers' star was on the rise. Bitter was their feud with the oologists. But the oologists had an advantage. Eggs come before chicks. To gain tactical advantage, the falconers climbed the cliffs as soon as eggs were laid and, to make them worthless to oologists, roughed the shells with sandpaper and daubed on India ink. "The birds don't mind," one of the vigilantes remarked. "They would as soon sit on doorknobs."

The aficionados of the peregrine had a gentlemen's agreement among themselves about taking young from nests along the Palisades and insisted that nests near big cities be left strictly alone. They took a special interest in seeing the young safely on the wing. Heaven help the egger they caught, particularly on the New York side of the line, where the peregrine was protected by state law. They even enlisted the aid of the park police who patrolled the highway along the cliffs.

✎

But all this had changed by 1960. Shortly after 1950 my friend Richard Herbert, who had shown Joseph Hickey and me many of the Hudson River aeries, noticed that although the birds were laying eggs, they failed to hatch. Eventually at aerie after aerie the birds disappeared. The famous Sun-Life birds in Montreal raised their last family in 1952. By 1960 no one knew of a single active aerie anywhere in the northeast, although passage birds from farther north still went through. It was not clear what was wrong, and many explanations were bandied about. Concurrently the peregrine was also in steep decline in Europe.

In 1965, Joseph Hickey, then teaching wildlife ecology at the University of Wisconsin, called together those who were most knowledgeable about the peregrine for a conference at Madison. More than forty participants and observers from North America and Europe presented papers or took part in discussions. These were published in book form in 1969 under the title *Peregrine Falcon Populations: Their Biology and Decline.*

Was it perhaps the requiem of a species? What was wrong? This ecological disaster was explored; a wide variety of adverse factors was examined, and the evidence pointed in an overwhelming way to

Peterson and Richard Herbert at the nest of a peregrine falcon on the Palisades, New York, in the 1940s. (Photographer unknown)

the widespread use of chlorinated hydrocarbons such as DDT, residual poisons that were passed through the food chain. Obviously the peregrine was a casualty of the subtle but deadly biocides.

In the years that followed, this was confirmed through further intensive work, and thanks to the banning of DDT, the environment was beginning to cleanse itself. But what of the peregrine? It had been completely extirpated as a breeding bird in eastern North America and was much diminished elsewhere.

Thanks largely to one of the Madison participants, Dr. Tom Cade of Cornell, and several others who attended that landmark conference, the peregrine is now on its way back. Using methods gained from their knowledge of falconry, raising young from the egg under captive conditions, and hacking them out at selected sites, they have saved this critically endangered species. This seed stock of wild breeding peregrines is now doubling its numbers every year or two in eastern North America, and the species is making a strong recovery in other parts of the world as well.

In November 1985, on the twentieth anniversary of the Madison conference, an even larger get-together of peregrine aficionados was held in Sacramento, California. It was hosted by the Peregrine Fund. Joe Hickey was specially honored for his own role in helping to save the peregrine, and more than seventy papers were presented, celebrating one of the most remarkable conservation success stories of our times.

—MAY/JUNE 1987

A Night in a Channel Lighthouse

THERE IS NOTHING LIKE spending a night in a lighthouse when the birds are flying, to see the hordes of small travelers pouring out of the darkness into the blinding beams.

I had my first chance when I was in England working on *A Field Guide to the Birds of Britain and Europe,* based on the system in my American field guides. My coauthor Guy Mountfort was an old hand at lighthouses. He said that St. Catherine's Light on the English Channel should be at its best about the third week in April. We decided to take time out from our labors on the book and go. Unfortunately Phil Hollom, my other coauthor, could not join us. But we had Keith Shackleton and his pretty young bride, Jackie; they offered to fly us in their small plane to St. Catherine's.

Keith was a protégé of that most famous of all wildfowl painters, Peter Scott, son of the Antarctic hero. He not only bears the name of that other famous Antarctic explorer Sir Ernest Shackleton but went to the same school as Sir Peter—Oundle—where the great humanitarian headmaster Kenneth Fisher, father of James Fisher, initiated him into the ways of birdlife. Keith was already painting seabirds and waves like a master, had sailed "fourteen-footers" against Americans and Canadians in championship races, and had recently published his first book, *Tidelines,* strongly reminiscent of Peter Scott's *Morning Flight.*

When we took off from Fairoaks, an aerodrome not far from London, our four-seater crammed with gear seemed like a flying sardine tin. The bird nets, which we planned to use for banding, would not fit inside, so the long bamboo handles were left to project through the

open window. This created a rattle and a turbulence that made the small craft rather difficult to handle. But Keith was a skilled pilot who had some RAF experience, and he had flown small planes for years in connection with his family's business.

The green English countryside, with its hedgerows, coppices, and old castles, was like a terrain model below us; we crossed the Solent, with its backwaters and tortuous estuaries on which swans rested, looking like little white specks. While we were fascinated by the moving panorama, time slipped by as quickly as the miles, until we found ourselves over the white chalk cliffs at the edge of the English Channel.

St. Catherine's Light stands on a bold headland of the Isle of Wight, a lonely light of a style that might be called "railway-station gothic," to use Shackleton's words. We carried with us a document from Trinity House in London stating that the "Elder Brethren" (whoever they might have been) had granted us permission "to visit St. Catherine's Light on the 19th April, 1952, for the purpose of observing bird migration." This we presented to the head lightkeeper, who showed us into the tower and up the winding steps to the lofty chambers where the huge rotating lenses magnified the relatively small light to something like 6 million candlepower.

Formerly, the keeper told us, when the light boasted 15 million candlepower, the destruction of birds had been much greater. In fact, he had seen no great numbers of birds on any night so far that season. We had timed our visit, however, to coincide with the absence of a moon, which would otherwise illuminate the shore. A small front was due to arrive, and the warm breezes from France would probably be blocked by cooler air. Conditions seemed right.

At eight o'clock the light went on, and the long beams, revolving in a clockwise direction, probed the increasing darkness. Although we knew it would take at least three hours for a small bird to make the channel crossing, we were impatient. We started our vigil at once. At 9:03 a swallow fluttered briefly before the lenses, but being normally a day migrant, it must have left the coast of France before dark.

Shortly after 11:00 a fine rain descended in a silky drizzle across the bright beams, and the foghorn down toward "The Needles" lowed like a lonely bull. Then we caught sight of our first real night migrant. Flickering and ghostly, it darted toward our high catwalk and swept over the top of the tower into the darkness. Soon another came in and another, like moths to a streetlamp. During the next two hours there must have been hundreds. Several that came close enough to be caught in our handheld clap nets proved to be whitethroats (not like our American whitethroats but Old World warblers with gray caps and white chins). We also caught two or three willow warblers—little olive-drab fellows, which, incidentally, are probably the most numerous summer visitors to northern Europe.

But this was the big night for whitethroats—a mass arrival. At least 80 percent of the birds were of this one species. Most got past the light safely, and we ringed with little numbered aluminum leg bands those few that fell to our nets. Not a sound did they make as they flew by (European night migrants are not as vocal as ours), and I was deeply moved by the silent drama that was taking place in this world of blackness, revolving white light, and rain. Weighing scarcely an ounce each, these tiny mites had crossed sixty to eighty miles of water by dead reckoning to be met by headwinds, turbulence, and rains. They were so tired when we scooped them from the air that they closed their eyes and fell asleep in our hands. This was the second sea crossing they had made on their northward pilgrimage from Africa. They had also crossed the much wider Mediterranean, and some would continue on across the North Sea. We award laurels to channel swimmers, yet every bird is a champion—an Olympic champion; it would not survive if it were anything less.

At one o'clock the stars came out, the shoreline was darkly visible against the lapping waves, and the birds no longer streamed in. I descended to the control room, where I tried to get an hour's sleep on the cement floor while the huge grinding cogs rotated the ponderous lenses above. When I returned, refreshed, the mist had thickened again, and a second great wave of birds was pouring in; thousands of birds, no fewer, must have passed during the night.

⤙

For some reason, our American lighthouses—most of them, at any rate—do not seem to take as great a toll on tiny travelers as the European lights. I believe there is a logical reason for this. In the spring there is no really massive movement of migrants up our Atlantic coastal plain other than those birds that nest there. The big waves from the tropics to Canada move up the Mississippi Valley and along the Appalachian ridges. In the autumn, however, when cold boreal winds from the northwest blow across these lands of travel, many birds are drifted toward the coast, like swimmers in a strong current. It is then that they jam up at coastal points such as Cape May, Cape Charles, and Hatteras. Such a wind from the northwest brings clear blue skies and starlit nights. It takes an easterly wind from the sea to bring the fogs that obscure the shoreline and cause bewildered birds to seek the beams that penetrate the mist and beckon them to their destruction.

In short, the mists and the major movements of birds seldom coincide on our side of the Atlantic. On rare occasions there is a catastrophe such as the one that took the lives of five thousand myrtle warblers at the Barnegat Light in New Jersey on a foggy autumn night some years ago. But these were undoubtedly the birds that normally wintered along the barrier islands. Myrtle warblers were decidedly scarce on the Barnegat strip for several years thereafter.

Europe, with its more complicated coastlines, is another matter. Some of the lighthouses along the channel, the North Sea, and in the Baltic take a great toll on birds, so great that racks of perches have been erected about the huge lenses to give weary birds resting places.

In the old days of fixed beams, mortality was much greater. On some mornings the rocks below certain lighthouses would be littered with thousands of birds, from tiny goldcrests to large waders, dead and dying, to be devoured later by the ever hungry jackdaws and gulls. The revolving beams of today are less lethal. Some Europeans have contended that many birds follow the revolving shafts of light round and round until they fall exhausted, but this is not so; the beams rotate faster than the birds can fly.

We were relieved to note that during our visit no birds killed themselves against the screen-covered glass. Under different wind conditions, when the eddies are strong, it might have been otherwise. Occasionally a bird rested momentarily on one of the perches, which I calculated could accommodate two thousand birds.

Some might have hit the unlit tower above, where there were no perches. The keeper told us that the perches above had never been replaced after the war—after the day at the close of spring migration in 1945 when the racks were being stored for the season. A Nazi dive-bomber, one of the last hit-and-run raiders, swooped across the channel, blew up the powerhouse and the shed where the perching racks were being stored, and killed all three lightkeepers. As the first light of dawn streaked the sky, our informant pointed out the spot where the tragedy had occurred.

And now for the unexpected sequel to our all-night vigil. At dinnertime the following day, Keith Shackleton called up so excited as to be almost breathless. After leaving us at Fairoaks, he had flown to another airfield, Biggleswade (about a hundred miles north of the Isle of Wight). There, while he and Jackie were taking the afternoon sun in a grassy meadow, he noticed two little birds working down the hedge nearby. He focused his binoculars on them. They were whitethroats, both of them, and one wore a shiny new band!

—July/August 1987

ORGY ON DELAWARE BAY

WHEN THE MOON is full, May 20 or thereabouts, and hide tides are at their highest, the shores of Delaware Bay just north of Cape May are invaded by legions of horseshoe crabs, *Limulus polyphemus*— and also by myriads of shorebirds. The spectacle has been likened to an invasion of miniature armored tanks, with the birds acting as the counterattacking forces. Actually, the whole cosmic affair is more like an orgy: the horseshoe crabs are mating and laying untold billions of eggs in the sand and spilling many of them into the shallows.

Knots, those robin-size sandpipers with robinlike breasts, compete with the laughing gulls, turnstones, sanderlings, and other waders for the goodies, which are about the size of No. 6 shot and look vaguely like uncooked tapioca. Fueling up, the knots may almost double their weight before making their next long hop of fifteen hundred miles or more to James Bay, en route to their nesting grounds in the High Arctic. Brian Harrington of Manomet Observatory, drawing on his years of banding and color marking, has calculated that the New World population of knots must be close to 200,000—lots of knots—but there are even more than that on the other rim of the Atlantic. Before I tell you more about what I saw last May in New Jersey, let me go back twenty-five years and reminisce about the knots on the British side.

Our horse, plodding into the cold wind and fine driving rain, pulled us in a gaily colored, two-wheeled cart over the vast stretch of water-sculptured sand toward Hilbre Island at the edge of the Irish Sea. At this point, where the Cheshire Dee separates England from the gray hills of Wales, the estuary is nearly five miles wide. Not far away is the great city of Liverpool. At low tide the combined estuaries

Laughing gulls (above), red knots, and ruddy turnstones (right) compete with other shorebirds for horseshoe crab eggs.

of the Dee and the adjacent Mersey form at least fifty square miles of exposed sand and mudflats, a feeding place for tens of thousands of clamoring shorebirds. But when the flood races in, these same flats may be covered by as much as thirty feet of rough water.

As we pushed on in the worsening weather, I thought of the legend of Mary, who went forth to call her lost cattle home, and how the "cruel crawling foam" of the rising tide racing across the sands of the Cheshire Dee brought her to a watery grave. As we pulled into Hilbre, I wondered what would be the fate of three little dogs that we had seen racing down the flats at half tide, unmindful of their peril. Would the rapidly widening channels eventually cut off their retreat?

Mine was the great good fortune to spend a week on Hilbre with a small group of photographers who made a holiday of it twice a year at the time of the highest tides. How I managed to crash the party when others had hopefully put their names on the list year after year, I am not sure. I was so involved in work on the European field guide that I missed the expedition in March, but in the slender hope that there might be room for me in October, I extended my stay in England. At the last moment there was accommodation for just one guest. I was the lucky one.

My hosts were "Big Bill" Williams, an amateur Cheshire ornithologist, and Norman Ellison, who was known as "Nomad" to millions of BBC listeners in the Midlands. Eric Hosking, England's legendary bird photographer, was there with his battery of cameras, and, most glamorous of all, Field Marshal the Viscount Alanbrooke, who had been the chief of staff of the Allied Armies in World War II. As one would expect of a military man, Lord Alanbrooke brought along his heavy artillery—a fourteen-inch lens mounted on a Kodak Ciné-Special. This was his seventh visit to Hilbre.

When the tide rises and the gray-green waters of the Irish Sea roll into the estuary, the battalions of wading birds are forced to leave their feeding grounds, where they have been gorging on marine worms and tiny mussels. Most of the curlews head inland, but the thousands of knots, oystercatchers, dunlins, and redshanks resort to the rocks of Hilbre and particularly to its satellite islands, the "Big Eye" and the "Little Eye."

A bird blind (or "hide") properly placed on either the Big or the Little Eye was almost sure to be surrounded by countless shorebirds at high tide. I put up my blind two hours before the "buildup" started. I might add that I have never seen any blind quite as practical or well made as a Hosking hide, unless it was the one Lord Alanbrooke had, which was an adaptation of the same design. Lord Alanbrooke let me work from his hide one morning; it had almost everything but hot and cold running water!

The important thing in estuary photography is the "buildup." If you do not withdraw from sight before the first few waders begin to gather along the creeping water's edge, a few hundred feet away, you may have no live decoys to lure in the passing flocks. The blind must be rigid, so as not to flap in the almost constant wind. As the waters rise, the birds increase in number and crowd in closer and closer. If by chance a clam digger elects to wait out the tide on your islet at this critical juncture, the flocks will clear out. Or if the local peregrine puts the mob to flight, you have had it. You might as well dismantle the blind and wait for another day.

Weekends are out. There is too much disturbance by fishermen and others—and there is also too much photographic competition. We did not bother to put up our blinds on Sunday. The big telescope showed us a strange new hide on the Little Eye, and one on the Big Eye as well. Sweeping the scope toward the mainland, we could see a blind on the Red Rock, with three cormorants sitting in front of it. Scrutinizing the Big Eye again, we could see a large flock of knots.

To an American, the oystercatcher is the star of the show. Oystercatchers (similar to ours but with darker backs) are much more abundant in Europe than they are with us. Those of us who live in New England think of them primarily as rather southern birds, which we travel to Virginia or the Carolinas to see in any numbers. In Europe they even spend the winter as far north as Iceland. The great flocks that winter on the Cheshire Dee can sometimes be seen walking about in snow. Audubon wrote of seeing oystercatchers in

Labrador. He might have been right. Perhaps we wiped out our northern population before other ornithologists were on hand to record the process.

I would not dare estimate the numbers of oystercatchers that crowded the eroded red sandstone of the Little Eye. At first there were dozens, then hundreds, then thousands. Closer and closer they crowded, *kleeping* and making an incredible racket while the buildup continued. At the very moment of high tide, a silence fell over the assembly, and every last bird tucked its long orange bill into the feathers of its back and went to sleep.

So busy had I been photographing the oystercatchers out of one side of my blind that I was quite unaware of what had been taking place on the other. Hearing a sudden rush of wings behind me, I peeped out. There, just a few feet away, was a great gray carpet of knots, close-packed as only knots can pack. There were thousands. More were dropping into the crowd, and some stood on the backs of others until they could find a spot where they might wedge in. I was told that sometimes the knots on the Dee exceed fifty thousand in a single flock.

Spectacles such as this must have inspired H. J. Massingham when he wrote, "A nation of knots spreading over the sea approaches the land like a gray rain-cloud, constantly altering its shape and shifting as the birds pursue their intricate mazes through the air. As the corporate legion draws nearer, the roar of its multitudinous wings is like the booming of high waves at the foot of limestone caverns."

＞━

Pete Dunne, in one of his aerial surveys north of Cape May, described a flock of knots so dense that he mistook it for a stretch of birdless beach until it lifted off and drifted away like a wind-driven cloud.

Pete invited me to come down to see this spectacle last May and also to be on hand for the windup of the "World Series of Birding," the birdathon that the New Jersey Audubon sponsors each year. Three years ago our team, "the Guerrillas," got 202, the highest score for New Jersey up to that time. However, our star, Bill Boyle, begged off this time, and because of other pressures Pete Dunne found little time to do any scouting himself. So he advised me not to join the team this year; we would not win. I agreed with him.

Pete had to take care of too many details that weekend, so he put me in the hands of Clay Sutton, captain of the *Bird Watchers' Digest* team, to see the shorebirds. A good photographer himself, Clay was well aware of the problems I would face trying to get close-ups. As I have confessed before, bird photography is my therapy; it is fun, a respite from the demanding days at the desk and drawing board.

Taking the wheel at Cape May, Clay drove us fifteen miles to Reed's Beach, one of a half dozen key spots on the lower reaches of Delaware Bay where the consortium of horseshoe crabs and shorebirds usually concentrates.

Horseshoe crabs, sometimes called "king crabs," are not closely related to crabs at all but have more in common with spiders and scorpions. These harmless, ancient, tanklike creatures have been around for 200 million years or more, long before there were birds of any kind to feed on their eggs.

Michael Male and Judy Fieth had already been at Reed's Beach for a week, sent by National Geographic to document all this on color film. They offered me the use of their blind, but I wanted to try out my own makeshift setup.

The Manomet team was there, too, with telescopes and rocket nets. From the shelter of the cottages, they scoped the mobs, hoping to pick up a bird they had color-marked previously, in Massachusetts, Cape May, Florida, or faraway Argentina. We did not wait to see them shoot off the sixty-by-forty-foot net, which is propelled over the resting or feeding shorebirds by five rockets, each of which weighs about six pounds. Startled by the loud boom, the birds spring into the air while the leading edge of the net drops in front of them, pinning them to the sand, sometimes as many as two or three hundred at a time. Then the biologists mark and release them, a process that may take three or four hours.

On the stretch of sandy shoreline between the cluster of cottages and the breakwall to the north, the horseshoe crabs formed a wavewashed roadbed of glistening brown carapaces, over which hundreds of laughing gulls walked or jockeyed for position as they gobbled the tiny eggs from the soupy water. The wavelets breaking on the shore tipped some crabs on their backs. Helplessly, they waved their claws about, and it seemed only humane to lift them by their spiky tails and toss them back into the water.

❧

Half a mile in the other direction, south of the cottages, our binoculars revealed a dense carpet of shorebirds gorging themselves on the goodies that had been deposited in the sand during the previous high tide. When we got out of the car and walked toward them, they lifted off and settled farther down the shore. Selecting a spot where they had been feeding most actively, I put down my folding chair and draped myself and my camera equipment with some camouflage material I had discovered at our local army and navy surplus store. Through the openings in the fabric, I could easily see what was going on around me, but I remained invisible to the birds; in fact, I looked like a bush. It was a lot simpler than putting up the traditional bird blind with jointed poles and all that. I could even change location by carefully lifting everything and slowly walking with it.

When I was properly set up, Clay circled the feeding flock at a reasonable distance and slowly edged the birds in my direction without putting them up. Soon they were out in front at minimum photographic range. Ruddy turnstones and sanderlings dominated the scene; the turnstones were in full breeding finery, the sanderlings in every stage of transition from gray winter plumage to bright rusty summer dress. How many plumages, I wondered, should I show in my new western field guide?

At the water's edge a lone willet preened itself but did not seem interested in feeding with the other birds. There were a few red knots in high breeding plumage, but the bulk of the knot battalions migrating from the southern tip of South America to their nesting grounds in the Arctic would probably arrive within the next three or four days, precisely when the egg laying of the horseshoe crabs would be at its peak.

❧

Shorebirds were so heavily shot in the bad old days around the turn of the century that it has taken decades for their numbers to recover. Knots bunch so tightly that they were particularly vulnerable. Back in the 1920s, I was with Alexander Sprunt and Burnham Chamberlain, of the Charleston Museum, when they were gathering material for a habitat group showing the Carolina shore. A large flock of knots flew by, and Sprunt took aim at a highly plumaged bird at the tail end of the flock. He wanted only one, that one; but thirteen birds dropped. He spent half the night marking up specimens.

Brian Harrington of the Manomet team points out that the avian titleholder—the long-distance champ—the arctic tern, when traveling from the Arctic to the Antarctic, feeds all along the way. By contrast, most of our knots, which travel about the same distance, may fly nonstop as much as four thousand miles in sixty hours, and according to radar studies they may go as high as twenty thousand feet—nearly four miles—to do it. Surely the red knot is the most spectacular migrant of all.

The turnstones, patterned like harlequins, were the stars of the show. Some were so close that through my big lens a single bird would fill the frame. There were frequent arguments when two turnstones contested their rights to a batch of eggs buried in the same depression. The sanderlings seemed to be more sharing, rapidly digging with a sewing machine motion, often with sand up to their eyes. By noon I had shot all of my film—ten rolls.

Although surveys show semipalmated sandpipers to be the most abundant of all the shorebirds on Delaware Bay in late May, they tend to congregate on the mudflats a few miles to the north, probably because they are unable to compete with their huskier relatives.

❧

There is no doubt that Delaware Bay, thanks largely to the horseshoe crab, acts as a magnet in spring to the greatest concentrations of migrating shorebirds in eastern North America. Ornithologists were not fully aware of this until recently. It is curious that Witmer Stone, who wrote the classic two-volume *Bird Studies at Old Cape May*, never mentioned this annual phenomenon. Nor did Audubon or

Wilson, both of whom knew Cape May, before him. Wilson, however, did mention concentrations of ruddy turnstones.

Now we must guard these critical stretches of shoreline. It is almost inevitable that sometime in the years ahead there will be a massive oil spill. Delaware Bay is the second most heavily utilized shipping lane in the country in terms of tanker traffic. Ships are constantly traveling to and fro between the sea and the great petroleum refineries around Philadelphia. A major oil spill or spill of toxic pollutants during spring migration would be disastrous.

On the brighter side: you must see this annual ritual for yourself; drive to Reed's Beach and nearby Moore's Landing in May at the time of the full moon. Stay at least a day or two and take in this ancient pageant of renewal, this mystical conjunction of planetary and biological forces.

—September/October 1987

FINDING THE IVORY-BILLED WOODPECKER

RECENTLY I was asked by George Harrison to tell readers of *Audubon* magazine about my most exciting bird experience. Was it the time, forty years ago (on New Year's Day in 1948), when Bob Smith, the Mississippi flyway biologist, flew me over the coastal marshes west of the Mississippi Delta in his two-seated patrol plane and showed me the last surviving whooping crane in Louisiana?

As we flew west from the Rainey Wildlife Sanctuary, named after Paul J. Rainey, Smith leaned back in his pilot's seat and pointed ahead. Over his shoulder I saw a white speck against the golden marsh, a huge white bird flying, not one of the numerous snow geese that were scattered like white flakes among the blues. It was a mile or more away when we first saw it, but our speedy little plane soon shortened the gap until, for a brief moment, we were flying not more than two hundred feet apart. I cursed the broken lensboard of the Graflex that rested idly across my knees.

Or was my most heart-stopping moment that time many years ago at the mouth of the Merrimac in Massachusetts when a lone curlew flew by? It looked small, and my glass showed its sickle-shaped bill to be very stubby—shorter than that of any immature whimbrel I had ever seen. Could it be an Eskimo curlew? Silhouetted against the low sunlight, it showed no color, nor did it call. It kept right on traveling until it was out of sight, and I had the uneasy feeling that I had muffed the chance of a lifetime. But there may still be a chance for me to see one. This past summer biologists found three nests in northeastern Canada.

Or how about the dozens of dusky seaside sparrows I saw on my earlier trips to Florida? No one could have foreseen that the dingy little sparrows that sang from the spartina across the Titusville Bridge on Merritt Island would become extinct. Some say it was because of ill-advised marsh manipulation. At the time, I was more interested in finding the black rails that had been reported there.

Condors no longer fly in the California skies, but they may eventually do so again if the two dozen captives in the San Diego and Los Angeles zoos cooperate by producing young under controlled conditions. In 1952, when I took my English friend James Fisher around the perimeter of the continent, we saw three condors in the Sespe ridges north of Ventura. Later, writing about this in our book, *Wild America,* we wondered "How long will it be before it joins *Teratornis,* the La Brea condor, the Grinnell eagle, the La Brea stork, the La Brea owl, and the California turkey?"*

➤

What then, *was* my most exciting bird experience? Without question it involved the ivory-billed woodpecker, which presumably is now extinct in the United States.

Fifty years ago, when I was on the Audubon staff, Lester Walsh (John Baker's secretary) and I spent ten days trying to settle rumors that were being whispered among ornithologists—rumors of ivory-billed woodpeckers in the wilderness of the Santee Basin of South Carolina. A well-known turkey hunter whose word was considered good had seen them there. As if that were not enough, he swore the Carolina parakeet was there, too. Several times small green parrots had come to the bait before his blind while he was waiting for turkeys. This sounded incredible, as the last good record of Carolina parakeets was a flock in Florida in 1920.

Even if the parakeets were not there, the ivorybills were worth a try. The Santee swamps were more extensive in those days; hundreds of square miles of cypress, sweet gum, and pine embraced the muddy yellow river, swamps known to few men other than a handful of hog herders and trappers.

After consulting maps with Alexander Sprunt, who knew the Car-

---

*Pre-Pleistocene birds whose bones were found in the La Brea tar pits nearby.

olina low country well, we decided to put a boat into the stream at a point far inland and drift toward the coast—a distance of about a hundred miles. Walsh and I would be the first birders ever to cover this section of river.

✦

Unpacking our folding boat, we stretched its rubber hull over the skeleton framework and eased the trim craft into the water. Food, enough to last several days, was stowed fore and aft, and with double-bladed paddles flashing, we slipped into the silty river. It was late in the day, and our better judgment should have held us until next morning, but we were eager to start. Darkness found us without a camping spot, but we welcomed this excuse to make a night of it on the river, listening to the night sounds.

With paddles across our knees, ready for quick action should a riffle betray a snag, we floated along. We pierced the darkness with the thin beam of our flashlight in the direction of strange animal voices but could see nothing. We drifted into little parties of wood ducks concernedly uttering their soft, finchlike *jeee*. At the stabbing flash of the light, they fled, the females almost screaming their terrified *who-eek!*

✦

The real bird of the night in the Santee is the barred owl. From everywhere came their baritone hootings—*Who cooks for you, who cooks for you all?* Two owls "talking" to each other in mellow southern accents would work up to a pitch that reverberated back and forth through the swamp. We counted fifty-five owls hooting in the course of a few miles.

Rather than pass by too much of the river country at night, we pulled up to the right bank and waited for morning. We eventually dropped into a sort of coma that certainly could not have been called sleep. Daylight seemed interminably long in coming. Awakening from a doze, we heard a cardinal sing. In a few minutes the air was ringing with the chants of cardinals, Carolina wrens, and titmice. The lesser voices were drowned out, but when the first burst of song had subsided, we could hear the weak, sibilant jargon of gnatcatchers, the sweet song of yellow-throated warblers, and the ascending buzz of the parulas. The striking blue-gray and gold prothonotary warbler was there, singing its emphatic *tweet-tweet-tweet-tweet-tweet* in the cypress sloughs.

During our first five days in the Santee, we saw more than twelve hundred wood ducks. From every bend of the river they flew, usually in pairs, the drab females always just in front of the males, as if by some inviolable rule of wood duck etiquette.

Although the swamp forests extended almost unbroken over hundreds of square miles, much had been cut years before, as the old stumps testified. But we found large tracts that had never known an ax, sweet gums fourteen feet in circumference, and loblolly pines with a girth of sixteen feet. Some of the cypresses had swollen buttresses that measured over thirty feet.

Turkey cocks could be heard gobbling at daybreak; woodpeckers of half a dozen species rolled out their tattoos. An eagle overhead, a glimpse of a swallow-tailed kite gliding above the live oaks, and ghostly egrets in a dark "gum slough" contributed to a picture of primeval beauty.

As we traveled down the yellow-brown river, we stopped where the trees were biggest to hunt for ivorybills; at night we dragged the kayak ashore over the slippery mud and slung our hammocks between cypress saplings. On the fifth day, sunburned and without water, we reached "the Bluff," where the ivorybills were originally reported.

During the next several days we covered the swamp for miles around by dugout and on foot, but if we had known as much about ivorybills then as we knew later, we would have bypassed the cypress and spent more time on the ridges, among the sweet gums and pines.

But our mission failed; we saw pileated woodpeckers wherever we went but no ivorybills. No one had further evidence that they were present, other than a few suspicious-looking diggings.

As for the parakeets—we had never quite believed the report in the first place.

Audubon wrote about the ivory-billed woodpecker; so did Alexander Wilson, but it began to look as though the last remnants of its clan would disappear from the earth before its life history and ecology could be properly recorded. In what proved to be the twilight of the species, the National Audubon Society set up a research project in collaboration with Cornell in the 1930s to study the bird and to see whether anything could be done to save it. For three years James Tanner devoted himself to the study, and when his painstaking work was completed, he was awarded his doctor's degree.

Tanner spent months in the swamps, following the birds around, recording their every action. He found that each pair required a territory of no less than six square miles of primeval wilderness and that an average of 36 pairs of pileateds could subsist in the same area and at least 126 pairs of red-bellied woodpeckers. The ivorybill fed mostly on trees that had been dead two or three years. It took about that long for decay to set in and nourish the fat, whitish grubs that tunneled just beneath the tight bark. In another year or so, these subsurface borers disappeared. Decay went deeper into the heartwood, but the ivorybill was no longer interested. The tree then became fodder for the pileated.

When Audubon voyaged down the Mississippi, he began to notice the ivory-billed at the point where the Ohio joins the Mississippi. He wrote, "I have seen entire belts of Indian chiefs closely ornamented with the tufts and bills of this species."

It was not, however, the Indians who eliminated the ivorybill, nor the collectors who came later. (There are between 200 and 250 ivorybills in museums and collections in this country. I even have a motheaten female that was collected in Florida nearly a hundred years ago.) The logging of the river forests decimated the species. These specialized birds were not able to adapt themselves to second-growth woodlands, as the pileated has done.

By 1940 there was good evidence of the presence of ivorybills in only three states: South Carolina, Florida, and Louisiana. Tanner estimated that there could not be more than twenty-four left in the whole Southeast. However, in three years of hard work he had seen only five—all of these on the Singer Tract in northeastern Louisiana.

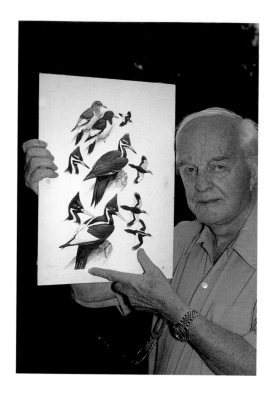

Peterson was one of the few field guide artists to have painted the ivory-billed woodpecker from firsthand experience.
(Virginia M. Peterson)

The Singer Tract had become a legend to me. It was the largest piece of virgin timber left in the East, the only spot that still retained nearly all of its original fauna—wolves, panthers, turkeys, even ivorybills— all except parakeets. The eighty thousand acres of low-lying wilderness would not last long. Already the ax was ringing against ancient buttresses. If I was ever to see an ivorybill, I would have to act, and so it was that in May 1942, at the little hotel in Tallulah, I joined my friend Bayard Christy of Pittsburgh. Mr. Christy, just turned seventy, said the ivorybill and the flamingo were the two birds he most wished to see before he died.

We had permits from the state of Louisiana to trespass on this forbidden ground where outsiders were excluded. To ensure our success, we searched out a local woodsman by the name of Kuhn, a modern Daniel Boone who had helped Jim Tanner with his work. Kuhn knew every foot of the great woodlands that extended along the winding Tensas ("Tinsaw") River.

We were in the swamp before daybreak, while the barred owls were still rolling their baritone hootings across the cypress bays. Waiting only until it was light enough to see, we struck out from the dirt road where we had parked the car. Setting the pace with his long, swinging stride, Kuhn led us toward a section where a pair of ivory-bills had roosted the year before. He urged us to step along because the best time to locate ivorybills was when they first left their roosting holes in the morning. "Then they talk more," he explained.

The vistas between the widely spaced forest giants were quite open, and the tangles of catbrier and poison ivy that barred our way were easily circumvented. We were in the higher, drier part of the swamp, the "second bottoms." The trees whose massive crowns towered 150 or more feet above our heads were sweet gum, Nuttall's oak, and ash. In the lower parts of the swamp grew the pale green cypresses, their knobby "knees" emerging from the dark, coffee-colored water. Never, said Kuhn, had he seen an ivorybill on a cypress.

We had gone half a mile from the road when Kuhn stopped short. He had caught a note on the edge of his sphere of hearing. I thought I heard it, but it could have been a chat. We had been told to listen for a voice that sounded something like a nuthatch. But there were plenty of nuthatches in these woods to confound us. We found ourselves starting at strange, unfamiliar notes that turned out to be squirrels and red-bellied woodpeckers. Kuhn assured us that when we heard the ivorybill we would know it all right. "Nothing in the whole world sounds like it."

Red-bellied woodpeckers seemed to be in every huge tree, calling *chiv, chiv.* Of pileateds there were any number, and we found a nest with a brood of young, buzzing like angry bees. We crossed and crisscrossed the best part of the swamp, where the John's Bayou birds once ranged. Deer leaped from our path and stood watching, wide-eyed, from the shadows. The tracks of turkeys and 'coon laced the mud, and we even found some large, round prints that Kuhn said were made by a panther. At least one or two of these large animals—

Louisiana cougars—still ranged through the Singer, survivors of a nearly extinct race of these big cats.

Later, when I hung back to investigate a Swainson's warbler in a tangle of cane and palmetto, from the corner of my eye I caught sight of a large, tawny form as it bounded silently across the wagon trail over which we had just passed. It was the panther, I knew, for no deer has a tail three feet long. It had probably not noticed me as I stood, half hidden, waiting for the warbler to sing. Hoping for a better look, I searched after it, but the wily cat had gone.

By early afternoon we must have covered fifteen or twenty miles within a block of woodland less than two or three miles square. As proof that ivory-billed woodpeckers were around, Kuhn pointed out some diggings and showed us how to tell them from the squarish holes made by the pileated. The ivorybills chip off the tight bark in great flakes, sometimes almost peeling a tree.

The next morning we started out on our own. Except for a small magnetic compass, we were unguided, but we had a good mental picture of the layout of this part of the Singer Tract. With this knowledge, we picked our way over the same ground as the day before, alert for rattlesnakes, camouflaged by the dry, silt-covered leaves. Our luck was no better, so we waded the turbid waters of the bayou and tried the woodlands on the west bank. We found wolf tracks in the yellow mud along the margin of the stream. It was here that ivorybills had been seen two weeks earlier. There were signs about, and many trees had been peeled, but we saw no birds.

By noon, we were back on the road, where we had seen so many diggings the day before. We would make another sortie before throwing in the sponge. Hardly had we gone a hundred yards when a startling new sound came from our right—a tooting note, musical in a staccato sort of way. For a moment things did not click, but then I knew—*it was the ivorybill!* I had expected it to sound more like a nuthatch; it was much more like the "toy tin trumpet" described by Alexander Wilson, or the "clarinet" of Audubon.

Breathlessly we stalked the insistent toots, stepping carefully, stealthily, so that no twig would crack. With our hearts pounding, we tried to keep cool, hardly daring to believe that this was it—the bird we had come fifteen hundred miles to see. We were dead certain this was no squirrel or lesser woodpecker, for an occasional blow would land—*whop!*—like the sound of an ax. Straining our eyes, we discovered the first bird, half hidden by the leafage, and in a moment it leaped into the full sunlight. This was no puny pileated; this was a whacking big bird, with great white patches on its wings and a gleaming white bill. By its long, recurved crest of blackish jet, we knew it was a female. We were even close enough to see its pale yellow eyes. Tossing its hammerlike head to right and left, it tested the diseased trunk with a whack or two as it jerked upward. Lurching out to the end of a broken-off branch, it pitched off on a straight line, like a duck, its wings making a wooden sound.

A second bird was a female, too. We had no trouble following the two, for as soon as they landed after a flight, they betrayed their location by their curious *henk, henk*. Whereas a pileated might call once and then remain silent for a quarter of an hour, an ivorybill, once heard, is easy to find.

We followed the big woodpeckers for nearly an hour before we lost them. During all that time they were in a partly logged section of the forest where some trees had been taken out, but others, less marketable, had been left standing. These birds, most likely, were the same two females that Tanner had seen in this place six months earlier. As mated ivorybills accompany each other throughout the year, it could be surmised that there were no males about. Six months after our visit, John Baker saw only one female in this spot. The other had disappeared. One ivorybill was seen in the Singer Tract as late as December 1946.

Unlike the last passenger pigeon, which officially expired at the Cincinnati Zoo at 1:00 P.M. Central Standard Time, September 1, 1914, no one knows the exact time of the ivory-billed woodpecker's passing.

We presume it is gone in the United States, but its continued existence in Cuba was recently confirmed by Lester Short of the American Museum of Natural History. The National Geographic Society is interested in a story, so they sent my former studio assistant Cuban-born Rob Hernandez (now high on the masthead of the *Geographic*), to meet with Fidel Castro and other officials to see if filming can be arranged. Good luck, Robbie!

—January/February 1988

Broley, the Eagle Man

When Charles Broley reached the age of sixty, he retired. He had been manager of a bank in Winnipeg for twenty-five years, and sixty is the traditional age for bankers to quit. It is also traditional for many senior citizens to go to the west coast of Florida, to Tampa or St. Petersburg or one of the other Gulf Coast towns, to enjoy the winter months during their golden years. En route south, at Audubon House in New York, Broley met Richard Pough, affable host to many of the visiting birders who stopped at 1000 Fifth Avenue. At lunch, Pough suggested he try banding a few Florida eagles.

It was only a casual suggestion, but Broley liked the idea. He was looking for some such project. All his life he had been an active man even though he had been a banker; he couldn't picture himself just sitting in the sun with all those old people. In the whole history of bird banding prior to this chance visit, only 166 bald eagles had ever been marked. In the ten years that followed, Broley himself banded more than a thousand.

The first season he banded forty-four eagles. To his great surprise, one of the bands was soon returned from Columbiaville, New York, eleven hundred miles to the north. Ornithologists took notice when other returns came from points equally distant. One bird banded at MacDill Air Force Base in Tampa was found shot in the province of New Brunswick, nearly sixteen hundred miles away from its birthplace. Another bird reached Prince Edward Island in the Gulf of St. Lawrence.

Broley's banding taught us that Florida bald eagles spent the winter months in Florida and the summer in the cool north. Normally, after fledging their young, eagles abandon Florida during the summer. The hawk watchers at Cape May and at Hawk Mountain see these same eagles returning southward in September. We had assumed this early autumn flight of bald eagles was of northern birds, but the bigger, more powerfully built northern eagles do not come down until much later, often not until winter, when they can be seen riding the ice floes that choke the Merrimac, the Connecticut, the Hudson, and the Delaware.

Originally Broley had not intended to do the rough work himself. Instead, he hired a boy to climb for him. The lad climbed the first tree; but when he raised himself over the rim of the net, the well-grown eaglet reared back, ready to strike with its big yellow claws. Frightened, the boy reached for a stick to strike. Broley could not allow this; he would have to find a way to climb the trees himself. So he devised a system of ropes and ladders.

It was early in 1946, not long after I was released from Army service, that *Life* magazine contacted me to do a color story on eagles; four pages of my paintings were to be supplemented by a page or so of black-and-white photographs showing Broley at his banding. Rather than send one of their staff photographers to Florida, *Life* commissioned me to take the photographs myself as well as paint the pictures.

When I wrote Broley that I was coming to photograph him while he banded his eagles he replied:

Bring your oldest clothes. I always have burnt-over territory to work in. Many of the trees are burned and black part way up, and with the pine rosin running on hot days I certainly am a mess. High boots are also a good idea. I killed a five-foot rattler last Tuesday, and last February I stepped right on a big one. If you intend to climb up to some of the nests with me, I would suggest that for three weeks before you come, you try chinning a bar until you can go up fifteen times. Work into it gradually—start by chinning yourself three or four times the first day or two.

We had no chinning bars in our apartment, so I used the bathroom door. I struggled up and down its smooth surface and thought,

What a man Broley must be! Although I was thirty years younger than he, I could hardly pull myself up seven times.

Broley had more than one hundred aeries under his watchful eye in the season of 1946, and we visited forty of them. Many could be reached by little, sandy roads, but often we had to park the car and pack the forty pounds of climbing equipment a long distance through the scrub palmetto and the pines. Most of the nests were in the virile, tortuous-limbed longleaf pines that give that part of Florida its semiopen, parklike look. I wanted to find an aerie where I could climb out on a limb so as to photograph Broley in the nest with a young eagle. Near Placida, in Charlotte County, there was just the right situation: A large horizontal branch at nest level would allow me to get out about twelve or fifteen feet from the trunk.

The first big limb was thirty feet from the ground, and the thick-set trunk with its rusty scabs of bark was impossible to shinny. Reaching into his sack, Broley took out a four-ounce lead sinker fastened to a cord. Placing the weight in a spoon attached to a broom-stick, he catapulted it over the limb. His accuracy on the first try was explained when he told me that he used to play lacrosse with the Indians in Manitoba.

When Broley started eagle banding, he pitched the weight over by hand, but one day he threw his arm out, so after that he used the broomstick. The weight, falling across the branch, dropped to the ground. To the cord was fastened a larger cord, to that a rope, and to the rope was attached a rope ladder. When the ladder was pulled into place, it was lashed securely about the base of the tree.

Don't think that a rope ladder is easy to climb. You have to know how. If you climb frontally, as on an ordinary ladder, your feet swing forward, and it is very taxing on the arms. The system is to climb the ladder *edgewise*, like a trapeze artist, grasping only one of the vertical ropes and going up "heel and toe" with one foot on either side.

Once one is up to the first branch, the rest is limb-to-limb climbing, using short lengths of rope to throw over limbs for hoists. Getting over the edge of the nest is often a problem, for the big platforms of sticks flare out like huge wineglasses. "Nest No. 23," at St. Petersburg, a "super nest"—twenty feet deep and nine and a half feet wide—was probably the largest nest in America, exceeding even the "Great Eyrie" at Vermilion, Ohio. That famous nest, which F. H. Herrick studied many years ago, was twelve feet deep and eight and a half feet across its flattened top before it crashed in a storm.

To step up to exceptionally deep nests, Broley threw a short rope ladder over the platform of sticks and anchored it. But for most nests he used a sort of shepherd's crook, an iron rod five and a half feet long with a broad hook that fitted over the edge of the nest. There was a smaller reverse hook at the other end, in which he inserted his foot.

Our tree was not a hard one to climb, and Broley went up first. As his head appeared over the edge of the flight deck, the young eagle, an eleven-week-old bird, grew panicky and launched off the other side. As it would have been another three or four days before the eaglet should have flown, it lost altitude rapidly. Broley yelled down to me to watch it. The bird crossed a deep creek and drifted a third of a mile until I lost sight of it in a low spot at the edge of a palmetto hammock.

Broley never left young birds on the ground. One day an eaglet jumped out and became tangled in a grapevine. It took an hour to get it back to the nest. Immediately, it hopped out on the stub where its nest mate was perched, then both lost their balance and came flopping into the lake below. They flapped ashore and hid in the dense scrub. By the time Broley got them back up the tree, he had spent seven hours. Because of such workouts he lost as much as seventeen pounds during a single week's banding.

This youngster from the Placida nest threatened to be another such problem. We found a way to cross the creek without swimming, but search as we might we could not locate the bird. At the end of two hours, by reorienting ourselves, we discovered it crouching under the fanlike fronds of a saw palmetto. It was a two-man job to get this vinegary, full-grown young eagle wrapped up in a piece of cloth so we could transport it back to the tree.

I followed Broley up the ladder, reached the nest, and, tense and puffing, edged my way out on the big limb. There was nothing between me and the ground to stop me if I fell. My admiration for Broley's simian abilities grew. He even went out to where I clung nervously and tied me on, so I could use both hands while I took my pictures.

My story appeared in the July 1, 1946, issue of *Life*, and because it was the week of the Fourth of July, I was asked to do a life-size head portrait of our national bird for the cover of the magazine. Before publication the idea was dropped for budget reasons. It would have been the first cover of *Life* in full color. Color reproduction had not fully recovered from wartime economics, but what really bothered me was what the editors had done to my full-page painting of an eagle diving on a rabbit. Without informing me, the art department painted out my rabbit and substituted a Disney-like bunny.

❦

It was exhilarating to perch on *Haliaeetus*'s high lookout. The two or three trees I climbed with Broley commanded magnificent views— great stretches of parklike pineland interlaced by winding tidal creeks or flanked by expansive salt flats, stretching out to the palm-studded shore of the Gulf. The only bald eagles' nest I have ever seen that surpassed these in grandeur was one the Craighead twins, raptor experts, showed me on the banks of the turbulent Snake River in Wyoming, where the alplike peaks of the Grand Tetons formed a dramatic stage backdrop for the king of birds. Although bald eagles' nests are to be found locally in the western mountains, these ranges are the realm of the golden eagle.

Very young baby eagles, still covered with pale whitish down, are too small to band, since the large aluminum bracelets slip off. Broley banded most of his young birds when they were between three and six weeks old. Then they are easiest to handle. But sometimes he was not able to visit an aerie until the eaglets were ten or eleven weeks old. These powerful youngsters, sleek in their new coats of glossy, dark feathers, were full of fight. Several times they sank their talons completely through Broley's hands, and he had to use his banding pliers to force them out.

Once, a young bird grasped his hand, and while he was intent on prying the talons loose, the bird suddenly threw its other foot into

Charles Broley, the Eagle Man, shows off a juvenile bald eagle in Florida.

Broley's face. Two of the sicklelike hooks narrowly missed each eye, and a third sank deep into his scalp. With blood streaming down his face, he managed to work out of that predicament. So the report was not far wrong that Broley was "scarred from head to foot" or, as one local newspaper stated, through a typographical error: "Mr. Broley is scared from head to foot."

He was never attacked by an adult eagle. Worried parents usually fly back and forth at a safe distance, muttering to themselves in a low *kak-kak-kak-kak* or in a high-pitched, creaking cackle *kqweek-kuk-kuk, kweek-a-kuk-kuk,* with the quality of an unoiled caster—hardly the defiant macho screams one would expect.

Great horned owls, by contrast, are more dangerous. Broley had several scrapes with owls that had taken over eagles' nests for their own use. One of these aggressive, silent-winged birds, striking him unawares, left the gashes of every claw in his back and nearly knocked him from the tree. Every year some of the aeries were appropriated by these big owls, which are very plentiful in the flat pinewoods.

One year, a horned owl was found brooding an eagle's egg with one of its own. Broley told of an even more fantastic situation. As he approached one of his nests, the female eagle flew off. Then, when he climbed to the great pile of sticks, a great horned owl flew off. There, less than three feet apart he found two eggs, one belonging to the owl and one to the eagle. We can imagine the fierce looks that must have been exchanged by the two stubborn birds as they incubated only an arm's length from each other! Torrential rains flooding the sandy backwoods roads made it impossible to revisit the nest, so Broley never knew the outcome.

Broley found that his Florida eagles ate little else besides fish, which made up more than 90 percent of their diet. But one pair—the birds in nest No. 35—were very partial to scaup ducks. This was an exception, not at all typical. Another family with unusual eating habits lived in nest No. 86. These birds had an appetite for brown pelicans and great blue herons! Hardly a year passed that Broley did not find the remains of one of the huge herons in the next. Both the pelican and the great blue have a wing spread nearly that of an eagle, but they weigh less, six and a half to seven and a half pounds (the limit an eagle can lift), against the eagle's own weight of eight to twelve pounds.

Like other winter residents, Florida bald eagles are great curio collectors. Broley had taken from their nests large electric lightbulbs, a bleach bottle, a tennis shoe, a child's dress, a gunnysack, a snap clothespin, corncobs, whelk shells, silk panties, and a copy of *The American Weekly*. A fish plug and a seventy-foot fishline were probably brought to the nest with a fish. In one nest Broley found a white rubber ball that the female did her best to incubate six weeks after her two young were hatched.

Broley estimated that at that time there were more than four hundred aeries in Florida. Formerly half of them were robbed each year by oologists who traded the eggs off to other oologists. A friend of mine, Bob Allen, who visited one of these oological kleptomaniacs many years ago, was shocked when his host drew from beneath a table a bucket brimful of eagles' eggs, the loot of one season's climbing.

Broley lost none of his birds to eggers because the practice had been stopped a few years earlier in Florida. He told me that 95 percent of the residents in Florida liked the eagles and wanted to protect them. As evidence of pro-eagle sentiment, I saw two or three nests in isolated trees on golf courses. In the center of a colorful gladiolus farm stood a lone tree, the only one spared when the fields were cleared, because it held an eagles' nest in its grasp. In a nearby town another pair of eagles occupied an aerial castle in a dead tree surrounded by houses. The town had grown up around it.

The most remarkable nest of all was one only a hundred feet from the back porch of a house. It reminded me of ospreys' nests I had seen on cart wheels atop poles near farmhouses in New Jersey. Directly beneath was a chicken pen, unscreened at the top, but the eagles did not bother the large white leghorns that strutted within, nor the numerous house sparrows that built their trashy nurseries in the sides of the eagles' own castle of sticks.

In Sarasota, I saw two large young eagles standing in a nest in a big pine behind the high school. Two boys were weeding their victory garden beneath the tree, and a neat white sign read:

BALD EAGLES
DO NOT DISTURB
ORDER OF CHIEF OF POLICE

When Broley first started his work, he was arrested several times before the police knew him. Once, while he was climbing to a nest, the defenders of the law received three phone calls from outraged neighbors who thought Broley intended nest robbery. So he usually checked in with the police before he started his banding. In due time local residents came to know him well, and a letter addressed simply to "Eagle Man," Tampa, Florida, was sure to reach him.

Richard Pough, who first suggested to Broley the idea of banding eagles, spent many a sober moment, hoping Broley would quit before he had an accident. But he was a careful man. He never trusted a rotten limb and tested each branch before he made a move. He was proud no nest had yet stumped him, even those in cypress trees 115 feet from the ground. "In fact," he told me, "climbing is getting easier each year instead of harder." Although he was very reticent about it, he did have one fall. It was at the end of a season of banding. He stood on a chair in the bedroom to put his equipment away on a closet shelf. The chair slipped; Broley hit his head on the bed and was knocked out!

Two years after my story for *Life*, approaching the age of seventy, in February 1948, Broley banded his thousandth bird. He then tapered off, much to Pough's relief, and spent more time watching individual pairs of eagles.

It was during those postwar years that Broley began to notice that his eagles were in trouble. Year by year they produced fewer young. He suspected it was because of DDT ingested with the dead fish that were killed by this residual biocide. It was only a hunch, but it proved to be prophetic. Unfortunately, soon after, Charles Broley died of a heart attack while fighting a brush fire near his summer home in Canada.

In 1954, when I moved to Old Lyme in Connecticut, there were approximately 150 occupied osprey's nests within a radius of ten miles of our new home. There was even an abandoned nest on the hill behind the house. The following season, when I surveyed the concentration of nests on Great Island at the mouth of the river, surprisingly few young were to be seen in any of the nests. It was the first week of July, and almost no young had been raised.

I recalled Broley's suspicions about DDT. Because their diet was exclusively fish, ospreys would be even more vulnerable than eagles. At my suggestion two biology students at Yale—Peter Ames and Tom Lovejoy—took up the investigation as part of their graduate studies.

So did Paul Spitzer, who eventually got his degree at Cornell. There proved to be no question that DDT was involved. Later I took part in the hearings in our state capital to have the chemical banned. Remember, if you will, that this was even before Rachel Carson published her landmark book, *Silent Spring*, in 1962.

Because DDT has been eliminated from the wetlands environment, eagles as well as ospreys are now recovering their numbers somewhat. Thank heaven!

—MARCH/APRIL 1988

THE CATTLE EGRET

THE NIGHT CLERK at the Southland Hotel in Okeechobee, Florida, glanced at our signatures, then looked up at us (James Fisher and I were on our epic journey around "Wild America").

"Glen Chandler has been expecting you," he said. "If you want me to, I'll ring him up; he should be home."

In a moment I was speaking to Chandler, the Audubon warden who patrolled Lake Okeechobee and the Kissimmee Prairie. He seemed excited.

"What are the chances of seeing cattle egrets?" I inquired.

"I have good news," he replied. "Sam Grimes and I were out at Kings Bar today and we found a nest. Sam says it's the first cattle egrets' nest for North America."

A prediction I had made the year before had come true.

In April 1952, Guy Mountfort and I, gathering data for our *Field Guide to the Birds of Britain and Europe,* had traveled from London to Spain to make the acquaintance of some of the Spanish birds and especially this beautiful ardeid, which the British formerly called the "buff-backed heron." South of Seville, on the road toward Gibraltar, we saw our first cattle egrets in the company of a magnificent black bull that was perhaps destined for the arena in Seville or Jerez. But there was no antagonism here. The birds walked inches from the beast's nose as he grazed. Perhaps the *toro* sensed the symbiotic relationship existing between himself and his white attendants. I contrasted this amiable tableau in the meadow to the grim encounter—man against beast—that I had witnessed at the Plaza de Toros in Madrid.

For as long as anyone can remember, cattle egrets have nested on the edge of the Marismas, the vast marshes that are formed by the delta of the Guadalquivir River. Our host, Mauricio Gonzalez (who was later to translate our field guide into Spanish), assembled a caravan of a dozen horses and mules and half a dozen horsemen and *guardas* for the eighteen-mile trek across the Sahara-like dunes and pinewoods. Our destination was the Coto Doñana. There Mountfort and I lived in the fabulous *palacio*, a hunting lodge of the Spanish aristocracy. My room was that of the Marques del Torero, while nearby were the quarters formerly used by King Alfonso.

The *pajarera*, or heronry, three or four miles from the *palacio*, was in several huge spreading cork oaks. We estimated the total number of birds to exceed four thousand, more than half of which were cattle egrets. The exact location of the colony could be pinpointed by the long ribbons of egrets flying to and from their distant feeding grounds.

The cattle egrets, standing on their twiggy nests, were still at the peak of nuptial beauty, with buffish plumes on their backs and breasts. Their bills were suffused with red, and their legs and eyes were garish puce-pink. Later in the season the red flush would leave the yellow bills and the legs, and they would lose their buffish plumes and become quite white.

On returning to the United States after my Spanish adventure, I learned of a most astonishing event: Cattle egrets, the first ever recorded in North America, had just been reported from three states.

The presence of these Old World birds had been known in the Guianas in northern South America for some years before their northward eruption. There they had found an ideal niche—herds of Brahman cattle with their Hindustani herdsmen, much as in India, where the bird is abundant. Did someone deliberately introduce them from abroad? Or did the first ones come as stowaways on a cattle boat? Most likely they were wind-borne wanderers. The distance across the Atlantic is much less between the bulge of Africa and northern South America than at other points. Vagrants assisted by strong winds could conceivably cover the expanse before they were

*Cattle egrets were first reported
in North America in 1952.*

completely exhausted. Other species, the glossy ibis, for example, must have reached our shores in such a manner in the past.

In a relatively few years, the original South American flock of cattle egrets increased to thousands. A correspondent in Georgetown in Surinam wrote me that part of the reason for their explosive spread was that they raised two broods each year.

William Drury, Jr., of Cambridge, Massachusetts, had seen the cattle egret at Aruba, in the Netherlands West Indies, when he was in the U.S. Navy. But the bird was far from his thoughts when he started out, on the morning of April 23, 1952, to make a check of the spring migrants in the Sudbury Valley at Wayland, Massachusetts. His companions were Allan Morgan and Richard Stackpole. They stopped at Mrs. Francis Erwin's farm to look over Heard's Pond. Morgan spotted a dark, heronlike bird with a decurved bill, which they identified through the telescope as a glossy ibis. This was certainly enough to highlight the day, because it was the first record of a glossy ibis in the Sudbury Valley in 102 years. As they started to leave, Morgan noticed a white bird alight among a herd of heifers. Their first reaction was that it was a snowy egret, but the binoculars showed that it was not. Drury, scarcely believing his eyes, correctly identified it.

Scientific ornithological tradition demands that the first record of a new species for a state be substantiated by a specimen. This was a "first" for the continent. Morgan possessed a federal collecting permit, but the bird, in typical leechlike fashion, stayed so close to the cattle that there was danger of shooting a heifer instead of the heron. Two shots were fired, but the bird did not lose a feather. Alarmed by these unfriendly actions, it flew quickly toward the next farm. There a herd of black Angus would act as decoys, it was thought, but neither herd nor heron could be located.

It was still rather early in the morning—about six o'clock. The frustrated ornithologists aroused a sleeping friend who owned a small plane; with this air support they soon located the missing bird. By shouting instructions through the open door of the low-circling plane to a Jeep below, the observers directed the ground party to their quarry. After several attempts, using the Jeep, then a tractor, as a blind, the bird was collected. The cattle egret was officially added to the North American list, and the specimen was placed in the Museum of Comparative Zoology at Harvard University.

Naturally, the first reaction was that it was probably an escape from some nearby zoo. A quick check revealed no clues. Then came astounding news from New Jersey. Two days after the Massachusetts affair, a cattle egret was discovered on a farm at Cape May. Later, a second bird appeared. Birders by the hundreds, from Philadelphia, Washington, New York, and even farther, poured in by car and by train to see these two distinguished visitors, which remained for months. Fortunately, the owner of the farm, Michael McPherson, was very interested in the birds and allowed no harm to come to them.

Then, on the first of June, Louis Stimson, touring the northwest shore of Lake Okeechobee in Florida with his wife, discovered *ten* cattle egrets, in two groups, of four and six!

In July, I returned to London to complete work on the European field guide. One afternoon, just outside the publisher's office, whom should I meet but Richard Borden, of camera-gun fame, with whom I had worked at the National Wildlife Federation. He invited me to his hotel for a cool drink, and full of gossip, I told him the news of the cattle egrets. I predicted, in all seriousness, that someday they would nest in the United States. "Dick," I advised, "if you ever see a small egret walking around the feet of cows, look twice at it."

"That reminds me," Borden replied, "I photographed some snowies with cows in Florida this spring." I suggested he look carefully again at his film. He did and discovered to his delight that he had unknowingly photographed cattle egrets, not snowies.

Borden's movies were taken on March 12, 1952. But there may have been cattle egrets in Florida even before that. Willard Dudley of Homestead saw a cattle egret at Clewiston in May 1948 but did not report it because he assumed that it was an escape.

There were other sight records during 1952, indicating a major invasion. Inasmuch as there was a whole flock around Lake Okeechobee, it seemed inevitable that they should nest. Late in the year they disappeared, to reappear in the spring.

Before James and I left Newfoundland on our 1953 odyssey, Leslie Tuck had asked whether we would care to see the skin of an egret in his office. The bird had come aboard a trawler on the Grand Banks, two hundred miles from St. John's, sometime between October 24 and 29, 1952. Tuck assumed it to be an American egret, but when he drew the specimen from the tray, I saw that something was wrong. The bird had a yellow bill and black legs; that added up to American egret if one tried to run it down in the field guide—but it was much too small. Was it a cattle egret? There was just a touch of buff on the crown—but those blackish legs, how to explain them? Every cattle egret I had seen in Spain had reddish or yellowish legs.

Cattle egret.

At my suggestion the bird was sent to Ottawa for checking. My suspicions were confirmed. It was indeed a cattle egret, the first record for Canada.

When James and I, continuing our odyssey, arrived at the Southland Hotel in Okeechobee, Florida, on the night of May 6 and heard the news, I was elated. Things had come full circle.

We were tired from our long drive through the Kissimmee Prairie, so we decided to turn in early. Our room was oppressively hot; not a breeze stirred although all the windows were open.

Glen Chandler was at the hotel the next morning before we had the sleep out of our eyes. No sooner were we on the road following Glen's car through the prairie south of town than we spotted fourteen white birds among a herd of cattle. They were small herons, about the size of snowy egrets. We put the telescope on them; snowies will sometimes consort with cattle, but these were cattle egrets all right, with pinkish or yellowish bills. I stalked them with my movie camera, and James stalked me with his Leica and got a shot or two of me photographing the cattle egrets before the nervous birds flew away.

Our destination was a large mixed heron and ibis rookery on Kings Bar out in the lake, where only yesterday Grimes and Chandler had actually found the cattle egrets' nest. As we drove along, we passed marshy ponds and rain pools. In one pool there was a big

Cattle egrets in breeding plumage have buff-colored plumes on the back, breast, and crown.

flock of handsome wood storks. At that time they were called "wood ibis," but, of course, they are not true ibis at all. The great white birds, their dark, naked heads down, busily sweeping for food, imprinted themselves on Fisher's memory more than anything else he saw that day. They were accompanied by another bizarre bird he had never seen before. Like knives, or scissors, a flock of black skimmers sliced the surface of the pond from end to end, charging in loose formation almost between the legs of the wood storks.

I assured James we would see many more black skimmers, but this first introduction to a graceful band, with vermilion beaks and poised and beautiful flight, contrasting so vividly with the long-legged wood storks, gave him great pleasure. I had never before seen a skimmer away from salt water. To see a flock feeding on a rain pool in a farmer's field was crazy.

At the fish camp we loaded a small boat with our camera gear and the blind. We gave the outboard a whirl and sped down the winding Kissimmee River to the vast, almost horizonless lake. Distorted by mirage, Kings Bar lay three miles offshore. We had some trouble landing, as there was no solid ground anywhere. Ibis erupted from the willows in great flocks, glossy and white ibis together. At that time, this one island must have harbored almost the entire U.S. population of the glossy ibis.

Chandler went ahead, keeping alert for poisonous water moccasins. Struggling through the bushes in two feet of water was quite a feat, especially because the surface was covered with an interlocking blanket of water hyacinths. We followed the junglelike trail that Chandler had hacked with his machete through the willows and buttonwoods the day before. Birds boiled up from the bushes by thousands: tricolored herons, snowy egrets, great egrets, little blues, even one or two yellow-crowned night-herons; and white ibis and glossies, of course. We came to a little clearing. Chandler hesitated a moment, then pointed with his machete to a platform of sticks. "I think that's it," he said. "There was just one egg yesterday, now there are two."

Chandler and James left me there while they explored the other end of the island. I did not use the wooden platform that Sam Grimes had placed about fifteen feet from the nest. Intending to disturb the birds as little as possible by using a longer lens, I erected my burlap blind in shallow water about thirty feet away.

Less than fifteen minutes after my companions had gone, the herons and ibis settled in the dense thickets on all sides. Coarse croaks were counterpoint to the bubbling *wulla-wulla-wulla* of the snowies and the rasping of the chicks. Then, through the coarse burlap, I saw a white bird swing in and walk deliberately down the branch to the two blue eggs. This was it! I ran off about ten feet of film. Then I peeped through the slit in the blind to confirm the identification. My heart dropped. The bird had black legs and bright yellow feet. The owner of the nest was a snowy!

I had no doubt that the cattle egrets were nesting nearby; a least two flew back and forth overhead among the disturbed snowies when James and Chandler returned. Unfortunately, to determine just which nest was theirs would have required more time than we had. The sky was threatening; we had to leave fast.

Sam Grimes, hearing the news, returned three weeks later. He discovered three more nests of cattle egrets and photographed the birds. He reported that the nest I photographed was indeed that of a snowy. The cattle egrets' nest that had been about five feet away had apparently fallen from its support before our arrival. It was in the water.

Snowy egrets have black legs and bright yellow feet.

During the summer of 1953, the cattle egrets returned to McPherson's farm at Cape May. This time there were six. Virginia and Maryland were added to the list of states where the species had been seen. Later in the year, on November 21, Stimson counted 1,521 cattle egrets on the south side of Lake Okeechobee. This was a far greater number than was hitherto believed to exist in Florida.

When Queen Elizabeth paid her royal visit to Bermuda, three adventurous cattle egrets also arrived at that outpost of empire. The distance from the Florida mainland is about a thousand miles. One bird stayed awhile and came to an ignoble end when it drowned in a rain barrel.

In May 1954, Alexander Sprunt estimated that two thousand birds were then in Florida—and spreading to adjacent states. In August, Mrs. William Keeling wrote me that she had just seen twenty cattle egrets among the other herons at Eagle Lake, Texas. At least ten pairs of cattle egrets bred in Texas in 1959. Twenty years later, a census revealed that there were a total of 644,640 breeding cattle egrets in the state.

It is now by far the most numerous heron in North America, having bred in all but a few states, including coastal Maine and the Pacific seaboard. Several strays have even reached Alaska.

Will the cattle egret taper off and decline as some predict, or will it continue to burgeon? It has now conquered all of the South American continent. When I was in the Falklands recently, I learned from Ian Strange that hundreds, mostly immatures, now visit that seagirt archipelago yearly. He predicts they will breed there soon. After hearing this, I was not surprised to see several in Teirra del Fuego.

Will they become a nuisance—sort of a trash bird? Apparently not. Being basically eaters of orthopteran insects, they do not compete with other herons for food. The idea that they specialize in ticks and other cattle parasites is not true. But according to Raymond Telfair, who made a fantastically detailed study for the Texas Agricultural Experiment Station, cattlemen just love these birds. Because of their diet of grasshoppers, they keep the range healthy. They are opportunists, of course, and in Africa I once saw a cattle egret grab a swallow as it came out of its nesting burrow (it could not swallow the swallow because its wings projected). I have also seen starving cattle egrets at the old fort in the Dry Tortugas try to snatch warblers at the birdbath.

Biologists are buzzing with conjecture about the cattle egret's "population explosion," which seems to be worldwide. This successful species has now established beachheads on every continent except Antarctica, where there are no cows. It is the first example, in our time, of an Old World bird invading the continental New World without our assistance (although the fieldfare colonized Greenland in 1937). It apparently got here on its own two wings and the wind. Its food habits, with the accent on insects, are in the main different from those of other herons. Although it shares heronries with snowies and ibis, there is no basic conflict. All seem to benefit. Predators (crows, raccoons, and other egg eaters) make fewer inroads, relatively, if the colonies are large.

The cattle egret, beautiful and beneficial, is a fine addition to the American avifauna. In Florida and elsewhere it has become a familiar sight along the highway verges. After all, the roads are game trails of a sort, and the vehicles are the herd animals.

—JULY/AUGUST 1988

HIGH SEAS
IN A ROWBOAT

"YOU WERE LUCKY, señors. You may not realize it, but your bones, *right now,* could have been down there with the fishes."

In truth, we had no idea how foolhardy we had been—not until we met Señor Mayer, an Argentine who spoke flawless English with machine-gun rapidity.

I will recount our adventure. Nearly thirty years ago, Dr. Philip Humphrey, leader of Yale University's Patagonian Expedition, and I were barreling south along Argentina's desert coast in our large Chevy truck when toward evening we reached the little windswept town of Camarónes (Spanish for shrimps), twelve hundred miles by road south of Buenos Aires and one thousand miles north of the Strait of Magellan.

Apparently the chief product of this bleak, tidy little town was a certain seaweed, exported to Japan for the breakfast table. We sought out the one small hotel, which, like most of the shabby hostelries along the coast of Patagonia, cost us approximately three dollars per day, including three meals. Usually such lodging was worth not one cent more, but in Camarónes the meals, at least, were good.

In those days the few Americans who traveled the Patagonian wasteland were usually connected in some way with the oil industry. The Argentines viewed them as a predatory breed with much too much money to squander. The hotel owner, spotting the obvious Americano, often upped his prices far above those extracted from the locals.

We were not oilmen, and we had to keep things on a shoestring budget. Furthermore, besides ourselves we had two helpers—

ayudantes—employed by Phil Humphrey to help make up the specimens he was collecting for Yale. Jose, a nineteen-year-old *Paraguayjo*, was an uncommunicative type who had never before been far from home. Atilio, a lad of twenty-one who, as a small boy, had fled with his father from Communist-dominated Hungary, was more a man of the world. His ten youthful years in Río Negro Province in the foothills of the Andes had transformed him into a very resourceful Argentine.

Our mutual strategy at the end of each day was to park the car near the hotel of our choice, then send Atilio ahead to dicker with the proprietor. When the deal was made, we would all file in.

At Camarónes, the proprietor was a bald, talkative Italian. We asked him about the birds—particularly, were there any seabirds near Camarónes?

"Sí, señors," he replied. "There is an island—Isla Blanca—about five kilometers off the shore." The name, Isla Blanca—"White Island"—sounded promising.

"What kinds of birds?" we asked. With an expansive wave of his hand he replied, "Muchos pinguinos—muchos cormoránes—muchas gaviotas [gulls]." Was there a boat to be had? There was, and after dinner he appeared with a strapping seafaring type—a man of about fifty-five with a handsome, weather-beaten face whose graying hair was kept in place by a black beret.

My Spanish has always been fragmentary, so Phil did the talking. Could the boatman take us out tomorrow? He said that he could. But we must be on the water by 4:30, at daybreak, before the wind was up.

We realized that the wind was a major problem and that throughout most of the day—and every day at this time of year (December)—an unrelenting gale blows. The winds, born of the Andes to the west, sweep unobstructed across the Patagonian plain to the coast. There are times when they reach hurricane strength, and the stones of the desert pavement become so sand-polished that they look as though they had been given a coat of lacquer. The winds blast through the town and blow out to sea, whipping up huge, white-capped combers.

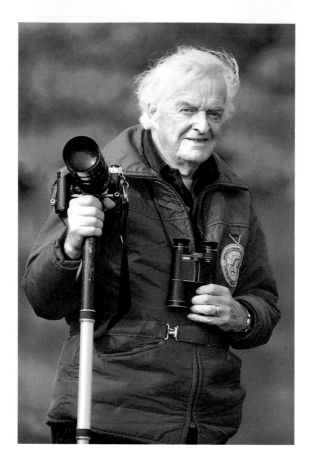

Peterson was rarely without his camera when in the field.

(Virginia M. Peterson)

At dawn we were met at the door by our boatman, who led us for two miles to the steeply sloping shingle where the boat lay bottom-up, safely above the high tide. It was just a dory, though a stout one, with two long oars and two smaller oars in reserve. We had not counted on rowing; we had expected some kind of an outboard at least.

At any rate, the sea was relatively calm, and on the horizon we could see the long, low island, at least half a mile long, with its three low, guano-whitened hills. There would not be room for the five of us in the boat, so Atilio and Jose were instructed to return to pick us up after the middle of the day.

There was no need for Phil and me to help with the oars. Our skipper's strong arms and the wind at our tail were sufficient. Giant petrels—*Macronectes*—large as albatross, flew by on stiff, flat wings.

One came close enough for us to see the tubed nostrils on its huge beak. Skuas hawked over the water like heavyset falcons and plundered the passing terns. The three miles did not take long, for the morning wind had freshened just enough to assist us.

A platoon of Magellanic penguins stood like a welcoming committee on the shelving rocks as we approached. When the boat grated on the cobble, the birds became panicky and scrambled on their bellies into the sea. These were our first penguins except for an oiled bird we had found on a beach two hundred miles to the north.

Penguins are made for bird photography. One roll of film, or two rolls, or even ten are not enough when a photographer is turned loose in a colony. This particular penguin, a spheniscid, one of the "jackass" group with a black-and-white bridled face, does not nest in close-packed colonies on open ground, as so many of the other penguins do, but scoops out a burrow, or at least a hollow, to hold its two stained, whitish eggs.

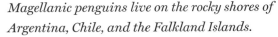

Magellanic penguins live on the rocky shores of Argentina, Chile, and the Falkland Islands.

There were many hundreds, perhaps thousands of penguins on this island. Wherever we went, they leered at us from their burrows. In a small shack of corrugated iron, a shelter used by guano workers, there were four nesting penguins—one in each corner.

I had been warned not to cuddle these engaging creatures, for there is nothing cuddly about the way they bite—not just with a nip but with a razor-sharp slash that can gouge out strips of flesh. And at close range there is nothing endearing in those fishy, watery-looking, bloodshot eyes as the bird wags its head from side to side as though to focus monocularly on the "super penguins" invading its island.

On the hill at the edge of the big colony of shags were scores of sacks of guano, hardened like sacks of cement that had been left in the rain. I assumed that this operation had been abandoned. In fact, I had never heard of guano harvesting on the Atlantic coast of South America.

The blue-eyed shag is also known as the imperial shag.

There were two kinds of cormorants: the blue-eyed shag—white-breasted and white-necked, with a curly crest and a ring of bare blue skin around the eye; and the rock shag—black-necked, with some red on its face.

The blue-eyed shags nested in dense colonies on the rounded crowns of the island. These birds would not leave their stained white eggs even when I shoved the camera almost into their faces. The rock shags, in smaller groups, clung to the more precipitous sites and vertical walls.

Wandering among the rocks at the water's edge were a score of dumpy, white, ptarmigan-like birds that at first glance one would take to be seafowl of some sort but that actually were aberrant shorebirds—sheathbills, *Chionis*. These snow-white birds, with their rather ugly faces and waddling walk, and the pretty Scoresby's or dolphin gulls lived on the offal of the nearby sea lion rookery.

Small sandpipers leaped from the tide pools, and by their icy squeaks, I knew them to be white-rumps, the commonest sandpipers on the Patagonian coast. Olin and Eleanor Pettingill, when they were in the Falklands, found them to be the most frequent sandpipers in those offshore islands. Certainly, this is the shorebird that habitually makes the longest journey of any in the world—longer than that of the golden plover (both use the same autumnal sea path from the Maritime Provinces of Canada).

Oystercatchers of two species attempted to distract me from their eggs. One was a white-bellied bird, a race of our own oystercatcher of the Atlantic Coast, the other a black species that pried mussels off the rocks while I shot it at point-blank range with 16-millimeter Kodachrome. Trying to document everything was like working in a three-ring circus. I tried to be systematic, shooting each species first with 16-millimeter movie film, then in 35-millimeter color with the Leica, and finally in both color and black and white with my two-and-a-quarter-by-two-and-a-quarter Bronica.

I did not notice the passage of the hours until the midday wind had risen to such a force as to make cinematography impossible. The sky held the threat of rain, and I ran back to my cache of equipment to make sure everything was covered. As the first drops fell, our boat-man studied the water and decided that we had better try to make it back. By this time the tide was low (it drops twenty to thirty feet here), and we wished for young Jose and Atilio to help us launch the heavy dory over the slippery rocks and seaweed. Only when we were afloat, with all equipment stowed in plastic bags and tarpaulin, did I realize that the row back was to be no picnic.

The skipper thrust an oar into my hands and gave one to Phil. He told us he had to have our help this time. Since Phil and I sat facing him, our arm action had to be the reverse of his. There was no place to stretch my legs, and at each stroke the oar handle banged my right knee. There was not much I could do about it. The problem was to pull away from shore.

The wind was kicking up again, and inasmuch as I had my back to the island, I could not see what progress we were making. However, with a slight turn of my head, my peripheral vision could catch one far end of the island or the other. As for our destination, a long, featureless line on the horizon, there was no way to establish scale.

The big waves now were beginning to comb over the bow, and there was no alternative but to hold our course and try to ride over them. It could be fatal to lose a stroke or two and get caught broadside.

Self-preservation spurs one to exhaustive effort, and in spite of the irritating banging on my knee, I matched Phil's strokes. I felt sure my back would break. Occasionally a roller far larger than the others broke over the bow, and for a moment or two we would actually be sitting in icy water. How I blessed the plastic bags that protected my equipment.

From minute to minute the wind seemed to wax stronger. The great waves now had their own pattern of smaller waves; even the wavelets had a crosshatch of riffles. The whole angry sea was moving upon us from the coast that seemed to remain forever distant. The spray that splashed our faces dried to form white patches of salt crystals. Swimming penguins outpaced us effortlessly, braying derisively, exactly like jackasses. They could escape the gale by merely diving into the windless depths.

At one point a black-browed albatross came knifing by—like a huge black-backed gull with saberlike wings, reveling in the very wind that we dreaded. This was the first time Phil had ever seen an albatross. In fact, I can recommend no better way to see your first albatross than from a rowboat in a high sea. You will never forget that bird.

And so, literally for hours, we struggled to cross those three miles. Raw blisters formed even on our skipper's horny palms. Finally, my peripheral vision could no longer catch the ends of the island, and I knew we must have gone at least halfway. I thought I could detect a

Black-browed albatross.

tiny, dark speck on the long horizon. It must have been the car.

The last mile went more quickly, either because the lee shore gave us some protection from the wind or because the wind itself had died down; I think the latter. At any rate, it was well past six when we beached. Atilio and Jose ran down to meet us, and while I hauled my gear up the slope and collapsed on the coarse sand, they helped the tired skipper roll the boat broadside up the cobble. They told us that several times as they watched us through the telescope the boat disappeared for minutes, hidden by the deep wave troughs, and they were sure we had gone down. By now leg cramps brought on by the cold, the wet, and the exertion were beginning to set in, and that night I lay on my cot in agony.

A month later we were quartered in the Grand Parque Hotel (another three-dollar-a-day deal) in Ushuaia, Tierra del Fuego, the southernmost town in the world. Phil and I were relaxing in the one congenial room—the tiny bar designated "nightclub"—when we were approached by Señor Mayer, who introduced himself.

"I have the room next to yours," he said, "and I couldn't help hearing you talk about birds. The walls are like paper. Well, it so happens that I am interested in birds, too—in a different sort of way. My company is in the guano business."

We talked about guano, about seabirds, and about Patagonia. The talk finally got around to Camarónes. I mentioned Isla Blanca. Señor Mayer shook his head. "Isla Blanca?" he asked. "That's our island. You had to have permission to go out there!" I said that actually we did clear our trip. The local harbor police knew we were going.

"Who took you out there? It must have been Hector Rodal, the man they call Tito. He would do anything for a few pesos." I told Señor Mayer that it wasn't all that bad. We had started out early before the wind had come up.

"But you had no assurance that you could ever get back," he said. "Two of our men tried it two months ago. The boat shipped water and went down just a quarter of a mile offshore. The older man went down almost immediately. The other man held on for a while, but fifteen minutes was his limit in the icy water, then he went under. There was nothing we could do about it. You were lucky!

"Next time," he said, "should you want to go out there or to any of the other islands, contact us in Buenos Aires. We will take you there in the big boat. In fact, we would welcome your advice about the guano birds."

That night I had a dream—a nightmare. I found myself again in the open boat, fighting the waves.

Now that time has passed, I realize that this experience, one of the most grueling in my life, and unpleasant at the time, was one that I wouldn't want to have missed. To take a chance once in a while and to get away with it is to feel alive.

—JANUARY/FEBRUARY 1989

Deceiving
the Experts

I confess that I have often played with the idea of planting a fake bird somewhere to deceive the experts. Years ago on one of the annual field trips of the American Ornithologists' Union, this mischievous thought first went through my mind. A well-painted wooden bird, a scarlet ibis or something even more improbable, could be placed far out on the marsh along the route of our boat. There it would be identified, but because of the treacherous mudbanks that would prevent our landing, no one would be able to check on it. What wild excitement!

It never occurred to me that I, myself, might someday be taken in by such a trick. Finally, it happened to me in the Bronx, on a Christmas Bird Census (now called the Christmas Count). One of the boys had a score to settle with Danny Lehrman. He knew that Danny was assigned to Bronx Park and that he would spend a half hour looking at the birds on Lake Agassiz. Using a block of soft wood, he carved out a dovekie, the little alcid that comes down from the Arctic to winter in the offshore waters of Long Island. He painted it, black above and white below, with the face pattern of the winter plumage. After much work and planning, he anchored it well out in the middle of the lake.

Danny reached the zoological gardens on schedule late in the afternoon, swept the pond with his binoculars, but did not spot the decoy. Either he was bleary-eyed from the day's concentration or his mind was on the gadwall that should have been there. A few minutes later I arrived. Bronx Park was not in my province, but I had exhausted the possibilities at Van Cortlandt Park and Riverdale, and we could not afford to miss the gadwall.

Starting at the right-hand side of the pond and moving toward the left, I scrutinized every tame mallard and every black. Right out in the middle, my glass paused on a small drifting object. My pulse jumped—it was a dovekie! Letting out a yell that the red howlers in the nearby monkey house could not have matched, I called Danny. This was the find of the day—not just a new record for the local Christmas Census but the first known record of a dovekie for the entire Greater Bronx region.

Other census takers arrived. We congratulated one another; we were exceedingly pleased with ourselves. But there was one thing that bothered us. The bird listed slightly, like a leaky toy boat. And it did not move much or dive but just stayed in one place, slowly turning in the current. I explained to my less experienced companions that its presence so far inland could be accounted for by the heavy wind and fog that had blown in from the ocean two days earlier. As an afterthought, I added that the bird looked rather sick and probably wouldn't make it through the night. Subconsciously one of the other fellows must have questioned the little auk's aliveness, for he cried, "See! See! I saw its head move!" "Yes," we agreed, "its head moved."

We could get no closer without scaling the ten-foot wire fence that girdled the lake. The question in my mind was not whether the bird was alive but whether it had reached Lake Agassiz under its own power. Perhaps someone had brought it to the park and Lee Crandall, the curator, had released it there.

At the long table during dinner that evening, we saved the dovekie till last. It was to be the pièce de résistance. We had carefully guarded our secret from the others. They, in turn, gave us no hint that they already knew about it. When the dovekie was announced, one after another of us was asked to stand and give the details. Were we sure the bird moved? We said we were. Then, at a signal from Joe Hickey, the chairman, the plotters roared in derision and the hoax was laid bare. In our chagrin we consoled ourselves with the thought that we had identified the bird correctly, even though it wasn't alive.

The dovekie experience paid dividends two years later on a field

A real dovekie, not a decoy.

trip to Cape May, held in conjunction with the annual Audubon convention. A whole platoon of Audubonites, eighty strong, led by three of us from the New York office, arose at 4:30 to watch the morning flight. It didn't come off; the wind was in the southwest. Few places can be as birdless as the dunes at Cape May Point on an off day. Everyone was ready to return to the hotel for breakfast when a rumor spread that there was a black-necked stilt on Lighthouse Pond. When our bus reached there, a crowd had already gathered on the dirt road where it skirts the south side of the marsh. There, at the edge of the cattails on the far shore, stood an honest-to-goodness stilt, its black back, white underparts, and long, reddish legs clearly visible through eight-power glasses. It seemed to be sleeping, with its slender bill tucked into the loose feathers of its back. Richard Pough, one of the leaders, drawing on his knowledge of New Jersey birds, pronounced that this was the first record of a stilt in the state since the early 1890s. But we were running behind schedule, he cautioned, so he advised everyone to take a good look and be back in the waiting buses in five minutes.

A species that had not been seen in New Jersey this century ought to be checked further, I thought, even though it was such an obvious bird as a stilt—the buses could wait. Furthermore, there was something about this inactive bird that did not seem right. For one thing, its legs looked too orange. Heedless of Pough's promptings, I plunged into the swamp with a teenager named William Fish and struggled through the thickets of cattails and pickerelweed. At one time I sank to my armpits in the mud and thought surely I would collapse from exertion and the sulfurous stench.

As we neared our goal, a deep channel we had not anticipated cut us off. We were close, but a thick patch of reeds hid the bird. There was nothing we could throw, so we clapped our hands. No result. Looking back helplessly at our crowd on the road, we saw Bob Allen poling a leaky rowboat through the pondweed. He would be able to settle the matter. Passing the mouth of our channel, he rounded the point and disappeared for a few brief moments. When he reappeared, he held something aloft for all to see. It was the stilt, stiff as a plank, a badly stuffed specimen that someone had planted.

Two or three in the crowd thought it was the poorest sort of humor. One less good bird for the list. I am sure one man held *me* accountable. Inwardly I felt pleased; it would have been much more humiliating if, after I had expressed my doubts, the bird had lifted its slim black wings and flown away.

A week later we ran down the story. During a housecleaning, the Academy of Sciences at Philadelphia had consigned a number of mounted specimens to the junk pile. Some wit from the Delaware Valley Ornithological Club had salvaged the stilt and set it up across the pond, placing it precisely where birders usually look for gallinules from the road. It was impossible to approach it closely, except by using the hidden rowboat; it was just near enough to be identified, but too far away to reveal its lifeless condition.

A fascinating literature could be built up on this topic of deception. In earlier days, when oology was a fad and museums were not yet glutted with egg collections, unscrupulous eggers palmed off fake rarities on their colleagues. One oologist told me that bona fide sets of wild turkey eggs were rare because there was no way of telling whether or not they came from the poultry farm. Even the curators at the Smithsonian often had their encounters with counterfeit eggs. Goose eggs were even offered as eggs of the California condor. Microscopic examination of the pitting on the eggshell by Dr. Alexander Wetmore quickly exposed the fraud.

In Britain, where oologists went to fantastic lengths to get what they wanted, a story is told about a pair of whooper swans, a species that breeds rarely in the British Isles, in the extreme north of Scotland. A watcher was stationed on the shore of the loch to keep his eye on the island where the birds nested, so as to head off nest robbers. Nevertheless, an egger swam to the island early one morning; but the guard, biding his time, waited till the thief returned to shore with his loot. While the scoundrel stood shivering with cold, the guard took the eggs from the collecting box and returned them to the nest. But the oologist had planned his strategy very carefully. The box had a false bottom, and the eggs the guard removed were eggs of the ordinary mute swan.

Practical jokes like this are embarrassing enough, but everyone knows how easy it is to be deceived by Mother Nature herself. One winter's day I was coming down the rocky trail on Mount Monadnock in southern New Hampshire with a group of teenage boys at my heels. My eye caught a dark shape with two ears, nestled close to a hemlock trunk about fifty feet up. I pointed it out to my charges and told them it was a long-eared owl. Here was a good example of natural camouflage, I informed them, and we could easily have passed it by as piece of bark. One of the boys was not convinced. Before I could stop him, he tossed a stone at it, but the bird stayed put. We walked over to the tree. Still the bird did not fly. No wonder—it *was* a piece of bark!

Everyone who hunts with a binocular knows how easy it is to make such mistakes. I remember the strange blue-looking bird one of the Bronx boys saw on a sand dune. It turned out to be a Bromo-Seltzer bottle. How many times have we put our glass on a fall webworm's nest silhouetted against the sky, thinking we had a hawk perched on a bare limb? Ludlow Griscom called these irritating webs "whisker-birds."

Whereas we sometimes see things that look like birds but are not, we constantly pass birds by because they blend with the landscape. Nature attempts to conceal and can be amazingly successful. In a general way, birds of the leafy forest crown—the warblers, vireos, and kinglets—tend toward yellowish greens, while those that rummage about the dead leaves of the forest floor—the thrushes, ovenbirds, and grouse—run to mottled browns. Birds of the grass country are streaked, while those of the beaches are dappled with muddy browns or sandy grays.

Although a few birds, like the tanagers and orioles, flaunt colors so bright that they seem to be saying, "I dare you," most are colored more like their surroundings. We call this form of deception "protective coloration." The bitterns not only are streaked with brown like the dead reeds they hide among but mimic them by standing rigid

Members of the Bronx County Bird Club, February 1978, in Florida.
(Virginia M. Peterson)

and pointing their bills toward the sky. It doesn't always work. Once I promised to show a least bittern to a schoolteacher friend. We glimpsed it as it slipped through the sedge, but it decided to "freeze" rather than fly. The only mistake the little buffy heron made was to freeze in the midst of bright green grass. Sneaking up slowly, I caught it. Another time I grabbed an American bittern in the same way, but this indignant bird struck me full in the face. To this day I carry the scar of its sharp bill on my upper lip.

Besides pattern there is another device of natural camouflage that obliterates form. Abbott Thayer, the artist-naturalist, called it "countershading." We have two little shorebirds that look much alike, the piping plover and the semipalmated plover. One is pale-backed, like the dry sand of the glaring beaches where it runs about. The other is dark-backed, like the wet sand or like mud exposed by the tide. Neither bird would blend with its surroundings were it colored the same below as above. The reason is that shadow on the lower part of a rounded object throws it into relief and gives it form. These two birds are white below, and the shadows cast on their underparts match their backs, causing the whole bird to disappear. The bright sand reflects light onto the breast of the piping plover, making the shadow lighter, just the color of the bird's pale back. The wet sand reflects less light, so the shadow on the semipalmated plover stays darker, matching its darker back.

Aware as I am of these things, I sometimes wonder why I should aspire to be a bird artist, for few things can be more difficult to paint than birds. This is the reason: An artist strives with his brushes and his pigments to create the illusion of form. Nature, in coloring the birds, whether with pattern or by countershading, attempts to obliterate it. How then can the artist succeed? First he builds the basic form of the bird. Then he eliminates it by superimposing the bird's pattern, thus winding up with a score of zero. That is why most bird portraitists seldom attempt to interpret nature literally. They follow in the tradition of Louis Fuertes, emphasizing feather patterns and overlooking the natural play of light and shade on the bird "in the round." However, a few artists who are more in the tradition of

Bruno Liljefors paint three-dimensional birds, playing with light and largely ignoring detail.

To get back to the plovers. They have another device that helps make them invisible—the black ring across the breast. This has been called "ruptive pattern" and helps to hide the bird by breaking up its shape into smaller pieces.

There are many other things about the pattern and plumage of birds that have set biologists to wondering—the flashy pattern of a willet's wing, or the white sides of a junco's tail.

William Vogt, the first editor of *Audubon* magazine, once played a mean trick on a yellowthroat while making a behavior study (behavior to most biologists seems to mean sex behavior). He put a mounted female yellowthroat in the territory of an ardently singing male. The male, as you know, has a black domino through his eyes. The female lacks this; she is just a plain little yellow and olive-brown bird. This male yellowthroat, overlooking the obvious fact that the female was not only inanimate but badly stuffed at that, courted and copulated as if she were the most desirable creature on earth. Two or three times he came back to repeat the performance. While he was away, Vogt slyly pasted a black mask on the female's face. The male returned and was about to resume relations as before when he suddenly noticed the mask. He bounced a full two feet in the air and dashed away as if completely mortified. Vogt concluded that unlike grouse, which use the trial and error technique, yellowthroats can recognize the other sex visually. Dr. G. Kingsley Noble of the American Museum got similar reactions when he pasted black mustaches on female flickers.

So the birds can be deceived as easily as we can. In fact, the ducks would not be as vulnerable if they were not so easily betrayed by decoys, which they have never been able to figure out. Surprisingly, decoys as we know them did not originate in Europe, even though the word comes from a contraction of a Dutch expression, *ende-kooy,* which means a duck trap. The earliest known decoys were founded by investigators who were digging in Lovelock Cave, in Nevada. There, in the rubble of a pre-Paiute civilization called the "tule eaters," they found some bundles of tule reeds carefully fashioned into the unmistakable form of canvasbacks. These decoys had been employed more than two thousand years ago, when the sea that lay in the Great Basin was far larger than the salty fragment that remains today.

Although there is some evidence that the Indians carried the scheme down through the years, the first mention of decoys in the white man's hunting, so far as I know, was made by none other than Alexander Wilson. In 1814, when discussing the mallard, he wrote: "In some ponds frequented by these birds, five or six wooden figures carved and painted so as to represent ducks, and sunk by pieces of lead nailed to their bottoms so as to float the usual depth on the surface, are anchored in a favorable position."

It was the rapid growth of market hunting during the last century that brought the wooden decoy into its own and made of its creation an art, albeit a homely one, practiced in between seasons by men with time on their hands. In those days they made "snipe" decoys too, and until recently you could still find them hidden under the gear, tarred ropes, and paint cans of many a Long Island fisherman's shanty, a reminder of days when shorebirds were shot all along the coast.

In recent years the hand-carved, hand-painted symbols of our much hunted waterfowl have become part of Americana and are sought by assiduous collectors who pay exorbitant prices, but probably some of the best examples still languish in dark corners of shanties on the salt marshes along the Chesapeake, the Jersey coast, the bays of Long Island, or in boathouses along lonely New England shores.

Whether decoys are inexpensive models from Sears, Roebuck or the best examples of the bayman's art, the ducks will be deceived—and so will the experts. One December afternoon I spotted a small flock of canvasbacks bobbing on the waves off Saybrook Point near the lighthouse. They were canvasbacks all right, and were as good as on my list. Just then a man rounded the breakwall in a punt and hauled them in—every last one of them.

—November/December 1989

Memories of
Sir Peter Scott

At the end of August, just a half hour before I left home for a month in Botswana, a phone call from England informed me that Sir Peter Scott had died.

That evening on the plane I had a disturbing dream. Two of my dearest friends, Peter Scott and James Fisher, now both gone, were standing there. They said nothing; they were just there, standing side by side. Surrounding them was a tessellation of crystals, rather large triangular crystals, shifting about, glittering. Half awake, I said to myself: "I must hold on to this dream." I repeated, "I *must* hold on to this dream." Then I awoke.

Peter Scott and I crossed paths for the first time in 1933, when we exhibited our paintings at an American Ornithologists' Union meeting at the American Museum of Natural History in New York. Peter's canvas of white-fronted geese was one of the hits of the show. How could one so young paint so well?

But it was not until some years later, in 1950—during the first postwar International Ornithological Congress (IOC), which was held in Sweden—that Peter introduced me to James Fisher, whose father had been Peter's headmaster at Oundle. While at this elite boys' school, Peter became hooked on birds, thus fulfilling his father's last words, written to Peter's mother, while he lay dying in the Antarctic: "Make the boy interested in natural history; it is better than any games." Peter not only was to champion the cause of wildlife protection worldwide and to become a great bird painter but also was to become a champion at several games. He was British figure skating champion while still a teenager and was an international champion of small boat racing by the time he was forty. When he took up gliding after the age of fifty, he soon held the gliding championship of England.

But to get back to the IOC in Sweden: One day at Uppsala, Peter, James, and I were having tea with Lord Hurcomb. Would it be practical, we wondered, to bring breeding ospreys and white-tailed sea eagles back to Scotland by hacking them? Whereas Sweden still had a good population of ospreys and sea eagles, both raptors had long been extirpated in Britain, wiped out by shooting and by egg collecting. Could eggs or young birds from Sweden or Norway be hand-raised at suitable sites in Scotland? Lord Hurcomb was enthusiastic about the idea, and so was Peter.

However, several years later, before the hacking experiment could be carried out, a pair of traveling ospreys, perhaps on their way to Scandinavia, dallied at Speyside in Scotland and set up housekeeping. The rest is history. Now there are more than fifty active pairs in Scotland descended from the original pioneers and augmented by hacking. As for the sea eagles, more than eighty young whitetails have been shipped from Norway during the last few years and released on the island of Rum off west Scotland. Reaching maturity, some of them have been laying eggs, and in 1985 the first native-born whitetail in seventy years took the skies over Scotland.

At the close of that memorable congress in 1950, many of us enjoyed a field trip to Lapland, where Peter acquired a pair of lesser white-fronted geese that he planned to bring back to Slimbridge. But somewhere along the way, the baggage crates with the captive geese were lost. I remember Peter's dismay at the railroad terminal in Stockholm, where he searched every obscure corner while cackling like a lesser white-fronted goose, hoping for an answer. The Swedish commuters who watched his strange behavior were puzzled and alarmed.

Geese had always been Peter Scott's favorites. The Hawaiian goose or "nene" was probably saved from extinction by his efforts. From a population of perhaps 25,000 a century ago, it dropped to a mere 30 known individuals by 1952, when he received several birds from Hawaii and through loving care started this strange little goose on its way to recovery. I was at Slimbridge the day after the first two goslings hatched and photographed them with their foster mother, a bantam hen. So well did they do that many of their descendants have become bums, begging for food at the picnic tables outside Slimbridge's reception center.

Guy Mountfort, who wrote the book *Rare Birds of the World,* is of the opinion that only because of the subsequent release of fourteen hundred captive-bred birds has the Hawaiian goose been able to maintain itself in the wild, but he is doubtful whether the species can continue to sustain the heavy predation pressure from introduced rats, cats, dogs, and mongooses.

Quite by coincidence, just after I returned to Christchurch in New Zealand after my first trip to the Antarctic (long before our trips on the *Lindblad Explorer*), I ran into Peter, who was about to visit the icy continent for the first time. I had just returned from McMurdo and was aware that he was in town because the billboard outside the motel announced, WELCOME PETER SCOTT. Later I spotted him at the Antarctic headquarters while he was being fitted out with a parka. When I tapped him on the shoulder, he turned around and looked at the mustache I had sprouted when I was at McMurdo. His first words were "I liked you better the way you were." Nearby in Christchurch there was a statue of Captain Scott in Antarctic gear, a rather heroic statue, created by Peter's mother, who was a talented sculptress. Some hooligan had placed an empty beer can in Captain Scott's outstretched hand. When Peter saw this, he promptly climbed up and removed it.

A reporter from the local press asked whether his visit to the Antarctic was a sentimental journey in remembrance of his father. He replied: "Not really. I simply want to compare Antarctic exploration the way it is now with the way it was then."

It was largely because of our mutual friend Lars-Eric Lindblad, and his great ship the *Explorer,* that Peter and I became such frequent companions, sharing our delight in the wild places of six continents. At McMurdo, I climbed with him to the cross that had been erected in his father's memory. In the Falklands we took part in ceremonies when we signed the Declaration of Conservation with the governor of the islands and Prince Bernhard.

Left to right: *Robert Bateman, Roger Tory Peterson, Peter Scott, and Lars-Eric Lindblad in Slimbridge, England.* (Virginia M. Peterson)

Both Peter Scott and James Fisher hosted innumerable television and radio shows for British Broadcasting. When I was in Britain, I was often asked to be a guest on their hour-long shows—so often that I was granted a membership in the club, free to have snacks at the studio in Bristol any time I chose.

I recall one broadcast in celebration of the life work of Ludwig Koch, the pioneer bird sound recordist. As a dry run, Peter posed the question "Which do you believe is the better singer—your mockingbird or our nightingale?" My reply: "I think that a good mockingbird is every bit as good as a nightingale."

At that point we put on a mockingbird recording, a rather run-of-the-mill mocker, I must admit. Then Koch put on his best nightingale—a virtuoso nightingale—a genius. There was no comparison. So when we went on the air we omitted that question. However, I still think that a really *good* mockingbird is better than some of those tiresome nightingales that sing all day long in the Camargue when you are listening for Savi's warbler.

Peter and his wife, Philippa, were frequent visitors to our home, both in Maryland and in Connecticut. I recall how interested Peter was in the pilot blacksnake that lived in the window garden of our living room at Glen Echo, gaining access by way of a chipmunk burrow that came in from the patio. And he was fascinated by the friendly skunk that came to our terrace in Old Lyme looking for a handout. By lying on the rug in the living room, with only the sliding glass doors between them, Peter confronted the little animal nose to nose (without the odor).

Whenever there was a convention of any environmental significance, Peter was always there. At a World Wildlife Fund meeting at Buckingham Palace, he even introduced me to Queen Elizabeth. When she asked me how many kinds of birds there were in the world, I answered: "About 8,600, Your Majesty."

And now all that is history. I have known no one who was more faithful in taking daily notes. Extracts from several of his logbooks, embellished with sketches, have been published.

Although most environmentalists think of Peter in connection with ducks and geese, his interests were far broader; they were as diverse as whales and sphinx moths. In later years he became increasingly interested in the colorful little fish that swarm around coral reefs, sketching them underwater with special equipment that he had devised. No living thing was unimportant to him.

We were all set to celebrate his eightieth birthday, and a number of artist friends and admirers had prepared a presentation album for the occasion. Each page would have a signed sketch or watercolor. But because of his heart problem, which he had endured for years, he just missed his eightieth birthday, by two weeks. Instead, a memorial service was held in November at St. Paul's Cathedral, with all the pomp and ceremony shown his father in those same vaulted halls many years earlier. As Lady Philippa commented: "Peter would not have known what to make of it all."

Although seemingly complex, Sir Peter Scott was basically a simple, direct, gracious man, but with far greater understanding of the natural world and how it fits together than most of us will ever have.

—MARCH/APRIL 1990

A Bar
in Botswana

A BAR? Not a *sandbar*—although I did photograph African skimmers nesting on a sandbar upriver. But a *beer bar* overlooking the Okavango River in Botswana. In this unlikely place I recently shot dozens of rolls of film.

Let me make this clear. I am not a barfly. I simply kept my film there in the fridge, but I soon discovered that this small, dilapidated structure was an ideal vantage point, a blind of sorts, from which I could photograph nine or ten species of birds at point-blank range without going outside.

Two kinds of swallows were actually nesting right inside the bar. Several pairs of striped swallows that had plastered their nests in the corners of the room flew in the open windows and out the doors, oblivious to the customers who were lined up for their drinks. These swallows, whose juglike nests of mud so closely resemble those of cliff swallows, are streamlined, more like barn swallows, but have strongly striped underparts. Rusty caps and rusty rumps contrast with the deep blue of their backs and wings. Several fully fledged young just out of the nest perched on the wall fixtures, begging to be fed by their parents.

Overlooking the bar, scarcely above eye level on the left-hand side, was the nest of a pair of wire-tailed swallows that also sported rusty caps but had clean white underparts. Their young were full-grown and flying, but when daylight faded they went back to the open, cuplike nest, where they were brooded by their parents while the bartender served sundowners only six feet away. The swallows inside the bar may have to look for another home in a year or two, because the insecure structure threatens to tumble into the river.

Already there were cracks in the ceiling, and the far corner of the room was beginning to project over the eroded bank, where the fast-flowing current had undercut the earth. In anticipation of the inevitable, the owners had constructed a new building farther back, where everything would soon be moved.

But at this point in time the steep banks below the open windows were a bird photographer's dream. Hundreds of carmine bee-eaters had excavated their burrows there. It was September, just before the rainy season; they had recently arrived in full force, and some were still digging. The carmine bee-eater has been called "Africa's most beautiful bird," and I won't argue the point.

There are twenty-four species of bee-eaters, an elegant family of birds that range across Europe, Asia, Africa, and Australia. None lives in the New World. Most of them run to vivid shades of green, but the carmine bee-eater is a shocking rose-pink accented by a bright blue crown, rump, and undertail coverts. Its slim form and elongated central tail feathers give it a streamlined look as it sails on the thermals.

Day after day I sat there on my folding chair while I shot roll after roll of Kodachrome and Fujichrome, sometimes with my 300-millimeter autofocus Nikon, at other times with a longer lens mounted on a heavy tripod. Because most of the nests were hidden below the lip of the bank, I worked on those birds that posed on branches and snags that projected over the water.

The carmine bee-eaters caught most but not all of their insects high in the air, climbing effortlessly to a height of two or three hundred feet. They seemed to be catching high-flying bees, which they deprived of their venomous stings by rolling them in their mandibles. This they did without interrupting their flight, or so it seemed. Returning to their perches after five or ten minutes aloft, they rested for another fifteen or twenty minutes before taking off again.

Unlike the little bee-eaters, which often cozy up to their neighbors, I never saw carmines snuggle. Three or four on a branch, perhaps, but usually several inches apart. When too close they threatened each other.

Carmine bee-eaters catch insects as high as three hundred feet in the air.

Occasionally there would seem to be a mysterious panic. The whole colony would fly out en masse, as though some phantom predator had appeared. But within minutes they were back, as if it had been a false alarm.

Late in the morning, activity around the clusters of nesting holes usually subsided, and suddenly a swarm of birds would take off, perhaps for a brush fire signaled by a wall of smoke two or three miles distant. Hawking around the edges of the flames and into the smoke, they seized the fleeing insects. One of their African names, translated, means "cousin of the fire." Returning in the afternoon, they decorated the nearby acacias like Christmas tree ornaments, bright pink against the blue sky. Later some of them came down to dust-bathe in the patch of dry sand beside the path.

Two young German photographers on a television assignment had already been on location for two weeks, filming from a burlap blind on one of the lower ledges near the bar. When I arrived they were digging a hole of their own a hundred yards downstream. Here they planned to film what went on inside one of the nesting chambers when the birds were incubating and feeding young. They would stay another month to film the whole sequence. Or so they hoped, if the birds did not desert. I never learned whether or not they were successful.

Among the very gregarious carmine bee-eaters were a few pairs of white-fronted bee-eaters, a species that I had filmed years ago near Lake Nakuru in Kenya. They were green-backed with a patch of red across the throat, as though they had been designed for color film, especially Fujichrome, which heightens the green and reds. They had started nesting earlier than their more numerous relatives and were already feeding young in the burrows. Their manner of catching bees, wasps, dragonflies, damselflies, and grasshoppers was quite different from the strategy used by the carmines, which foraged aloft. The whitefronts spotted their prey from their favorite perch, then sallied forth only a short distance before returning with the bee or wasp, which was whacked vigorously against the branch. It is believed that this battering removes the toxic stings from these hymenopterous insects before they are swallowed. As if taking no chances, the whitefronts gave the same rough treatment to dragonflies, damselflies, and even to the occasional butterfly.

Early in the morning, and again later in the day, noisy companies of gray louries or "go-away birds," long, slim birds with bushy crests, came to the water's edge apparently to eat pellets of mud, or so it seemed. They were obviously getting something they needed.

Three kinds of kingfishers cruised along the river and sometimes perched on a snag only fifteen feet away. The tiny, jewel-like malachite kingfisher posed for me, and so did the larger pied kingfisher; but the giant kingfisher eluded me until we took the boat upriver.

A pair of African pied wagtails had a nest somewhere nearby. They tripped along the edge with food in their thin bills, their tails bobbing nervously up and down. I got some pictures, but from my vantage point I could not see where they had their young.

Offshore a pair of reed cormorants swam in the strong current and took turns drying their wings on the snag while I took shot after shot. What a setup!

Malachite kingfishers are common along slow-moving rivers and ponds.

Exactly where is this special place? If you examine the map of Africa, you will find a landlocked country, Botswana, in the southern part of the continent. Formerly called Bechuanaland, it is embraced by the sands of the Kalahari. Because of its aridity, Botswana supports a relatively small population of people, including the primitive bushmen. However, because of a lucrative diamond mine, it is not a poor country. Nor is it plagued by political dissension or tribalism as are its neighbors. It is comfortably peaceful.

It is difficult to define the extent of the Kalahari. Dominated by a blanket of sand, it is said to be the largest continuous stretch of sand in the world, extending at least fifteen hundred miles from the forests of Zaire to the Orange River in South Africa. The farther south, the more arid the terrain becomes, but where we are in northern Botswana, deep in the heart of the golden Kalahari, there is a strangely different landscape, an anomalous green jewel. The Okavango River, flowing southward from the mountains of Angola, abruptly fans into a broad delta, at least one hundred miles across, dividing and subdividing into countless lesser streams until their blue waters disappear into a deepening sea of sand, the dry bed of a huge ancient lake. Thousands of islands are isolated by the meandering water, especially after the rains, a mosaic of green islands and islets in the midst of the brown desert. Some are scarcely more than sandbars decorated with a few palms, while others are blanketed by waving marshes of papyrus. Here and there larger islands are clothed with rich forests of acacias and tropical hardwoods, where owls and nightjars hide by day and announce themselves in the moonlight.

To get from one isolated camp to another required a small plane, a three-seater piloted by Tim Liversedge, who took Wes Henry and me from place to place, usually landing on dirt runways. Our favorite place was Shakawe, a fishing camp where the bar was located. The owners had found that birding groups, such as those led by Victor Emanuel, are also profitable.

However, I am not a lister; I had already ticked off most of the East African and South African birds. I go for the photography, and I have found no part of Africa more fulfilling than the Okavango, especially Shakawe, although there are several other fishing camps in the delta that are also popular with birders and that have their own unique specialties. The big mammals are in the Okavango too, perhaps not as many as in the Serengeti, farther north, but the birding is richer, whether you are a lister or an obsessive photographer, as I am.

—MAY/JUNE 1990

IMMORTAL AUDUBON

WHEN I WAS a teenager, more than sixty-five years ago, I painted a kingbird that had been killed by a car. My eyes were far more acute then, and with a fine 00 brush I tried to paint in every barb of every feather as I imagined John James Audubon had done. I spent a week on that drawing, but it was a disaster; far too "tight." I did not know then that the extremely fine detail I saw in the Audubon prints had been added by Robert Havell, the engraver who made the copperplates from which the printers were struck. It was not until I went to art school in New York that I saw Audubon's original watercolors and realized this.

My early role model remains a force and an influence today, for the name of Audubon has become synonymous with birds, and he has been all but canonized in American natural history. Whereas many once-famous men have faded from memory, Audubon's mystique has been kept alive and growing, largely because of the conservation organizations that bear his name. His original watercolors for *Birds of America* are often still on display at the New-York Historical Society on Central Park West. Of the 435 originals, only 2 are missing—the blue-gray gnatcatcher and the black-throated blue warbler; where they are remains a mystery.

The collection of paintings, almost intact, was acquired from Audubon's widow twelve years after his death in 1851 for a modest $4,000. Today these paintings are beyond price. At Sotheby's gallery in New York in June 1989, a single print of the great blue heron—not the original painting—went at auction for $66,000. Several years earlier the full set of 435 prints was sold individually to bidders for a total of $1,716,660, more than 120 times the cost of the bound set of plates that was on display at the National Audubon Society's Fifth Avenue home when I worked there fifty years ago. It was on loan from a Virginian named Duncan Reed, who told me that he paid $14,000 for it.

Jean Jacques Fougere Audubon was the son of a French seaman, also named Jean, who owned property in Les Cayes on the island of Santo Domingo (Haiti), where he fathered a boy and a girl out of wedlock. The mother of the boy, a French woman, a Miss Rabin, died less than a year after her son was born.

Audubon's father returned to his home in France in 1791 with the young boy, Fougere, and his half sister, Muguet; how he explained things to his legal wife is not known. Mrs. Audubon apparently was a very forgiving woman, and being older than her roving husband and somewhat beyond the age of childbearing, embraced the children as though they were her own. If this suggests that Audubon's origins were humble or disadvantaged, it is far from the truth; he was all but spoiled by his overindulgent adoptive mother and was given a young gentleman's tutoring. His father's attempt to give him a naval education was a fiasco; the young man hated it. However, he did gain the artistic skills that would determine the direction of his life's work.

When Audubon reached the age of eighteen, his father sent him overseas, perhaps to avoid conscription in Napoleon's army, to Mill Grove, near Philadelphia, where he owned property. By then birds had become an obsession from which the young man would never free himself. He watched them and drew them, much as he had done as a teenager in France, but here in America everything, including even his name, which he Anglicized to John James, was new.

The first American birds to attract his serious attention were a pair of phoebes that lived along the creek near his new home. Because of these tame little birds, he performed an experiment that marked a first in the history of ornithology. He wrote that he placed "silver threads" about the legs of a brood of young for identification, seeking to learn whether they would return the following year. Two of them did, building their own nests farther up the creek. Thus he became the first American bird bander.

At Mill Grove, he met Lucy Bakewell, a neighbor, whom he married, and they settled in the frontier town of Louisville, Kentucky, where his father had set him up in business as a merchant. After a discouraging start, the young couple moved westward to the Mississippi and eventually downriver to Louisiana. Because he met with a succession of business reverses, he has often been judged "impractical." But in fairness we must realize that investment was risky during those years;

Peterson saw original Audubon watercolors such as this one at The New-York Historical Society. (Greater Flamingo [*Phoenicopterus ruber*], 1838, by John James Audubon, accession number 1863.17.431 in the collection of The New-York Historical Society.)

the War of 1812 had brought the country to the brink of bankruptcy.

Nevertheless, we can argue that Audubon spent too much time afield with his beloved birds, exploring the wilderness, shooting, and painting. Later he wrote, "I drew, I looked on nature only; my days were happy beyond human conception."

Eventually forsaking business, he devoted more and more time to the birds, often staying away from home several months at a time eking out a living as an itinerant portrait artist, dancing master, and fencing instructor. During these hand-to-mouth years, Audubon's devoted Lucy, who had borne two sons, Victor and John, was both motive power and the balance wheel that kept home and hearth together. She ran a small private school, taught, and acted from time to time as a governess, freeing her husband for his creative endeavors. As Francis Herrick, Audubon's biographer, commented: "Without her zeal and self-sacrificing devotion the world would never have heard of Audubon. His budding talents would have been smothered in some backwoods town of the Middle West or South."

It is not clear whether Audubon had in mind eventual publication when he embarked on his grandiose plan of painting all the birds of North America. Perhaps it was the unheralded visit of Alexander Wilson at his shop in Louisville that stirred him to action. Wilson was trying to get subscriptions for his pioneer work on American ornithology and was dumbfounded when Audubon showed him his own portfolio.

Audubon had an advantage not shared by Wilson, or his predecessors who drew birds with such archaic stiffness, as though they were museum mounts on pedestals. He took birds out of the glass case for all time and gave them the illusion of life. His method was to wire freshly killed specimens into lifelike positions on a gridded board. He describes the first time he tried this:

> One morning I leapt out of bed . . . went to the river, took a bath and returning to town inquired for wire of different sizes, bought some and was soon again at Mill Grove. I shot the first kingfisher I met, pierced the body with wire, fixed it to the board, another wire

held the head, smaller ones fixed the feet . . . there stood before me the real kingfisher. I outlined the bird, colored it. This was my first drawing actually from nature.

Inasmuch as Audubon wired his models in this fashion, the end result sometimes looked it; even so, his birds remained the most lifelike representations for many years. All of his birds, whether hummingbirds or eagles, were painted and reproduced the size of life. To fit the great blue heron onto the page, he drooped the neck gracefully so that the bird's bill nearly touched its feet. To hasten the project, many of the backgrounds were painted by his assistants, Joseph Mason, George Lehman, and Maria Martin.

Although he displayed his portfolios to prospective printers in Philadelphia and New York, he could find none who would risk the capital necessary for publication. Therefore in 1826, at the age of forty-one, with money he had scraped together by doing portraits, and from Lucy's savings as a teacher, he set sail for England to try his chances there.

He was an immediate sensation abroad. The once bankrupt businessman proved to be a master salesman. Just as Benjamin Franklin had played his part well at the French court by wearing plain Quaker garb, Audubon knew the public relations value of acting the role of the "American woodsman" in the salons of London, even to his long, bear-greased locks. It is well known that he admitted to an inordinate fondness for elegant attire when he was in the fine homes of Philadelphia and New Orleans.

With subscriptions assured, he began production with an engraver in Scotland, William Lizars; but after only ten plates had been engraved, the colorists went on strike. Things dragged on for weeks until Audubon, exasperated, switched to Robert Havell, in London, who was to become one of the greatest engravers in aquatint the world has ever known. However, from time to time Havell added touches of his own to Audubon's work, improvising branches or backgrounds when they were needed to complete a composition. Approximately two hundred sets of the Double Elephant Folio were bound

Audubon's influence on Peterson can be seen in works such as this Peterson painting of greater flamingos.

and distributed. They were priced at one thousand dollars each.

Although Audubon received high honors and accolades during the last two decades of his life, he became much more famous in the century that followed. Because he sparked a latent national interest in America's wild heritage, especially its birds, his name has been perpetuated in innumerable parks, streets, and towns across the land. A mountain peak in Colorado bears his name. In the Washington Heights neighborhood of upper Manhattan, where Audubon spent his declining years and where I once lived as an art student, there was an Audubon Avenue, an Audubon Theater, and translated into digits, an Audubon telephone exchange. A local group of painters called themselves the "Audubon Artists," even though they did not draw birds.

Before the turn of the century there were even "Audubon gun clubs," which, in a sense, reflected Audubon's predatory nature more accurately than the noble fiction that gave rise to the Audubon movement and the National Association of Audubon Societies, now simply called "Audubon." Far more birds fell to his trigger reflexes, his obsession with shooting, than he needed for his drawing and research, and most of the early ornithologists who followed him were equally fond of the gun. They had to have the specimen "in hand" to establish base lines of morphology, classification, and anatomy. At the turn of the century, even that venerable bearded nature writer John Burroughs counseled the serious young bird student: "Don't ogle it through a glass, shoot it." But by the 1930s, with the advent of modern field guides and better optical equipment, the binocular replaced the shotgun.

Audubon never really concerned himself with environmental matters, although in his later years he began to worry a bit about the future of certain birds because of direct persecution.

We often speak of the "Audubon ethic" as though Audubon was the first to practice what we now preach so fervently. True, he came to America with a fresh eye when it was still possible to see some of the virgin lands, but his writings tell us little of the rapid changes that he must have witnessed during his lifetime. Still, we find frequent references to the palatability of birds and their availability in the market. He comments like a gourmet about the relative tastiness of not only owls, loons, and crows but also robins, white-throated sparrows, and other songbirds.

But as he grew older, a conscience began to surface in his writings. Of a pair of least sandpipers he wrote: "I was truly sorry to rob them of their eggs, although impelled to do so for the love of science, which offers a convenient excuse for even worse acts." After his first meeting with arctic terns he wrote: "Alas poor things! How well do I remember the pain it gave me to pass and execute sentence upon them."

Audubon's real contribution was not the conservation ethic; it was awareness. Awareness inevitably leads to concern, and because he opened the eyes of others, it is understandable that he has become the father figure of the conservation movement in North America, even though he himself never dreamed of current preoccupations such as recycling and air pollution. As one cynic put it, "What if his name had been Joe Bloke?"

His own eyes must have been almost as sharp as those of a hawk. Not merely 20/20 vision, but perhaps 20/5. But his hearing seems to have been poor, even though he played the violin. Although he wrote glowingly about the ebullient song of the mockingbird, he apparently could not hear the sibilant voices of some of the warblers. He claimed that the parula warbler had no song. Yet, when I visited Oakley house at St. Francisville, Louisiana, where Audubon lived and painted for a summer, I found the parula to be the most persistent singer in the live oaks around the plantation. Audubon had been banging away at birds so incessantly that his eardrums, I suspect, had become as insensitive to the high register as those of a rock musician.

A great many artists and illustrators have painted American birds since Audubon, but it was not until Louis Agassiz Fuertes appeared that anyone could challenge his preeminence. Fuertes dominated bird illustration during the first quarter of this century just as Audubon had done nearly a century earlier. His own career was sparked by Audubon, and like him he was basically a delineator rather than a painterly painter. Although Fuertes's paintings show more subtly and accurately the character of the birds they depict, they are not as dynamic as decorations on the wall as the Audubon prints. Audubon reflected Audubon in everything he did, whereas Fuertes mirrored more of the character of the bird, less of himself.

My own initial influences lie somewhere between Audubon and Fuertes; from Audubon a sense of design and spice; and from Fuertes knowledge of how a bird is put together—the personality of a species. My field guide drawings, however, are primarily an invention of my own, a different art form, if you will. They are a teaching device in which I have reduced things to an abstraction of form and pattern, with little arrows pointing to the key field marks. By contrast, most of my limited edition prints, published by Mill Pond Press, are more in the Audubon tradition; they are portraits arranged in bold patterns against open backgrounds. But my training, many years ago at the Art Students League and the National Academy of Design, under masters such as Kimon Nicolaides, John Sloan, Edwin Dickinson, Raymond P. R. Neilson, and Frank Vincent DuMond, was of another sort. It was in the more painterly, academic tradition. I plan to return to these origins.

—JULY/AUGUST 1990

CAPSIZED
BY A ROGUE WAVE

HERE COMES A BIG ONE! Because our eyes were on the cormorants lined up onshore, only one of us was aware of the rogue wave—even momentarily—before our boat was rolled over, a couple hundred yards off Western Egg Rock, in fifteen or sixteen feet of water. I was wrapped in eye-dazzling foam one moment, in murky green depths the next, with dark objects sinking around me— thousands of dollars' worth of camera equipment. But no time to panic; another gulp or two of seawater could send me choking to the bottom, where I could just drift away . . . to nothing.

Struggling to the surface, I had just time to take in some air and hold it as I went under again with the next comber. I repeated this several times, and had it not been for the courage and strength of young Bob Bowman, who helped me keep my head above water, I would not have had my eighty-second birthday.

Our twenty-three-foot vessel was floating upside down, and I dog-paddled desperately to reach it; once there I clung to its round bottom with my five friends. After a breather of a minute or two—at the most three or four—another outsize comber rolled over us, and it was the same all over again. My eyeglasses had washed away, and so had the contact lens in my right eye. Everything was blurry.

This time we were closer to shore. Momentarily between waves I could touch bottom, only to be thrown off balance against the barnacle-encrusted rocks. This time it was Michael Male who held me up and insisted I could make it. Too weak to stand, I was dragged ashore by the others, then laid on some dry rocks warmed by the afternoon sun. It was about 4:30.

There I lay, sorely bruised, with arms scraped raw and bleeding by barnacles. Was my left hip broken? Or my ribs? It felt as though they were. Retching to get rid of the salt water, and shivering—shuddering—I was grateful for the wet garments that were put over me. Hypothermia was setting in, and again had it not been for Michael, who added his own body warmth and positive encouragement, I might not have pulled through.

Earlier his wife, Judy, a good swimmer, had saved Michael himself when he was being pulled under by his heavy television equipment, which had become snagged on his battery belt. Later, after we were ashore, and still dripping salt from her sinuses, she salvaged a tent from a duffel bag that drifted in. With the help of Steve Kress and Jerry Skinner, both of whom were near exhaustion, it was put up, and I now had some protection from the damp wind and the chill while we awaited rescue by the Coast Guard. But how to reach them?

Bob Bowman, fortunately, had a pocket cigarette lighter with which three fires of driftwood were started, one at each end of the island and one on the highest rocks. This attracted the attention of the *Hardy III*, a passing tour boat full of puffin watchers who had not expected to add RTP to their list under such unusual circumstances. They spotted our upturned boat and the fires. With their binoculars they could see our distress signals, conveyed by a reflector that had been salvaged and a large blue tarp that was waved wildly about. Getting our message, they immediately radioed the Coast Guard.

While this was going on outside my tent, I fell into a deep sleep. Then awakening, with my one functioning eye I made out the shadow of a monarch butterfly as it alighted on the canvas above— but *was* it a monarch? The shape was more like that of a red admiral or an anglewing butterfly, but it was much too large. Was it the magnifying effect of the late sunlight on the canvas? Or, hallucinating a bit, was I seeing an *angel* wing? Too drained to get up and check, I dozed off again.

It was reported in the news that we were lifted off by helicopter. Actually, it was three or four hours after we were stranded that the Coast Guard arrived in a big cutter, the *Wrangell*. Four men in a rubber landing boat beached nearby, soon had me wrapped in a warm blanket, and debated whether or not to walk me down over the slippery rockweed. It was rapidly becoming dark, so to be safe they put me on a stretcher, strapped me firmly across the ankles, hips, and shoulders, then carried me down the slope to the water's edge. All very professional.

I felt strangely peaceful; it was surreal. Lying on my back, helpless, unable to move and gazing straight up into the darkening heavens, I thought I saw a Leach's storm-petrel as it flew out of the mist. There would be more of them later.

From the rubber boat I was winched, still strapped to the stretcher, onto the *Wrangell,* and well before midnight I was safe in my hospital bed in Boothbay Harbor, where I remained two days for observation of my vital signs—because of my age, I suppose. The final verdict: no heart problems, no broken or fractured bones.

Now, how did all this happen? And just where is Western Egg Rock?

Let me first explain about that "rogue wave." As I understand it, an occasional big wave well offshore, perhaps a remnant from a previous storm miles and even days away, may rhythmically build up a towering force as it nears an island. There if it is met abruptly by a strong countercurrent, it may unite into a giant comber that, peaking under a boat at the right moment, could easily roll the boat over. This, I must admit, is a rather clumsy explanation of a mysterious and little understood phenomenon. One report said that a "rogue whale" had done it!

Was Muscongus Bay in Maine trying to tell me something? It has been suggested that returning to a place to savor old memories can be dangerous.

I described my affection for Hog Island earlier, in "The Maine Story" (see page 83), and in July 1990, I wanted to go to Muscongus Bay again to stay a few days on my beloved islands and to see what Steve Kress and his helpers had been doing with the puffins and terns. Puffins, storm-petrels, and terns of three species had been the focus on Eastern Egg and three other key islands offshore.

Judy Fieth and Michael Male of Blue Earth Films were making an hour-long film for PBS. Although it was to be primarily about some of the spin-offs of bird watching, they planned to accent the positive effect that our concern has had on the seabirds along the New England Coast. They had already filmed sequences on the herons at Ding Darling in Florida, the horseshoe crab and shorebird spectacle on Delaware Bay, and the return of the ospreys in Connecticut.

At the turn of the century the seabirds along the Maine coast were at their nadir, their colonies destroyed by egging, the millinery trade, and insensitive target shooting.

The Atlantic puffin was declining fast even in John James Audubon's day. Although Audubon is reported to have shot puffins himself, they were being destroyed at such a rapid rate all the way up to the Labrador that he wrote in 1833, "This war of extermination cannot last much more. . . . They must repent their trade." Two years later, he stated that in the islands at the entrance to the Bay of Fundy there was not one bird "for a hundred that bred there twenty years ago." By 1900 almost no puffins—or a very few—still bred south of the Canadian border except for the colony on Machias Seal Island (which is arguably in Canadian waters).

After driving the van from the cottage on the hill, where Steve and Evie Kress spent the summer, down to the old boathouse, we stowed our gear in the launch. Several pairs of nesting cliff swallows protested our invasion of their place, just as they did many years ago when they displaced the barn swallows. We planned to go straight out to Eastern Egg Rock and would drop in at the Audubon camp on our return.

As we approached Eastern Egg, the light *slip-slap* of the waves gave way to a choppier movement, for we were at the threshold of the open sea. Far off to starboard at one portal of the bay stood Pemaquid Light, a sleepless eye that guards the coast during the night. The foghorn at Monhegan Island moaned to the south, where the fog was probably denser than it was here at the mouth of Muscongus Bay. The gray overcast showed no sign of burning off, but we hoped for better conditions for photography during our three-day stay.

Steve Kress managed to land us in the dory without too much difficulty; he had done this many times. We were met by three young women, this year's keepers of the island; they were the nurturers, the nursemaids who kept tabs on the young birds and documented their growth. Following them up the rough trail, I had to use my monopod to steady myself as I stepped from boulder to boulder, but at one point I slipped and went flat on my back. This did me no good whatsoever.

Judy, Michael, and I pitched our tents outside the cabin shared by the three women. Barbara North, a ginger-haired young woman from Idaho State University, ran wildlife seminars and rafting trips on the Snake River. Debbie Zombek was at SeaWorld in Florida, and Tracy Tennant had been involved with the endangered least terns in California. During the past seventeen years more than one hundred students and researchers such as these have been involved in Steve Kress's puffin (*Fratercula*) project, which now includes terns and petrels.

It started with the puffins, which as tiny chicks were flown peeping and pooping all the way from Newfoundland, a thousand miles away. Since 1973 more than two thousand chicks have been transplanted and nursemaided till they fledged and could fly. Now as adults a growing number have returned to Eastern Egg and are raising young of their own without human help.

By the ingenious use of wooden decoys and tape recordings, Steve Kress has attracted not only the puffins and petrels but more recently the terns, rehabilitating them on islands they had deserted some years ago.

To accomplish this, a certain amount of gull control has been necessary. Ironically—because the Audubon Society saved the last viable herring gull colonies on the Maine coast at the beginning of the century—they posed an unforeseen threat to the terns. Now protected, the gulls prospered, their winter survival enhanced by the proliferation of garbage dumps and skewer outlets up and down the coast. But the reverse side of the coin was that when summer came they varied their diet with the eggs and chicks of the terns whose islands they invaded. While the gulls increased, the terns took a nosedive.

That first night on Eastern Egg, as I lay secure in my sleeping bag, protected from the fog and drizzle outside, I could hear the purring notes of Leach's storm-petrels as they made contact with their mates. Some apparently were nesting in burrows under the cabin, and at least one bird seemed to be trying to get under the floor of my tent.

The next day, photography was out of the question, but the young women were out anyway, making their rounds, and the cries of laughing gulls and terns were constantly in our ears. Laughing gulls now numbered about two hundred pairs, and although they often tried to take fish away from the terns, they were tolerated and allowed to nest; but not the more predatory blackbacks. It was the best year ever for terns. Common terns had built up to more than 1,100 pairs; arctics to about 100 pairs; roseates to at least 40. All had been lured by decoys and tape recordings. As for the puffins, there were at least 40; a goodly number had chicks.

After lunch, while it was raining outside, Barbara North bade us be quiet—not a word—while she read to us from one of the *Alice* books, *Through the Looking-Glass*, which I hadn't read since I was a kid. Although seemingly written for children, is it really a gentle satire on the adult world, as scholars suggest?

The next day started out the same (in Maine you have to play the waiting game), but by late afternoon I got some fairly decent pictures through the light overcast.

Our last morning turned bright and clear. From my pop-up blind erected on a flat rock studded with pink feldspar, I quickly exposed at least a dozen rolls—more than four hundred transparencies of common and arctic terns and a few of black guillemots—all at point-blank range; the birds were oblivious to my presence.

After lunch we took down our tents, packed everything, and carefully worked our way down the trail to the landing while the terns and laughing gulls noisily saw us off. Barbara North rowed us out to the launch where Steve Kress, Bob Bowman, and Jerry Skinner took us aboard.

We would head directly back to the Audubon camp. I would have

Peterson was able to get close to black guillemots on Eastern Egg Rock Island in Maine.

liked to have gone out to Old Hump Ledge, where in the mid-thirties Allan Cruickshank and I photographed the nesting cormorants. Cruicky and Helen visited the ledge yearly to check on the burgeoning numbers that had built up from zero prior to 1931, when our friend Bob Allen recorded the first several pairs.

However, we would pass close to Western Egg Rock, a ledge that had been taken over by the cormorants and the gulls. Although herring gulls and blackbacks were not tolerated on Eastern Egg, they were free on Western Egg to work out their own survival problems.

As we headed across the open water, a Manx shearwater scaled by at close range, the first that Steve had spotted all summer. We can almost predict that this Old World tubenose will be found breeding in Maine before the century is out.

We had no intention of landing on Western Egg; we would skirt it at a safe distance. But through forces beyond our control, land we did!

A day after the accident Mike Reny, a lobsterman out of Round Pond, found my Lindblad bag floating on the water. It was two miles from where we had gone down, and several rolls of my exposed Fujichrome of guillemots and terns were okay, protected by their plastic canisters; but most of my film was ruined. Michael and Judy lost about fifty thousand dollars worth of television equipment, which was insured. However, they salvaged most of their exposed film but not the sound. None of my own equipment was insured. My new 500-millimeter Nikon lens, for which I paid nearly four thousand dollars, had gone to the bottom, as had four camera bodies, flash equipment, and a number of automatic lenses. The few pieces that were retrieved were irreparably ruined by salt water.

But thank heaven I was alive! I still have several books to finish.

The boat was later salvaged by twenty young people from the Audubon camp. It suffered only one bad crack.

A month after the accident, on August 28, when my wife, Ginny, and our staff celebrated my eighty-second birthday with a cruise up the Connecticut River, I wore my life jacket!

—November/December 1990

Memories
of Manhattan

THOUSANDS OF BIRDS over Manhattan's desert of skyscrapers at daybreak! Most people in the city are sleeping too soundly at that early hour to be aware of the faint chips, chirps, and lisps that shower from the dim but lightening sky. The heart of New York City is hardly the place where one would expect to find large numbers of birds. Actually, most large cities have some green areas—Chicago has its Lincoln Park and Boston its Public Garden. But New York boasts the most famous urban bird trap of all—Central Park. This two-and-a-half-mile-long park, set like a narrow, oblong emerald among Gotham's towers, is at times an amazing place for birds, as I discovered when I lived in New York, back in the 1920s and '30s.

Winter can be quiet in the park, but sometimes an unusual bird strays in. For two winters while I was living in the city a barred owl perched every day in the same tree above a squirrel box, near Seventy-seventh Street. It became one of the sights of Fifth Avenue, and bus conductors pointed it out to their passengers. My best find in winter was among the ducks on the Fifty-ninth Street lake. In an ice-free patch of water, roped off from skaters, several hundred wild black ducks gathered to share the food thrown to the swans and tame mallards. Sometimes a wild wigeon, pintail, or shoveler dropped in, creating a striking picture of wildlife against the towering skyline then dominated by the Sherry-Netherland Hotel.

One January day I noted a strange new duck, something like a mallard, but grayer, with a green crown and tan cheeks. I passed it by as one of the innumerable domestic hybrids that mingle with the wild birds on the pond. Later I realized this was the same duck that

Audubon had painted and that he called the "bemaculated" or "Brewer's duck." Audubon had picked up a specimen that had been shot in Louisiana, and what he had was a hybrid between the mallard and the gadwall. The bird of the Fifty-ninth Street lake was Audubon's "bemaculated duck," feather for feather, a hybrid so rare that there is not a single specimen in the vast collection of Anatidae in the American Museum of Natural History.

The payoff came in late February, when the imminence of spring manifested itself in gonadal disturbances among the ardent drakes, who would soon leave for more northern ponds. The bemaculated duck, a natural hybrid, chose as his inamorata a wild hen black duck. He rushed this way and that, chasing all male blacks away. After much maneuvering, I took a good picture of the blissful couple with my four-by-five plate camera. What wouldn't I have given to see what their offspring were like!

Strange birds, escaped from zoos, pet shops, and aviaries, sometimes roam the park. Brazilian cardinals, waxbills, and even parrots have been seen. A European chaffinch once spent the winter with a flock of house sparrows. One day a curator at the American Museum of Natural History came across a bewildered group of birders staring goggle-eyed at a pied hornbill from India! On another occasion Allan Cruickshank rushed into my office and announced excitedly that a strange duck had dropped into the small lake behind the Metropolitan Museum. In all his years of birding he had never seen anything like it. Together we hurried to the pond. The "duck," which puzzled us both for a while, turned out to be a maned goose from Australia, free-flying but obviously an escape.

Birds turn up in odd spots all over the crowded island of Manhattan. Guy Emerson, Edson Heck, and other residents of Greenwich Village made surprising lists of birds around their homes, where hardly anything but a ginkgo or an ailanthus tree would grow. One November there was an invasion of dovekies, the little auks that usually spend the winter far at sea. Easterly gales had forced them inland, and several were found swimming in rain-flooded gutters. I once saw a barred owl outside City Hall, a tiny saw-whet owl on

Riverside Drive, a great blue heron flying down Fifth Avenue, and a flock of whimbrel over Greenwich Village.

One morning a woodcock came to rest on a fourth-story ledge of the General Motors Building just outside my window in the former offices of the National Audubon Society. Cynical newspaper photographers who had been sent to cover the story thought the bird had been "planted" for the sake of the publicity. But anything can happen in New York. John Kieran told me of an old-squaw that fluttered from under the seat of an inbound Coney Island subway train.

At least a dozen peregrine falcons spent the winter each year among the skyscrapers of Manhattan, taking tribute from the flocks of fat, lazy pigeons that befouled the ledges. Now peregrines once more inhabit the city, having been released in Manhattan and in a number of other eastern cities as part of the Peregrine Fund's restoration project, which Tom Cade initiated at Cornell University.

One winter a young red-tailed hawk spent two or three months around the Metropolitan Museum, perching above the ornate façade, where I could watch it from my office window across the street.

On some misty evenings I saw hundreds of small birds fluttering through the brilliant lights that illuminate the tall towers of Radio City. During spring and fall many birds came to the Gardens of the Nations high up on this modern Tower of Babel. On autumn nights, when the wind was in the northwest, I sometimes took the elevator to the observation platform, sixty-odd stories above the street. There, far below, the city lights were strung like jewels to the hazy horizon, while close about me in the blackness I could hear the small voices of southbound migrants. For a few brief moments I could feel as if I were one of them.

On a warm fall day many years ago, a southward-bound hermit thrush, weary of picking its way through the bewildering canyons of the city, descended to the sidewalk on Madison Avenue at the southeast corner of Sixty-third Street. The display of palms and flowers in the shop of Christatos & Koster must have suggested to the thrush its tropical destination, and it flew in through the open transom, taking refuge in a secluded corner.

All through the winter the bird led a happy existence and finally became so tame it would alight on anyone's hand to secure a mealworm. Marco, as he was christened for no accountable reason, had many admirers who would drop in to pay their respects. The following spring he was restless, and one day, when the transom windows were open, he departed. His friends hoped that he had gotten safely out of New York to join his fellow hermit thrushes in their flight to cool northern woods.

Two years later, during the fall migration, a hermit thrush appeared in front of the very same shop. He allowed himself to be picked up and brought in, and the proprietor and his employees insisted it was Marco who had returned. I myself saw the bird, and it really seemed as though it must have been the same Marco, for he had already fallen into his old habits, coming to the hand for food. But if it was Marco, why did he skip a year before returning?

Most small birds migrate at night. In the spring, clear, warm nights in late April or early May are best, evenings with a gentle breeze from the southwest, especially after a spell of poor weather. These are the nights when birds by the hundreds of thousands sweep northward up the continent, unseen. When dawn approaches they drop into the nearest trees. But imagine the predicament of those reaching New York's metropolitan area at daybreak; what a discouraging outlook for a small, tired bird! By the weak eastern light, nothing can be discerned but a vast, arid jumble of steel and stone, cut by sterile gorges and steep canyons. In the distance a blur of green—Central Park—becomes dimly visible. Some nearly exhausted birds may drop down to the few bushes in Washington Square or even to a scraggly ailanthus in a Greenwich Village courtyard; but most of them struggle on toward the more promising oasis of the park.

The park policeman and the homeless unfortunate sprawling on a bench are not the only human beings astir at that hour. There are often bird watchers, and if it is the month of May, scores of them. The calls of the birds shower out of the purplish half-light, weakly and from a great height at first; but as visibility increases, the birds drop lower, and an occasional dim form can be seen pitching into the nearest trees. During the minutes that follow, the chorus of song gradually swells until the voices of scores of birds are blended to greet the morning sun as it rises and glows from the direction of Fifth Avenue.

The biggest concentration point is the Ramble, two verdant acres threaded by winding paths and a trickling stream between Seventy-second and Seventy-seventh Streets, near the American Museum of Natural History. More remote from the main automobile boulevards and with a heavier growth of trees, it is the logical place for a bird to wander into.

Many people take a turn or two about the Ramble before office hours. The binocular is the badge of the clan, and anyone with a pair can be confidently approached on a basis of friendship. Bird watchers are as gregarious as the flocks they follow, although some find more pleasure in scouting alone.

Once when a prothonotary warbler, a bird of southern swamps, put in an appearance, it remained for days and could always be located by a large ring of admirers. Their unabashed enthusiasm had its effect on some of the casual strollers. Because of that one golden bird a number of people took up birding.

In those days the record for Central Park was seventy-nine species in one day. Once, soon after I had come to New York to study, a blanket of fog hanging low over the city at dawn had confused a horde of birds that would otherwise have gained Van Cortlandt Park or the woods of Westchester County. Early in the morning, when I left my lodgings in Brooklyn, I could hear and see many small birds flying low in the fog, barely clearing the tops of the buildings. Late that afternoon, after my classes at the Art Students League, I hurried to the park to find it jammed with birds—not only in the Ramble but from Fifty-ninth Street all the way to the north end of the park. At 110th Street, where they had been stopped in their tree-to-tree wanderings by the forbidding wall of buildings, the branches buzzed with birds.

Overawed, bewildered observers could only look about and gasp.

Imagine half a dozen scarlet tanagers in a single tree and four smart-looking rose-breasted grosbeaks in another! In the row of bushes outside the old Casino, later torn down, I saw all five species of brown thrushes. Even the woodcock, that long-nosed recluse, was there. One flushed from a bridle path, and four others were found in other parts of the park.

Rarities often remain in the park for several days. I once saw a dickcissel, far from its home in the Midwestern prairies, consorting in a patch of ragweed with a flock of house sparrows. The first Bewick's wren ever recorded in New York State was seen in the park. For several days it passed as a Carolina wren (there were many of these on the Palisades across the river), until its sibilant, song-sparrowlike melody was heard. Few singers have risen to fame so rapidly.

One day an excited woman reported a chicken-size bird with a purple breast, greenish wings, yellow legs, and a red and blue bill. It swam, and climbed along the branches of the willow trees, she said. Investigation proved her fantastic description absolutely correct. It was a purple gallinule, the first recorded in New York State in forty-nine years. We were so excited when we heard about it at the Linnaean meeting that the whole Bronx County Bird Club hurried up to the 110th Street lake, even though it was 11:00 at night. We saw the bird silhouetted against the reflections of Harlem's streetlights on the water, pumping its head as it swam, in typical gallinule fashion.

The ever-present gulls have adapted their ecology to the cities along the coasts and the Great Lakes. At any time of day gulls—herring gulls and ringbills in winter, laughing gulls in summer—may be seen floating over New York's buildings trading between the East River and the Hudson, or merely flying over Central Park to the Eighty-sixth Street reservoir to take a freshwater bath.

The very best spot for gulls when I lived in New York was the sewer outlet at Ninety-second Street in Brooklyn. For several years a little gull (*Larus minutus*), a tiny European species with smoky-black wing linings, was seen with the buoyant Bonaparte's gulls, snatching tidbits that welled up in the sordid flow. There in the Narrows, where European immigrants got their first view of the Statue of Liberty, I often saw both this and another foreigner, the black-headed gull. At that time the only other place on the Atlantic Coast where these two rare Laridae from the other side could be depended on was also at a sewer outlet, at Newburyport, Massachusetts. There, for many years, the black-headed gull, which looks like a largish Bonaparte's gull with a red bill, could be found off the end of the pipe that dumped its waste into the Merrimac.

Hundreds of thousands of herring gulls have been banded on this side of the Atlantic. In one great color-marking project, young gulls in nine different colonies from Long Island Sound to the Gulf of St. Lawrence were banded. The birds of one colony were marked with a black band on one leg and a red one on the other; the birds of another colony with a blue band above a yellow one, and so on. The next year each colony was given a different combination. By the end of the third year it was possible to see gulls with anyone of twenty-seven different combinations of colors on their legs.

The first person to spot one of these marked gulls around New York City was John Kieran. On his way to the subway one autumn morning, he put his glass on some newly arrived gulls that covered the field at Van Cortlandt Park and discovered that two of them wore colored bracelets. In the weeks that followed we could always find three or four color-banded gulls along the waterfront at Fulton Fish Market in downtown Manhattan, and one day in early winter, Joseph Hickey (who promoted the scheme) and I found sixteen, representing six different colonies, on the garbage dump at Floyd Bennett Field near Brooklyn.

That was the first time all bird watchers could take part in a banding project. Much was learned about the sequence of plumages, from brown young birds to pearly adults, and something about the pattern of their migration; but less than ten years later, not a single color-banded bird could be found. This did not mean that all the thousands of birds were dead, for we knew of a captive herring gull that lived for forty-nine years. What happened is that in due time the celluloid bands disintegrated. Gull banders had not yet found a more permanent plastic or metal that would withstand the corrosive action of salt water and garbage.

It is a standing jest among bird watchers along the coast that there is no place like a good garbage dump for birds. Among my favorite sites in years past were the dumps at Dyker Heights in Brooklyn, at Newark Bay, and at Hunts Point in the Bronx. There have been others, too, but these in particular bring food, though odoriferous, memories. During one of their cyclic eruptions, there were four snowy owls at the Hunts Point dump. Some might say they frequented the place for concealment, because they resembled packages of garbage wrapped in newspaper—white with black print, but a more likely reason was the abundance of rats. One winter we had twelve short-eared owls in the marsh adjacent to this dump, and that, mind you, was deep inside metropolitan New York, along the bustling East River, with gas tanks and apartment houses crowding in on all sides.

Even where urbanization has locked the green world into a sarcophagus of cement and stone, there are opportunities to watch birds—if only house sparrows or starlings. But most cities compromise with nature a bit more than New York and Chicago do. Washington is virtually a city in the woods. John Burroughs wrote of it in *Wake-Robin*: "There is perhaps not another city in the Union that has on its very threshold so much natural beauty and grandeur, such as men seek for in the remote forests and mountains." Theodore Roosevelt, during his term of office in Washington, kept a list of the birds he saw on the White House grounds. If anything, there are more birds in the nation's capital now than when these men lived. Burroughs spoke of the cardinal as a shy bird—an uncommon sight. And the mockingbird was almost unknown in Washington then. Now both can be found among the ornamental plantings of the government buildings in the very heart of town.

These days, on my occasional visits to the Big Apple to examine the specimen trays at the American Museum, I take pride in knowing that I had a positive impact on nearby Central Park. Fifty years ago, as a staff consultant at National Audubon, I was asked by the park authorities to help restore three key spots in the park. Three off-path peninsulas were fenced off and replanted, one at the north side of the Fifty-ninth Street lake, another near the Ramble, and one at the 110th Street lake. Today they remain verdant oases in a much used park, places reserved for the birds.

—JANUARY/FEBRUARY 1991

ECOTOURISM—
THE NEW BUZZWORD

BIRD TOURS are not new. In America they put down their roots more than fifty years ago, and during that half century I have often been involved with them in one way or another.

It started in the late 1930s, when John Hopkinson Baker, then the executive director of the National Audubon Society, initiated tours to Lake Okeechobee and the Kissimmee Prairie in Florida. These were led by Audubon's sanctuary director, Alexander Sprunt, Jr., and one of the wardens, Marvin Chandler.

The original purpose was to help several birds that were in trouble because of irresponsible gunners—the "Everglade kite" (now called the snail kite) and the limpkin, which in our country were largely confined to the marshes of Lake Okeechobee. Caracaras and the Florida race of the sandhill crane on the nearby Kissimmee Prairie were also vulnerable.

The idea was to fill the local hotels at Okeechobee, Moore Haven, and Clewiston with bird watchers, thereby helping the local economy. If the residents of those towns saw money coming in from people who wanted to watch birds instead of to shoot them, they would be willing to cooperate. It worked. Those endangered birds are now secure in Florida, and the locals are proud of their role in saving them.

I am not sure who started to lead bird tours outside of the United States, first to the West Indies, then elsewhere. It may have been "Major" Bowes and his wife, Anne La Bastille (of Guatemalan flightless grebe fame). Or it may have been C. Russell Mason, who invaded the Caribbean before 1960 with members of the Florida Audubon Society.

The first organized transatlantic bird tours were not attempted until 1961—thirty years ago—when Orville Crowder escorted a group to Europe for the sole purpose of bird watching. Crowder undertook 32 trips in 1972 and racked up a twelve-year total of about 150 tours, reaching every continent except Antarctica. His groups were limited to fifteen or twenty people, which is all that a single leader can reasonably cope with.

In my opinion the person who has done the most to bring nature and wildlife tourism—as distinct from bird tourism—to the rest of the world is Lars-Eric Lindblad, a Swede who is now a U.S. citizen.

Lindblad has been called the high priest of cultural tourism, a sort of modern Vasco da Gama. He was the first to transport tourists to Antarctica, and (feminists, please note) he claims to be the one who integrated the frozen continent by bringing women there. Now women are included among the scientific personnel at some of the stations.

Because he had his own ship, he was able to offer tours to places that hitherto could not be visited without mounting full-scale expeditions. We could follow the trails of Darwin, Cook, Scott, or Shackleton without the hardships. His vessel was like a floating hotel, eliminating the necessity of shore facilities or camps that would mar the wilderness.

Many tourists contribute handsomely to conservation causes. The Seychelles robin would probably not exist were it not for Lindblad and his followers. Passengers raised at least twenty thousand dollars for the Cousin Island project in the Indian Ocean, thousands more for the Charles Darwin Research Station in the Galápagos. They gave numerous donations toward an island off the British coast that was purchased as a memorial to James Fisher. As a follow-up to an Antarctic cruise, a British passenger purchased one of the Jason Islands in the Falklands where a million rockhopper penguins and hundreds of thousands of black-browed albatross make their home. I don't think Lars-Eric Lindblad has been given nearly enough credit for what he has done.

Although Lars is linked in most people's minds with the *Explorer,*

Tourists watching chinstrap penguins.

which he no longer owns, oceanic travel has been but a portion of his worldwide network of tours. Not only did his ships drop anchor at hundreds of islands where no tourist had previously set foot but he was always a leap ahead of his competitors, until a combination of events two years ago forced him into bankruptcy. He is still active in tourism through his Intrepids Club.

Lindblad, a devout conservationist, believes that tours should be led by the best available talent, guides who not only interpret but also instill in the traveler a code of behavior and a reverence for life. In fact, a roster of his tour guides and guest lecturers reads like a who's who of exploration, natural history, and the humanities.

On one of our cruises to the Galápagos we had onboard at least twenty Italian tourists, all of them obviously well-heeled, if one could judge by the Pucci clothes worn by the women at cocktail time. Only two or three spoke English; this posed a problem for my evening recap and briefing. Fortunately, my Argentinian assistant, Francisco Erize, spoke Italian fluently, so while I gave my lecture to the English-speaking passengers, he presented a similar one in Italian in the other lounge. Many of the Italian group had never thought of conservation before, nor of the "rights of wildlife," but before the cruise was over Francisco had made a convert of everyone. One woman remarked: "This morning I found a moth in my desk, and I didn't kill it."

I have been amused that many a soul who wouldn't walk two blocks in the rain at home would willingly accept all sorts of discomfort and indignities under the guise of adventure. When we landed at Campbell Island, 450 miles south of New Zealand, the weather was appalling. The peaks were socked in, but up there in the fog were several thousand royal albatross. The nearest nesting pair was an hour's walk for a teenager, two hours for an older person—and almost straight up the mountainside. Even so, one spirited woman in her eighties made it. I forged ahead with the more obsessed birders while another staff member stayed with the laggards, cheering them on as they slithered through knee-deep pockets of mud between the rocks and tussock grass. After an hour of scrambling, one of the dear ladies, drenched, muddy, and tired, picked herself up from a puddle, looked up the soggy trail, and said quizzically: "And we're paying for this?"

Recently I asked my studio assistant to go through my bird magazines and jot down on cards the tour agents, organizations, and clubs that advertised wildlife tours. We soon had a stack of more than three hundred!

Victor Emanuel Nature Tours (VENT) has taken tens of thousands of people on feather quests. Victor, with whom I have long been affiliated, continues to expand his agency in spite of strong competition from companies like Field Guides (the Rowletts), Wings (Will Russell), Bird Bonanzas, Joseph Van Os, Questers, Wood Star, Caligo Ventures, Dan Guravich, Kingbird Tours, and innumerable

Ecotourists with king penguins in the Falkland Islands.

others of varying expertise. However, they all cooperate, exchanging ideas freely.

Some clients stick loyally, like members of a family, to one agency; others play the field. Traveling takes time and money, so understandably a large portion of bird tourists tend to be affluent retirees. But others save frugally for a precious two or three weeks of birding.

The term *ecotourism* is relatively new. I had not heard it before 1987, when it was used by my friend Hector Caballos and Mario Ramos, who translated my Mexican field guide into Spanish. Last year when I visited Brazil, I found the term widely used, especially in the Pantanal and the Mato Grosso. The concept, put into practice, may yet be the solution to saving large parts of the rain forest.

This buzzword has now crossed the Rio Grande, and in the months ahead we will hear about ecotours sponsored by the Socorro County Chamber of Commerce in New Mexico. They will concentrate on the nearby Rio Grande and especially the Bosque Del Apache National Wildlife Refuge, where binocular addicts can watch vast congregations of snow geese and sandhill cranes and, if lucky, perhaps a whooper.

Photographers—the really good ones—often use their slides or films in lectures when they get back home. We must never underestimate their contribution. Photography is a very important spin-off of bird travel.

All in all, bird tourism—or ecotourism—or whatever we choose to call it—has had an enormously beneficial effect in saving our birds. And if there are any problems or negative aspects, they can easily be solved with common sense.

—JULY/AUGUST 1991

Long After Columbus

Columbus was the first bird watcher to keep notes on American birds. After he left the Canary Islands, birds became the most important entries in the ship's log. As he sailed west into the unknown, his men grew sullen and threatening. At this crucial time, flocks of migrant birds coming from the north and making for the southwest gave them heart. Columbus turned his course in the direction the birds were flying and in due time reached the Bahamas.

Had Columbus not followed the birds or had he left the Canaries two weeks later, after the heavy fall migration was past, his first landfall might have been the coast of Florida—if indeed there had been a landfall. His men were so close to mutiny that the extra two hundred miles might have made the difference between success and failure.

Every obsessed birder I know would give his soul to step back in time about five hundred years and walk the continent in the historic year 1492. It was virgin country then, with trees centuries old and the native grass waist high on the prairies. Many birds may have been more abundant in primeval America. In 1614, six years before the pilgrims landed at Plymouth, John Smith sailed down the coast of Maine. He wrote of the incredible abundance of "eagles, gripes, divers, all sorts of hauks, cranes, geese, brants, cormorants, ducks, sheldrakes, teals, meawes, gulls, turkies, dive doppers, and many other sorts, whose names I know not."

In early colonial days there were no game laws, but it did not take long to realize that there would have to be a brake on the killing. The first legal regulations were imposed in New Netherlands more than three hundred years ago. At the close of the colonial period, twelve of the thirteen colonies had some sorts of game laws. Since then restrictions have multiplied. An army of millions of Americans now goes out with guns each year; 2 million purchase the federal duck stamp. The wildfowlers have grown legion, even though there are now only a fraction of the ducks that swarmed the flyways when John Smith cruised the coast.

The ducks and some of the other wetland birds may be down, but many other birds are doing well and even climbing. Let us look briefly at the score sheet and see which way the avifauna seems to be going.

Today most of the marsh birds, not just the waterfowl, are in the red. Every day plans are made somewhere to drain a lake, a swamp, or a marsh. Upward of 100 million acres of land have been drained in the United States for agriculture alone. Other millions were ditched to control mosquitoes. Considering that a marsh or swamp may harbor nine or ten nesting birds per acre and most farming country an average of fewer than three, this means that at least half a billion birds may have been eliminated from the face of the continent by the process of digging ditches.

The birds of prey—hawks and owls—are much reduced. One summer day nearly fifty years ago, I paddled a rubber boat down the Snake River in Wyoming. There, in the dome of the sky that vaulted the breathtaking Teton Valley, hawks were never out of sight—circling redtails and Swainson's hawks, swift-flying prairie falcons, a few eagles. It gave me an inkling of what the normal conditions must have been like in aboriginal America. Yet the gunners often blamed the growing scarcity of game not on themselves but on these natural predators, which had lived in adjustment with their prey for thousands of years. They were "vermin," competitors to be shot and destroyed. Most raptors are now protected, but the skies still do not enjoy their full complement.

Vultures, by contrast, have spread. The turkey vulture, pushing northward in the Appalachians, followed the return of the deer to the Northeast and can now be seen rocking on the thermals as far north as Maine and Quebec. Its intelligent, aggressive cousin, the black vulture, has bypassed Washington, D.C., and has now penetrated southern Pennsylvania and New Jersey.

When a land is settled as rapidly as ours, it is harder for birds to roll with the punches. So we have lost the Labrador duck, the Carolina parakeet, the passenger pigeon, and probably the ivory-billed woodpecker and Bachman's warbler. When the heath hen faded out, we lost merely a race of the prairie-chicken that had become isolated along the Atlantic coast. Recently, through mismanagement, we lost the dusky seaside sparrow of Florida, a race teetering on the brink of speciation.

Evolutionary processes are so slow that it is sad to lose even a subspecies or a local population. We shall probably forfeit very few additional species, although birds like the Eskimo curlew and California condor are close to the lethal threshold. Once gone, no power on earth can bring them back. The whooping crane and the trumpeter swan were snatched from the edge just in time.

Human beings, the ultimate primates, are the only check on themselves. There is no higher predator to keep us under control—not since our cave days, when we played hide-and-seek with saber-toothed tigers. We are at the peak of the pyramid. When we go hog wild with the exploitation of our domain and ominous signs appear, we can look for no outside help. We seem to sober up at the eleventh hour, so we establish laws, game regulations, soil conservation practices, national forests, national parks, sanctuaries, and wildlife refuges. It is our better self trying to rebuild, to safeguard for our heirs what is left.

Today, millions of acres in the United States are bird sanctuaries in name or effect. This started in 1900, the zero year, when the National Audubon Society snatched the last few gull colonies on the Maine coast from eggers and the millinery trade. The society still patrols a long string of sanctuaries from Maine to Florida and along the coast of Texas.

Most of the society's sanctuaries give haven to the ornamental water birds that have no value as game—gulls, terns, pelicans, cranes, egrets, ibis, and spoonbills—glamour birds that concentrate in large, vulnerable colonies. When you see your next great egret, white against the green marsh, or the little snowy, shuffling in the shallows, take off your hat to the National Audubon Society.

The first federal bird reservations were set aside in 1903 by executive order of President Theodore Roosevelt. Now there are more than 350 administered by the United States Fish and Wildlife Service. They aggregate more than 20 million acres, and all forms of wildlife are protected. More than two thirds were created primarily for waterfowl.

I have never visited one of these superrefuges that did not prove to be the best place for birds for miles around, and that was not fully ten times as good after it had been scientifically managed for a few years.

The National Park Service administers more than 357 parks and other units, which are, in effect, bird sanctuaries. They total more than 80 million acres. Besides all these, there are the national forests, embracing 176 million acres, and although hunting is not prohibited, wild creatures find in them reasonable havens. In addition, many states have "wildlife refuges" that are breeding reservoirs for game species, assurance to sportsmen that there will always be enough "seed stock" to ensure "harvesting" in the surrounding country. So, with federally owned lands, state lands, and countless inviolate estates, private parks, and sanctuaries, we are trying to take care of wildlife.

Aldo Leopold observed that all civilizations seem to have been conditioned upon whether the plant succession, under the impact of human beings, gave a habitable assortment of vegetative types or an inferior and uninhabitable assortment. He pointed out that "Caesar's Gaul was utterly changed by human use—for the better. Moses' land of milk and honey was utterly changed—for the worse." Both changes were unforeseen.

Whether we abuse the land or use it wisely, there will be birds—but far more on well-managed land. Whereas many farms average fewer than three birds per acre, this ratio can be doubled with good management. Every last one of the fifty or more standard practices of the Soil Conservation Service—strip cropping, hedgerows, gully dams, and all the other devices to check erosion—also helps birds. This hardworking government agency, whose job it is to ensure our daily bread, has undoubtedly increased American birds by millions. Beauty and bread often grow best together.

The farmers' fields have favored the westward spread of bobolinks, meadowlarks, dickcissels, and vesper sparrows. Conversely, those farms that bridged the Great Plains became stepping-stones for western birds now invading the East. Western meadowlarks have bred as far east as western New York; Brewer's blackbirds have reached Ontario. Because groves of trees were planted around the ranch houses, the yellow-shafted flicker of the East met the red-shafted flicker of the West, and now we see "orange-shafted flickers," or flickers with one red whisker and one black, suggesting that systematists were wrong when they formerly designated them as two distinct species. After all, the birds should know.

More birds have adapted to a changing world than have failed. Few have the narrow tolerance of the ivory-billed woodpecker or Bachman's warbler. I have never, in all my years of birding, seen a chimney swift nesting in its ancestral site, that is, in a hollow tree. In the Northeast more nighthawks lay their eggs on the flat gravel roofs of buildings than on the bald ground. Today phoebes use bridges or rafters; only a few still favor rocky ledges.

As a family, the swallows seem to be completely won over to our way of life. Cliff swallows and barn swallows plaster their mud nests on our barns; martins, tree swallows, and violet-green swallows accept our bird boxes; bank swallows and roughwings live in road cuts and sand quarries. The Hirundinidae are opportunists; they will never allow civilization to displace them.

At least fifty North American birds will nest in bird boxes. These are the species that in less manicured terrain use secondhand woodpecker holes or natural cavities. Hole-nesting birds of prey—barred owls, barn owls, screech owls, saw-whet owls, and kestrels—can be attracted to nesting boxes. Even the B-29 bomber, in the nose of which a friend of mine found a great horned owl's nest, could be called an artificial nesting site.

Among the nesting devices for raptors are the trays put out for peregrine falcons on the ledges of office buildings, and the cart wheels on poles that support the osprey's castles of sticks. A variant of the cart wheel idea was tried on Shelter Island, New York, and in Connecticut by the electricians of the power commissions. They were tired of having ospreys short-circuit the wires on utility poles with their bulky nests, so they erected substitute poles with platforms nearby. The ospreys took the hint and switched.

The shorebirds—"snipe" in the gunner's language—nearly faded from our beaches; but after they were excluded from the game bag, most of them (but not all) returned. One would not look for shorebirds in the heart of Washington, D.C. Yet, for a few brief weeks in the late summer of 1928, when the ground was being cleared for the Department of Commerce Building, shorebirds flocked to the muddy pools on Fourteenth Street. The curators and ornithologists of the Smithsonian and the U.S. Biological Survey paused on their way to work to see what new shorebirds had dropped in. The rain-filled excavation, known as "Hoover's Lake," was one of the best spots for shorebirds the District of Columbia has ever known, second only to the golf course at Potomac Park.

Golf courses and airports—who would think they would often be hot spots for rare waders? The Newark Airport in New Jersey was a first-rate spot for golden plovers before traffic got too heavy. Flocks of these long-distance fliers would drop in like squadrons of transports arriving on schedule.

Some of the best shorebird areas I have known were found not on clean beaches but where sewage polluted the mud. Even pollution, if it is organic, not chemical, can attract birds.

Gulls, of course, like such places. They are scavengers; they always have been, but sewer outlets, garbage dumps, and fish wharves now make it possible for more of them to survive the lean months of winter. On the big municipal dumps they swarm by confusing thousands—brown gulls, gray gulls, white gulls, young ones, middle-aged, and old ones, rising in windrows at our approach and dropping to the rear among the grapefruit rinds, chicken bones, and coffee grounds.

Now protected, and their winter survival enhanced, gulls are nesting in greater numbers on the offshore islands, while terns are losing out. The posturing and displaying of the terns, so important to their mating, is disrupted by the dominant gulls.

The fortunes of the black-capped, fork-tailed terns have gone up and down like the stock market; they are sensitive to change but adaptable. Some of the largest colonies of least terns I have visited have been on land where real estate developers pumped shell and sand over the marsh. Other successful colonies are established on the flat gravel roofs of supermarkets and shopping malls, where they are relatively safe.

On the one hand, gunning, when it was not well regulated, marsh drainage, and beach development have been among the most damaging factors that civilization has imposed on the birds.

On the other hand, we believe our manipulation of the land has made most of the countryside more suitable for songbirds. Civilization has created enormous amounts of "edge," has scrambled the plant communities, and has kept the green growth in such a constant state of succession that there may be far more songbirds now than in the days of the Pilgrim fathers—perhaps a billion or two. We can only guess. Let us look at the older countries of Europe, where these processes have gone on longer. In rural and suburban England, orchards and gardens may average more than thirty to forty times the number of birds that are found in wild country such as deer forest and ungrazed moorland.

In earlier days songbirds were caged; they went into potpies; boys made collections of their eggs. Although they are now free from all this persecution, some species have declined because their environment has changed. But for every one of these, others are more common today. Wherever human beings go, down comes the wilderness. The ringing ax starts plant succession all over again. The majority of the songbirds find their niche in the developmental stages of plant growth; relatively few are obligated to the mature forest.

Audubon found the chestnut-sided warbler only once in all the years he roamed America. "In the beginning of May, 1808," he wrote,

I shot five of these birds on a very cold morning near Pottsgrove, in the state of Pennsylvania. I have never met with a single individual of this species since. Where this species goes to breed I am unable to say. I can only suppose it must be far to the northward, as I ransacked the borders of Lake Ontario and those of lakes Erie and Michigan without meeting it. I do not know of any naturalist who has been more fortunate, otherwise I should here quote his observations.

At that time unbroken woodlands still covered much of the Northeast. A century later the chestnut-sided warbler had become a common bird, its bright song ringing from every brushy slope and clearing. On many a farm, this little sprite with the yellow cap and rufous sides became numerous when abandoned pastures were reclaimed by low shrub. It spread down the Appalachian plateau and became common in Audubon's Pennsylvania, and following the thickets under the blighted chestnuts in the mountains, it made a spectacular appearance as far south as Georgia.

In primeval America, when trees were big, birds like the chestnut-sided warbler must have depended almost entirely on windfalls and lightning-ignited forest fires. These acts of God were their vehicles of survival. In a partially deforested landscape, there is much more room for them. But there are all sorts of lumbering practices. Selective cropping of the timber is better for wildlife than the policy of "cut out and get out."

I am willing to wager there are many more indigo buntings now than there were in Audubon's time. As I drive across the Appalachian hills in July, through the open windows of my car I often hear more of these bright blue finches than any other birds. In addition to indigo buntings, we undoubtedly have far more song sparrows, field sparrows, robins, catbirds, orioles, cardinals, mockingbirds, phoebes, kingbirds, waxwings, prairie warblers, goldfinches, and towhees.

Having stepped up five hundred years from Columbus to the present, let's leap ahead another five hundred years to the year 2492.

Awakening like Rip Van Winkle, will we find more birds because

Northern mockingbirds are undoubtedly more numerous now than they were in Audubon's time.

of our improved understanding of wildlife, or fewer because we have not controlled our own burgeoning numbers? Although the DDT syndrome is behind us, at least in this country, how many other chemicals will prove catastrophic to wildlife? What about the hole in the ozone layer? Or the "greenhouse effect" caused by the destruction of forests? Are the recent reports of local declines of songbirds an ominous sign?

—SEPTEMBER/OCTOBER 1991

Memories of
Ludlow Griscom

MORE THAN THIRTY YEARS have gone by since Ludlow Griscom saw his last warbler migration from his garden in Cambridge. At the end of May, about the time the last blackpolls were going through, he was laid to rest in Mount Auburn, the cemetery in Cambridge where he had spent so many hundreds of May mornings.

Ludlow Griscom was the first ornithologist I ever met when, as a lad of seventeen, I came to New York in 1925 to attend my first meeting of the American Ornithologists' Union. I arrived a day early, and to get my membership sponsored I climbed the stairs to the bird department on the top floor of the American Museum, where a well-made young man of thirty-five signed my application. The young man was Ludlow Griscom, and I was to see him in action the following Saturday, when he led the field trip to Long Beach on Long Island, a barrier beach that had not yet been given over to condominiums. On that day thirteen new birds went down on my life list, and I particularly recall the murre that flew over near the inlet. It was the first record, Griscom stated, of a Brunnich's murre (thick-billed murre) since the days when Eugene Bicknell worked the beach with his handheld telescope.

Returning to New York a year later to take up my art education, at the Art Students League, I often saw Ludlow Griscom at the bimonthly meetings of the Linnaean Society, which he dominated. He was always a good show and just a bit austere in keeping in line a group of young upstarts, a half dozen eager beavers known as the Bronx County Bird Club (Joseph Hickey and Allan Cruickshank were charter members). Although he had a particular fondness for these young men, his cross-examinations were ruthless when they reported three-toed woodpeckers in Bronx Park and other unlikely finds. This was good training, and only a few years later I witnessed both Joe and Cruicky giving similar merciless grillings to other upcoming teenagers at Linnaean meetings.

I was accepted as the first non-Bronx member of the very select Bronx County Bird Club, mostly because I hung around so much. Griscom was our god, and his *Birds of the New York City Region* was our Bible. Every one of us could quote chapter and verse. We used his terminology and even his inflection when we pronounced something as "unprecedented" or "a common summer resident." The leader of our little group, Jack Kuerzi, even parted his hair in the middle in the approved Griscom style.

It was quite logical that we should choose Griscom as our role model, for he represented the new field ornithology. He bridged the gap between the shotgun ornithologist of the old school and the modern field observer with a binocular. He recalled:

> When a veteran ornithologist of an older generation wished to add birds to his collection, he drove out on a lovely May day from New York City to Van Cortland Park and was perfectly free to shoot as many warblers in the morning as he could skin in the afternoon. When visiting a friend in Connecticut, and wanting to add a warbling vireo to his collection, he was taken by his friend on a Sunday Morning to the home of a well-known lady in New Haven, in whose shade trees a pair of warbling vireos was nesting. By first ringing the doorbell, hat in hand, and courteously asking permission, it was entirely possible to blaze away and shoot the warbling vireo out of the treetop onto the lawn in the city of New Haven on a spring morning.

In those days records would hardly have been valid without the dead specimens. When Ludlow Griscom was a young man developing his field techniques, he was challenged by one of the older men who made all his own identifications through the sights of a shotgun. Griscom pointed out a female Cape May warbler high up in a sycamore. The old boy blazed away. He picked up the bird. It *was* a female Cape May. After several repeat performances, he became convinced that Ludlow knew whereof he spoke.

Griscom became the high priest of the new cult of split-second field identification, and the Bronx boys were his most apt pupils. My field guides owe much to Ludlow; certainly the philosophy and fine points of field recognition I learned from him and my young Linnaean friends. Being trained academically as an artist, I was able to give things form. The visual presentation, particularly the use of the little arrows and the working out of comparative patterns, was a contribution of my own.

We know the techniques so well today that they are taken for granted, but I find that wherever I go throughout the fifty states, the sharpest field experts can usually be traced to Griscom's influence either directly or indirectly, through some eastern club in New York, Boston, Philadelphia, or Washington, where his influence and that of his disciples was felt most strongly. He was indeed the dean of field ornithologists.

In 1927 Ludlow Griscom left the American Museum of Natural History for a position on the scientific and administrative staff of the Museum of Comparative Zoology in Cambridge, Massachusetts, and it was not until I went to Boston in 1931 to teach school that our paths again crossed. It was there, sixty years ago, that we got on a first-name basis and became close friends.

He introduced his high-pressure methods to the leisurely bird watchers of the Nuttall Club in Cambridge, the oldest bird club in the country, whose members soon rivaled the New Yorkers in their skills. Notwithstanding that he had once stated it was a physical impossibility to see 250 species in a single year in the New York City area or anywhere else in the Northeast, he eventually was attaining totals of more than 300 every year around Boston. He developed a statewide grapevine that had not yet been equaled anywhere else in North America, not even in New York, Philadelphia, or Washington, where there were already rather good communication systems among the members of the field glass fraternity.

How wonderful were those Saturday and Sunday field trips when

Ludlow Griscom was the dean of field ornithologists.
(Edwin Way Teale Papers, Archives & Special Collections at the
Thomas J. Dodd Research Center, University of Connecticut)

we met before dawn at the cafeteria on Harvard Square! Like a commanding general, Ludlow took charge. A council of war had been held the evening before. The weather maps and tide tables were studied. Each hour was mapped out so that the most productive places would be visited at the best times. From dark to dark our forces invaded the realm of the birds with military thoroughness. Crossing a field, we deployed our ranks on a wide front so that no bird slipped by. Fast travel between strategic areas with a tankful of gas and good brakes was part of our tactics. Twice, on round-the-clock "Big Days," starting with owls and ending with owls, we broke the all-time record for Massachusetts. Our top count was 161, but this was exceeded in later years.

Very few North American birds eluded Ludlow Griscom. His world life list was well over three thousand. Even during his long illness he insisted upon expanding his world experiences, and virtually against doctor's orders he set off for Mexico and Africa. After somewhere between ten and eleven thousand field trips, he had learned to call off birds in a split second so quickly and surely that his academic colleagues sometimes had their doubts.

What gave him this edge? Let us look at his early background. Brought up in a family with a tradition of international diplomacy, he crossed the Atlantic fifteen times before he was twenty-eight. He spoke French and German, not as an American speaks them but as a European. All told, he learned to speak five languages fluently, could read ten easily, and could translate up to eighteen with little help. As a youngster, he played the piano so proficiently that by the time he was mature he had to make a choice between the careers of concert pianist and ornithologist. There came a time when he could further his art only by devoting eight hours a day to the keys instead of four; this meant he would have to give up the birds. The birds, his true passion, won out.

Languages and music both demand the control of masses of detail, so organized that they can be sorted out with unconscious speed. Griscom's achievements in these fields undoubtedly conditioned his way of thinking and, in addition to his training as a first-rate biologist, helped make him the field man he was. The mind of a good field observer works like a kaleidoscope, the gadget of our childhood, wherein loose fragments of colored glass fall quickly into symmetrical patterns. We see a bird. With an instinctive movement we center it in our glass. All the thousands of fragments we know about birds— locality, season, habitat, voice, actions, field marks, and likelihood of occurrence—flash across the mirrors of the mind and fall into place— and we have the name of our bird. Griscom's reactions in assembling these varied fragments were exceptionally fast.

Today, when birders have seen all the local birds and have enjoyed the sport of it, they may go on to explore the further vistas of birding and ornithology. The point of transition may be reached by the observer's early twenties, or it may come later. Whereas it once might have taken a lifetime to learn to recognize and name all the birds, now it can be done in a crash program in a mere four or five years. The period of basic training has been shortened.

Ludlow Griscom did much to make this possible, and in this way made one of his most significant contributions to the science of ornithology. Even though his more formal publications on faunistics, systematics, and migration led to the highest honor in his profession, the presidency of the American Ornithologists' Union, and although his efforts in the field of conservation made him the logical choice as chairman of the board of the Audubon Society, those who knew him will always remember Ludlow Griscom as the great virtuoso of field identification.

—JANUARY/FEBRUARY 1992

THE FESTIVAL
OF THE CRANES

FOUR YEARS AGO, Socorro, that historic old settlement south of Albuquerque on the Rio Grande, celebrated its first "Festival of the Cranes." Last autumn (if it could be called autumn) the event took place from November 22 to 24, and I was invited to speak my piece on "Ecotourism," show some slides, and sign a lot of books. I suspect that *Bird Watcher's Digest* may have had something to do with this, because the Thompsons, among others, were involved in the planning. I jumped at this excuse to get away from my slavery in the studio, where I was still working on the update of the *Field Guide to the Birds of Britain and Europe*. What could be more fun than aiming a lens at tens of thousands of snow geese and sandhill cranes—and perhaps now and then a whooper?

In recent years my forays into the Southwest have been during the spring and summer, not when the geese and cranes were there. I usually bypassed New Mexico for the nearby hot spots in southeastern Arizona, where birders converge from all corners of the land to add hummers of a dozen sorts, and perhaps a trogon or two, to their lists.

I remember that nearly forty years ago, when I drove across New Mexico with James Fisher on our *Wild America* adventure, we spotted some great-tailed grackles in the town square at Lordsburg, just short of the Arizona border. They were the first great-tailed grackles ever to be recorded in any of the western states outside Texas. Since then, this flamboyant Mexican icterid, adapting to the cattle ranches, has become widespread in the Southwest, having extended its range far into California, Nevada, and Colorado. Casual strays have even reached Oregon and British Columbia. I predict that these adaptable blackbirds will eventually take over the entire West, wherever there are cattle. The wasteful artificial feeding of these bovines ensures the bird's survival. But at the time of our visit to Socorro this last November, when the dry leaves were still falling, the grackles had already moved south to milder latitudes, and so had some of the geese and ducks. But the snow geese and sandhill cranes were at their peak, tens of thousands of them.

Bosque del Apache means "Woods of the Apaches," referring to the groves of cottonwoods that line the stream banks. These riverine woodlands, so important to certain songbirds, such as yellow-billed cuckoos and Bell's vireos, are in trouble because of the invasion of the salt cedar, an alien that threatens to crowd out the cottonwoods and other endemics.

The Bosque comprises 57,000 acres (ninety square miles) that were purchased by the federal government in 1939 for only $2.17 an acre! Without modern game management practices, the mobs of waterfowl would not be there. Only a part of the Bosque del Apache is managed, the water levels being manipulated up or down with the seasons. The rest of the vast area remains as it is, forever wild. Farm crops on the refuge provide supplemental food for the winged visitors. The farmers in the surrounding area are allowed to plant corn and other cereals in the refuge on a sharecrop basis. After harvesting, one third of the crop is left in the fields for wildlife. It is a cooperative system that works.

Every year, nearly 100,000 people visit the Bosque del Apache National Wildlife Refuge, outnumbering the cranes and possibly even the geese (but I'm not sure). Whereas the avian hordes may stay there for weeks or even months, the people come and go. On any given day there are far more birds than people.

The Festival of the Cranes is sponsored by the Socorro Chamber of Commerce, which believes that "ecotourism" can have a dual meaning—economic as well as ecological—bringing money into town, supporting local hotels as well as bed and breakfast places (often called "bird 'n' breakfasts"). Anna Appleby and her partner, Tom Harper, host one of these, the Eaton House. This year it was the

Sandhill cranes are abundant during fall migration at Bosque del Apache National Wildlife Refuge in New Mexico.

energetic Anna who chaired the festival committee, and it was she who put us in the hands of Phil Norton and Pat Basham, who saw to it that Ginger and I had a double dose of sandhills and snow geese.

Phil Norton, manager of the refuge, took us in his own van along roads that were less frequented by the touring public. He knew which water impoundments were visited by the geese at certain hours of the day, and which fields of corn to visit when the birds were feeding. A few sandhill cranes, family groups, could be seen on almost any piece of cropland, but in certain fields and marshes they assembled by the thousands. They were mostly greater sandhill cranes, but there were also a few lesser sandhills from the far north, distinctly smaller and usually stained with rust. Sprinkled here and there among the snow geese were a few darker blue geese and also some Ross's geese, a smaller species that seems to be on the increase. There were surprisingly few Canadas.

At one water impoundment where several thousand geese and

cranes were feeding, a lone coyote was trying to get himself a meal. This offered me an opportunity, because it was against the rules of the refuge for me to step out of the car and flush the birds. Then how was I to get mass flight shots with my Nikon 4 or my Canon EOS? The coyote helped me out; the rules did not apply to him. As he walked along the water's edge between the cranes and the geese, they would flush, then settle down again in a blizzard of wings while I shot roll after roll of Kodachrome. The coyote, an inexperienced young male, never did catch a goose.

Phil Norton told us that he had plans for more nature trails and perhaps an observation blind or two. At the present time most goose watching at the Bosque del Apache is done from the car along the network of roads that loop in and out of the fields, marshes, and impoundments. I asked him, "Why not one or two strategically placed blinds like those at Slimbridge in England that were designed by the late Sir Peter Scott?" A walkway over the marsh, camouflaged on each side with canvas, reeds, or brush would make it possible to reach an elevated blind unobserved, and to be right among the geese or cranes for close-up photography. I saw such blinds in New Zealand that were patterned after those at Slimbridge. Mr. Norton thought well of this idea, so perhaps in another year or two there will be something like that at the Bosque. Then I will be back!

Most whooping cranes go from northern Canada down through the Plains to their winter home along the Texas coast, but here in New Mexico there is a separate flock of thirteen birds that migrate from Grays Lake National Wildlife Refuge in Idaho, where they were raised by sandhill cranes that acted as surrogate parents. Because of behavioral problems (not being imprinted in childhood by their own kind), they were not yet reproducing successfully. Dr. Rod Drewien, who has worked with this experimental flock for more than fifteen years, told us about the subtle difficulties.

A lot was going on at Socorro during the festival—not only were there early morning bird tours of the refuge and the nearby Cibola Forest, but during the three days there were demonstrations of all sorts and exhibits. These were put on by the raptor rehabilitators, the

Snow geese are at their peak during fall migration in Socorro, New Mexico.

New Mexico Wild Turkey Federation, the Rocky Mountain Elk Foundation, Hawk-Watch International, Rio Grande Bird Research, the Rio Grande Zoo, and several other groups. The Rio Grande Woodcarvers put on their own show, as did a number of other artists. Doug West exhibited his fabulous silk screen serigraphs of southwestern landscapes. Julie Zickefoose, our former neighbor who lived up the road in Connecticut (and whose work often appears in *Bird Watcher's Digest*), gave three classes in field sketching, and later she shared the podium with me at the banquet. After I held forth about "ecotourism" and showed my slides, she talked about her bird drawings, the rehabilitation of injured birds, and her work with endangered least terns and piping plovers. She is a dedicated, talented young woman.

The weather was perfect, and the geese and cranes did their part. So if you haven't seen the Bosque, put it on your calendar for next fall.

—MARCH/APRIL 1992

INTRODUCED SPECIES

AT THIS VERY MOMENT there are hundreds of species of foreign birds on display in our zoological parks. Once in a while one escapes. Then we may have reports from the binocular toters of a blue-gray tanager in the Brooklyn Botanic Garden or a Brazilian cardinal at a feeding station in Hartford.

Before 1900 at least 150 species of birds from other parts of the world were set free in North America, released in the hope that they might become part of our avifauna. Everything from flamingos to Japanese titmice were tried, but with all of our continent for an ark, only a handful of species survived.

Ecology was an unknown word in those days, and little was understood about a bird's relationship with its environment. Birds of the desert were set free in the humid Northwest. But even when some judgment was used, most transplants soon died out.

It is hard to duplicate in the New World the exact niche a bird occupied in the land of its origin, where over the centuries its survival problems have been worked out within the framework of its environment.

But a city is a city the world over. So is a barnyard. Look down the lists of "pests" and see how many of them came from cities and farms across the sea: insects such as the gypsy moth, Japanese beetle, and cabbage butterfly; vertebrates such as the Norway rat, rock pigeon, house sparrow, and European starling. Through the centuries they had already adapted themselves to the cities and farms of Europe and Asia. Sparrows and starlings had little difficulty here—and almost no competition until a few of our native birds adapted themselves to city or suburban ways.

The early settlers frequently commented on the seeming scarcity of songbirds, of which they had so many in the homeland. Nostalgic German-Americans imported hundreds of birds from the fatherland: bullfinches, linnets, even European dippers. Transplanted British, attempting to bring something of their environment, imported robin redbreasts, skylarks, and nightingales.

In the 1870s and 1880s, "acclimatization" societies sprang up. One in Cambridge, Massachusetts, called itself the "Society for the Acclimatization of Foreign Birds" and released all sorts of unlikely species in Mount Auburn Cemetery. I can imagine Ludlow Griscom's bemused reaction in this favorite stalking ground of his, had he lived in Cambridge at that time.

Another group, in Ohio, the "Cincinnati Acclimatization Society," spent nine thousand dollars between 1872 and 1874 and liberated three thousand birds of twenty species—but in vain. In the late 1880s, the Portland, Oregon, Songbird Club was established "for the introduction of useful songbirds." It set free thirty species, but none took hold, although the skylark did well for a while.

To the "American Acclimatization Society" in New York City can be attributed the starling's success. Oddly enough, several previous attempts to get this well-known alien started were failures. In 1890, Eugene Schieffelin, leader of the society, brought 80 starlings from Europe and set them free in Central Park. The following year he liberated 40 more. These 120 birds multiplied a millionfold. Their growing armies crossed the Great Divide, successfully laid siege to the fortress of the Rockies, and then became established along the Pacific Coast from Alaska to Mexico. (I remember seeing some of the first ones to reach Seattle.) They have even flown aboard ships far at sea.

Fifty years ago as I sat at my desk on the sixth floor of Audubon House, then at 1000 Fifth Avenue in New York City, it seemed incredible that the black blizzard of birds that swarmed to the ledges of the Metropolitan Museum across the street could be descended from a mere ten dozen birds released in that very neighborhood hardly more than fifty years earlier. On several cold winter afternoons I put on my overcoat and stepped onto the small balcony to watch the evening flight.

The vanguard straggled in shortly after 4:00 P.M. By 4:30, large flocks began to sweep in. During the next half hour, flock after flock, three or four hundred at a time, poured through the gap in the buildings above me. Most of them had come from far out on Long Island, where commuters saw the city-bound flocks twenty miles or more from Manhattan. Other flocks came down Fifth Avenue from the direction of the Bronx. A few arrived from the west.

It was like watching a three-ring circus; yet there was an orderliness. Each flock handled itself with military precision, like a squadron of fast aircraft. When one bird turned, they all turned. When a flock passed in front of another flying in a different direction, the sky was cross-hatched with a moving pattern of birds.

I tried counting, but the starlings pitched onto the ledges so fast that I had to guess at the numbers in each incoming flock. At times the sky was a swirling storm of wings, and even the broadest estimate was pure guessing. The first evening when I totaled my figures, the count came to 24,000. A week later, when I tried again, I got 36,000. The din from the thousands that shoved and jostled on the ledges could be heard far into the night; they never seemed to sleep. When I passed by on a Fifth Avenue bus at midnight, they were still squealing.

The directors of the museum, prodded by complaints of residents up and down the avenue, stationed four men on the long, flat roof to frighten the starlings off. Each carried a long pole from which cloth streamers trailed, like the tail of a kite. When the starlings were routed from one end of the long building, they flew to the other, three or four blocks away. For weeks the uneven battle went on while icy winds whipped down the avenue. The birds won out. The museum directors, unwilling to concede defeat, were reported to have thought of trying the aluminum owls that an enterprising manufacturer had put on the market.

This roost was not the largest. The swarms along Pennsylvania Avenue in Washington exceeded 100,000 when I lived in our nation's capital. If such a snowballing of numbers were to continue, simple mathematics indicated that eventually we would be knee-deep in starlings. But as time went on there was a leveling off.

After its initial success in this country, the house sparrow actually went into a steep decline. In most cities there are nothing like the numbers of fifty or sixty years ago—in many places there is probably only one sparrow today as against twenty or more earlier in the century. Henry Ford, some contend, had much to do with this. Oil droppings from motor cars are a poor substitute for horse droppings. But the sparrows in one city I passed through had turned things to their advantage. At the Greyhound bus station they awaited the arrival of the buses and picked off the insects that were stuck to the grilles of the radiators—roasted grasshoppers, grilled butterflies, fried bees.

I *admire* house sparrows—and also rock pigeons and starlings. I really do. What would our cities and towns be like without them? They manage to live with us on our terms—and there is no denying that, as a species, *we are difficult.* "But," you may ask, "aren't house (or English) sparrows foreigners that shouldn't be here?" My answer is that most of us are of foreign origin, too. When my own parents came from Europe, sparrows were already well established on this side of the ocean. They are thus as American as I am.

I am not worried about the house sparrow. Although we can still see noisy roosts in some towns, it is on the ebb. The house sparrow must now be accepted, and so must the starling. Furthermore, their food habits are not bad. How many other birds will eat Japanese beetles? Both may have put pressure on bluebirds, martins, and one or two other natives, but the crest of their tide has leveled off and subsided. Actually, our native tree swallow can be much more aggressive than the house sparrow in taking over bluebirds' nesting sites.

As for the flowers, the alien plants we often call "weeds" make up at least 40 percent of the species that line the roadsides and highways throughout the East and Midwest. The list includes lovelies such as daylilies, daisies, dandelions, chicory, orange hawkweed, and Queen Anne's lace. What would our roadsides be like without *them*? They have adapted to the disturbed soil of roadsides ever since the old Roman days in Europe.

The rock pigeon (or domestic pigeon, if you prefer) is another city dweller that finds no difference between New York and London. Under domestication it became adapted to the buildings in cities, but some rock pigeons still nest in the ancestral way in caves and rocky ledges by the sea not only in Europe but also in the New World. On the headlands fronting the sea at Nahant, in Massachusetts, I could always find several pairs nesting among the rocks. I have seen viable pairs and colonies living ferally in sea cliffs as far south as Patagonia.

The house sparrow and starling invasions put an end to free-for-all acclimatization efforts in America. In 1900, the Lacey Act was passed. From then on no one was permitted to bring in birds from elsewhere without permission from the U.S. Fish and Wildlife Service. Although Henry Ford liberated four or five hundred birds on his estates at Dearborn, Michigan, in 1930, songbirds are not intentionally imported nowadays.

In spite of the law, there has been one recent introduction that has taken a strong hold—the house finch. Originally from the Southwest, the house finch looks very much like the related purple finch but acts more like a house sparrow. Few American birds are more adaptable, and when our West was settled, they moved from the deserts and dry canyons into the cities. Illegally brought to New York as cage birds, they were released in 1940 on nearby Long Island as game management agents closed in on a pet store dealer. At that time I predicted they would not survive. I was wrong; they have been raising three broods a year ever since and have expanded westward until they have all but bridged the gap with the western population of house finches. Today in downtown New Haven there are more house finches than house sparrows. My feeders at home are dominated by these fidgety little birds; I have no house sparrows.

A number of other aliens almost made the grade; they prospered for a while, then died out. A few gained a hold locally but did not seem to spread. The European tree sparrow, which looks like a house sparrow with a chocolate crown and a black spot behind the ear, did

House finches were illegally brought to New York
as cage birds, and released in 1940.

well around St. Louis, where twelve pairs were set free in Lafayette Park, in 1870. It would have spread more widely had not the more aggressive house sparrow arrived in St. Louis about the same time. There still are European tree sparrows near St. Louis, but you have to know where to look for them.

The sky lark, the bird of Shelley, is another species that almost made good in the United States. It survived for twenty-five years around Flatbush, Long Island, until the growing city swallowed the little colony. It was also the one bird that the Portland, Oregon, Songbird Club nearly succeeded in transplanting. For twenty or thirty years a few sky larks could be seen near Portland.

The sky lark was also introduced around Victoria, in British Columbia. Initially it did not do well, but the Victoria Natural History Society was not discouraged. The people of Victoria are as traditionally British as any on our continent. They longed for the touch of the old English countryside that only the sky lark could bring. So they decided to try again. They sent a man to England to find the place where the climate was most like that of Victoria. They then imported their birds from that locality.

Today there are still plenty of sky larks near Victoria, but they will probably never spread beyond the well-kept farms of the southern tip of Vancouver Island. There, on a winter's day, several members of the Victoria Natural History Society showed me a flock of thirty. Some of the birds hovered low over the grass, flashing their white outer tail feathers like pipits. While a herd of cows crowded around us in idle curiosity, I gazed in fascination at the birds made famous by the English poets. It was late January, but as we watched, several of the larks climbed into the gray sky and sang.

The European goldfinch, a little tan bird with a red face and a yellow wing patch, so often portrayed in medieval paintings (a symbol of the soul and resurrection), was also imported by homesick Europeans. One lot, liberated at Hoboken, New Jersey, in 1878, prospered. They became common around Englewood and in Central Park in New York City and appeared on Long Island. Then they vanished.

Yet there must have been a few of these goldfinches holding on to the thin thread of existence somewhere; in the 1930s they reappeared. For a few years many nested around Seaford, Massapequa, and other towns along the south shore of Long Island. Edwin Way Teale and I made a special trip to see them. We searched where John Elliott, the local authority, had seen one the day before. A suspicious bird darted into a maple. I hurried over, and there, its red face peering at me from the green leaves, was my first European goldfinch— sitting on a nest!

This species had never been photographed on this side of the Atlantic, so it was worth a try. An old wooden door placed across two sawhorses made a platform for my heavy tripod and my big four-by-five-inch Graflex. Standing on a stepladder, I focused on the nest and wired a remote control release to my flash equipment.

The motorcar patriots driving along the Sunrise Highway that Sunday reported my suspicious actions to the Seaford police, and a patrol car pulled up just as I was waiting for the bird to come back. In those early war years, everyone along the south shore of Long Island was nervous about spies. Only a week before, several German spies had been captured after coming ashore from a submarine a few miles to the east.

When I told the officer I was trying to photograph goldfinches, he inquired: "British or American?" "British," I gasped in surprise.

He then told me he already knew about these birds. Earlier in the day, he had picked up a man and his wife, and to explain their suspicious actions they showed him a book that said Seaford was the best place to look for British goldfinches. The book was a copy of my field guide!

Occasionally, exotic birds seem to have appeared from nowhere. Some years ago the crested myna, a sociable starlinglike bird from the Orient, appeared in the city of Vancouver in British Columbia. No one really knows how it got there, but it spread rapidly until it nested even in the downtown business section. It was another urban bird on the move. As it approached the U.S. border mile by mile, there were predictions that it might become the most numerous bird on the West Coast. But that did not happen; it seems to have gone into a decline, perhaps because of competition with its European relative the starling.

The mute swan, the graceful park swan with the orange bill, is the only exotic waterfowl species that has taken hold. Originally these swans were bred as ornaments on the big estates of Long Island and Dutchess County on the Hudson. The young birds, unpinioned, wandered off, and now there are several thousand mute swans of feral stock in the Northeast. I have often seen a hundred or more in a flock at the mouth of the Connecticut River near my home. The native tundra swan, or "whistler," is almost unknown in these parts. It bypasses New England on its way from the Chesapeake to the Great Lakes en route to the Arctic.

The American Ornithologists' Union has officially given the mute swan a place on the list of North American birds, but there are those purists who insist we should "control" mute swans by shaking (and thereby ruining) their eggs. I cannot agree; my advice is to leave

Europeans brought mute swans to North America in the nineteenth century.

them alone. They give pleasure to a great many people and pose no real threat to other waterfowl.

Of course there are also a number of game birds that have been introduced from abroad, and "managed" for the benefit of the hunting fraternity. But that is another story.

—JULY/AUGUST 1992

SEVENTY YEARS
BEHIND THE CAMERA

WAS I THIRTEEN years old or fourteen when I got my first camera? I am not sure. To earn it I delivered papers, the *Jamestown Morning Post,* riding my bike with the bag of newspapers slung over my shoulder.

Getting up at 3:30 in the morning to pick the papers up at the printers and delivering them from door to door to the elite residents on the north side of town took a lot out of me. Shortchanged on sleep, I often dozed off at my desk in school. Because of this I was not the best of students, so finally my teachers forced me to give up my paper route. By then I had saved enough for a four-by-five-inch plate camera, a Primo No. 9, that cost me somewhat more than a hundred dollars, a lot of money in those days. It was one of those old-fashioned jobs with bellows, and it used glass plates, which I developed in the basement darkroom of my cousins' home on North Main Street.

The Primo No. 9 was strictly for the birds. I did not even shoot my friends with it; I wish I had. My first avian subject was a screech-owl that had been carefully pulled from its roosting hole by my friend Clarence Beal, who also had a camera. So that the bird would have no choice but to sit for us, we tied a string around one leg and posed it in such a way that the string would not show.

"That's not the thing to do," my father chided. "Birds are meant to be free; that is why they have wings."

Clarence and I were just kids, but we learned fast. We soon developed a code of ethics for whenever we intruded on the private lives of our bird subjects.

There were no remote controls for cameras in those days, so I used a cord attached to the shutter release. By setting up the camera on a wooden tripod, focusing through the ground glass, and disguising things, I was able to shoot birds at close range, at the nest or at the birdbath, while I was twenty or thirty feet from the camera.

Somewhere along the line I graduated to a bulkier box camera, the four-by-five-inch revolving-back Auto-Graflex, to which I added old-fashioned flash equipment with bulbs. Allan Cruickshank, one of the Bronx boys who became perhaps the best bird photographer of his day, working in black and white, had a similar camera, but at first he did not use flash. He argued that it was not a natural source of light. Skeptically he examined my setup at the birdbath in the Roosevelt Sanctuary on Long Island, then tried it himself. From that point on he would not be without his own flash equipment.

That was before the days of 35-millimeter color transparencies. I was still using the four-by-five-inch format for my lectures to local garden clubs, painstakingly coloring the black-and-white slides with watercolors. I recall my first really big public lecture. It was on a Saturday afternoon at the auditorium of the Brooklyn Academy of Sciences, where fifteen hundred kids filled the hall. They had to sit through my presentation before they could see a much publicized Douglas Fairbanks film. Halfway through my talk, while I was facing my audience, the kids burst into laughter. Turning to look at the screen, I was appalled to see the chestnut-sided warblers on my slide melting away. I had been talking too long, and the heat of the projector had melted the waxy surface of the slide! From that point on I took no chances and kept my commentaries short.

When I was a sergeant in the Signal Corps of the U.S. Army during the early 1940s, I was still using the large four-by-five-inch black-and-white format, but it was with sheet film, not glass plates. At Fort Belvoir I was assigned to do the artwork (if it could be called that) for training manuals—how to build Bailey bridges, how to defuse land mines, et cetera. The lads and lasses next door who were doing the photographic work often used the new color film, Kodachrome, in four-by-five-inch sheets. It was relatively slow (ASA 10?). Although it was not yet readily available in the camera stores, the corps had so much of it that from time to time my captain let me have a few sheets for my own use.

A half mile from the nearby National Airport, on a lake not far from the Potomac, tame, well-fed mallards attracted at least two hundred wild pintails, which allowed themselves to be photographed at point-blank range if I tossed out popcorn. Today I no longer see them there.

In 1948 Dodd, Mead published my *Birds over America*, a celebration of my black-and-white photography. To embellish my essays, one hundred photographs were selected from more than ten thousand negatives that I had exposed during the previous twenty years.

Peterson took more than ten thousand photographs in the 1930s and 1940s. (Photographer unknown)

Only a few had been published before. Most of them had been taken with my big Auto-Graflex, which some of my friends teased me about because of its bulk. They quipped that it was large enough to use as a darkroom in which to develop my films. At that time my goal was ten new species photographed each year; my "life collection" had already passed two hundred species.

The Auto-Graflex was equipped with a ten-inch Protar VII lens with an old-fashioned "compound" shutter. This between-the-lens shutter was synchronized with a Mendelson flash gun that allowed a speed of one two-hundredth of a second at f/32. Most of my pictures of small songbirds at the nest and at feeders were taken with this setup. Water birds and other larger birds I photographed in normal daylight without flash, using a seventeen-inch Dallmeyer lens.

When this collection was published, forty-five years ago, I was getting into movies for the Audubon Screen tours. It is difficult to handle both movies and stills at the same time, so my still photography was somewhat neglected for a few years until I stopped lecturing for Audubon. Then I gradually retired my Bell + Howell movie camera and my Arriflex and went more exclusively into stills.

It was after the end of the war, in 1946, that *Life* magazine commissioned me to paint four pages in color of bald eagles. In addition they wanted some action shots of Charles Broley, who banded eagles in Florida. Rather than send one of their own staff photographers to Florida, they asked me to do it, handing me a four-by-five-inch Speed Graphic, which was less bulky than my Graflex. Thus the Speed Graphic became my camera of choice for a while, and then came the smaller-sized two-and-a-quarter-by-two-and-a-quarter-inch Hasselblad, which originated in Sweden, and its Japanese counterpart, the Bronica. I tried them all.

I had the privilege of knowing Victor Hasselblad, who was addicted to bird photography and who used the Swedish edition, *Vara Fagler,* of my European field guide. In 1977, when I was named "Swedish-American of the Year," he entertained Ginny and me at his country home near Stockholm. While we were in the library he took pictures of us at his desk. Then, when I asked whether he minded if

Peterson's black-and-white exposure of a singing female evening grosbeak.

we took pictures of him with our mini-Rolleiflex, he replied: "Go ahead, I'm on their board of directors too." He was, indeed, international.

With the smaller, more convenient 35-millimeter cameras getting better and better, it was inevitable that I, like most other wildlife photographers, should switch to them; not the simple "point and shoot" variety (although I still have a couple) but the more sophisticated models with their zooms and long lenses that cost so much one thinks twice before making the investment.

For several years I worked solely with Leicas; then Olympus seemed to be the answer to some of my problems. I tried them all—Pentax, Nikon, Canon—accumulating so much equipment and accessories in the basement of my studio that Ginny said I could open a camera shop.

I have no idea what the future holds, but right now I favor my automatic Nikons and Canons. Even when I boiled things down to these two, I often got confused when changing lenses or filters. So I put red stickers on all my Canon equipment and left them off my Nikon stuff. Will I finally settle on one—either Nikon or Canon? The decision has yet to be made; I like certain things about both.

Why automatic focus? Many old-timers had become so used to their manual systems that they were reluctant to change. But to me autofocus was a godsend. Now that I am in my mid-eighties, my eyes are not what they used to be. Cataracts have been removed; the left eye has an implant, the right eye a removable hard contact lens. And because of facial surgery after a car accident, I have so much astigmatism that it takes an extra pair of eyeglasses to pull things together. This lack of quick flexibility of my eyes slows me down when taking photographs. I can still see a good picture and can compose it, but when using the manual mode I must fiddle too long with my lens to get sharp focus; thus I lose many of those "grab shots." Automatic focus is quicker and more reliable than my own eyes.

Whenever I get a new camera, new lens, flash, or a new batch of film, I test things on the tame ring-billed and herring gulls that patronize the restaurant at the mouth of the nearby river. I now have at least ten thousand transparencies of ringbills—flight shots, head shots, foot shots, everything!

Last October, two months before I sent the color plates for the new European field guide off to London, I took a three-week breather. This time it was along the coast of Texas with my friend Seymour Levin, who shares my passion for bird photography. While he was at the wheel, we used beanbags on the partially lowered windows. When you rent vehicles these days, it is hard to find one where you can lower the windows sufficiently to give enough play for the beanbags and cameras. The idea of the auto designers was to safeguard small kids who might otherwise fall out. But photographers with cameras are not small kids.

This time I had two Canon bodies with me, the EOS-1 and the EOS-10. My lens of choice was a spanking new 300-millimeter Canon f/2:8 autofocus with a 2x extender, which at 600-millimeter f/5:6 is surprisingly sharp and just right for roadside photography.

Birds seem to regard the car as a big, harmless beast with round legs, but if you open the door and step out, off they fly. In effect, the car is a good blind.

October in Texas is a bit late for the best flights of passerines and migrant hawks, and a month too early for the mobs of cranes, ducks, and geese. So we concentrated on shorebirds. Greg Lasley, Gail Luckner, and other Texas friends started us off on Bolivar Flats, where at high tide there was a fabulous congregation of pelicans, skimmers, terns, and waders.

On a cold, windy day in one of the refuges, we had an upland sandpiper that was probably tired after its thousand-mile flight from the northern prairies. Protected from the wind by the bushes bordering the narrow strip of grass that lined the road, it was reluctant to fly. We could take all the frame-filling portraits we pleased; I shot six rolls of Fuji and Kodachrome, nearly all of which turned out well. Later, along the outer coast, we had similar luck with marbled godwits and long-billed curlews. The important thing was to jockey ourselves into position so we would not be bumped by passing cars.

Along the beaches, tame willets and other shorebirds ignored the joggers, while sanderlings and turnstones closely approached any fisherman who might offer a discarded shrimp or other bait. Even great blue herons and egrets are becoming excessively tame. Some white pelicans are now becoming as trusting as the brown pelicans; they know where and when the fish gutting takes place. From pier 37 near Snoopy's restaurant on South Padre Island, Seymour and I shot at least a dozen rolls of close-ups of these big, stunning birds.

At Bentsen State Park on the lower Rio Grande, where bird-feeding winter visitors park their house trailers, we took a lot of pictures of green jays, chachalacas, and other south Texas specialties. Seymour and I were on track this time in spite of the uncertain weather. With today's upgraded films, lenses, flash, and the increasing cooperation of the birds, we did very well.

—MARCH/APRIL 1993

EXTINCTION
IS FOREVER

FORTY YEARS AGO, in 1953, when my English friend James Fisher and I made our special trip around the perimeter of the continent, we saw a bird that has since become extinct—the dusky seaside sparrow. Indeed, we saw quite a few. Let me quote James from our book *Wild America*:

> After a detour of thirty miles on the back roads of Merritt Island, we picked up a rare sparrow with a curious fizzing song, the dusky seaside sparrow, *Ammospiza nigrescens*. It is confined absolutely to Florida, to the marshes at the northern end of the Indian River, the great lagoon which runs along the east coast of that state, where it can only have a few hundred individuals. There is another very rare species, a greenish bird, the Cape Sable seaside sparrow, *Ammospiza mirabilis*, which even Roger has never been able to find. In several days we will be within a few miles of it. This species probably numbers only a few score individuals, now believed to be confined to the south of the Tamiami Trail near Ochopee. It was the last new species of bird described from the United States (in 1919). Actually, we are sure that these eccentric sparrows, the dusky and Cape Sable, are no more than very well-marked geographical races of the ordinary seaside sparrow, *Ammospiza maritime*, because they do not overlap the ranges of any of the races of this species, which lives locally in salt marshes all the way from Massachusetts to Florida and Texas. Roger believes that hurricanes in times past could account for the numerous well-separated forms of this rather sedentary bird by having wiped out great sections of the population as well as their environment.

Back in 1934, when Houghton Mifflin published my first *Field Guide to the Birds,* the book had only four color plates. The sparrows were not included in these four color plates; they were shown in black and white. Although the widespread seaside sparrow was illustrated, the closely related Cape Sable and dusky seasides were mentioned only in the text.

In 1947, when I revised the book for the second time, I included the two rare seaside sparrows in a color plate of "Florida Specialties." The Cape Sable seaside was considered endangered, and to examine a specimen at the American Museum, I had to get a key to the well-guarded "first collection." However, the dusky seaside was not yet in trouble. The trays in the general collection were full of these dark passerines, and I was free to take specimens home to draw. This I did not need to do, because I already had in my possession three birds that were collected in 1876 by C. J. Maynard. Although Maynard himself shot the first specimens known to science, Robert Ridgway was the taxonomist who actually named the bird, giving it a trinomial, correctly regarding it as a subspecies of the seaside complex. Maynard, by contrast, insisted that it was a full species, which he called the "black shore finch." (The "lumpers" and the "splitters" have been battling back and forth for more than a century, to the annoyance of the bird listers.)

Not so many years after James and I visited Florida, the fortunes of these two sparrows changed dramatically. The locally thriving dusky faded away, while the Cape Sable sparrow survived; you could still tick off the latter on your list if you knew where to find it. But many birders lost interest; going by their rules, subspecies do not count on the life list.

What happened?

A fascinating book, *A Shadow and a Song: The Struggle to Save an Endangered Species,* by Mark Jerome Walters, has recently been published by Chelsea Green Publishing Company, and I urge you to read it. It tells a complex and depressing story, first about the spraying of DDT and then about the bungling mismanagement by the U.S. Fish and Wildlife Service of the marshes adjacent to the Canaveral Space

*The dusky seaside
sparrow is now
extinct.*

Center (which had been turned over by NASA to become the Merritt
Island Wildlife Refuge). What should have been salvation of the
sparrows became their undoing. Bowing largely to the duck-hunting
fraternity, the service created impoundments that changed the salt-
water marshes to a freshwater habitat more suitable for dabbling
ducks. By the late 1960s the environmentally specialized dusky seaside sparrows could no longer be found where James Fisher and I
had seen so many in the early 1950s.

Even though dusky seaside sparrows were no longer to be found
on Merritt Island, there were still a good number in the nearby
marshes along the St. Johns River adjacent to Titusville. By 1980,
however, because of mosquito control, uncontrolled fires, and explosive suburban development around Titusville, the St. Johns birds
were reduced to four known males. These were captured in the hope
that they could be crossbred in captivity with female Scott seaside
sparrows, a race found commonly along the Gulf Coast of western
Florida. Through selective breeding, workers hoped to replicate the
dusky strain. But before this could be accomplished, the last aging
males gave way to the ghost of extinction.

However, a few of their offspring, with varying amounts of dusky blood, survived at Disney World, where they had been housed. But through neglect their cages fell into disrepair; Norway rats and rat snakes got in, and that was the end.

In 1990 the Fish and Wildlife Service removed the dusky from the endangered list. A bird that had been on the road to speciation was officially extinct.

In 1984 a nature trail around a part of the Merritt Island Refuge known as Black Point was dedicated to the memory of an old friend, Allan Cruickshank, who was the first to suggest that Merritt Island become a federal refuge. His wife, Helen, was there, and I gave the commemorative speech to a small gathering of Allan's friends and admirers. But there were no longer any dusky seasides to hear me speak or to add their own lisping comments. Their voices on Merritt Island had been silenced forever.

A Shadow and a Song, eloquent and well researched, is a book as much about people as it is about the sparrow—the conflicting cross-currents between people of passionate ideals and those involved with self-protecting bureaucracy. As Mark Walters puts it: "The sparrow's history is a constellation of individuals' mistakes and fortunes, of their sorrow, their pain."

Tears came to my eyes when I read about the death of "Old Orange," age twelve, the last surviving pure-blooded male. It breathed its last on June 15, 1987.

Extinction is forever.

—MAY/JUNE 1993

RTP's Perspective: Birding Today

JUST AFTER *Bird Watcher's Digest* began publication (in September 1978), the publishers asked me for my reaction to the first issue, and I wrote the following:

I was delighted to receive the copy of your first issue of the *Bird Watcher's Digest*. You asked for a critique of your new magazine.

I think it is a great idea, and would like to see it aimed not so much at those who are not yet into bird watching, but rather at the vast numbers who are already confirmed addicts.

General articles about species or subjects that bird watchers can find easily in their reference books should probably be skipped—articles about certain species that merely give the well-known facts, as well as those articles that extol the joys of bird watching (which we all know).

I do not think that your digest will serve a real function unless it excerpts the really newsworthy stories—and you had many of these in the first issue, articles that were newsworthy and had immediacy: "The Red-cockaded Woodpecker," "The House Finch on Long Island," "The Finch Connection" (an amusing, offbeat story), "The Bald Eagle in Florida," "Bird Counting," "Hawk and Hare Are One" (a good philosophical article), "Shooting 645 North American Birds" (with a camera), "Why Can't the AOU Leave Our Bird Names Alone" (this was a controversial article to which one could easily give a good reply), "Great Smokies, Paradise for Bird Watchers," "Lost Song" (Bachman's warbler), "How Do These Noteworthy Exotics Reach Us?" (a good theme), etc.

As we can see, the articles in the first issue fell into two basic categories: (1) articles for the uninformed who won't be very likely to take the *Bird Watcher's Digest* anyway. These articles have no real news value but are simply space-filling essays at an unsophisticated level. And (2) articles that have immediacy and are of interest to the ever-growing fraternity of birders.

Others may disagree, but I have stated what I would like to see. You can have a magazine that is unique and that fills quite a different niche from *American Birds,* which monitors bird trends, or *Birding,* which is for those addicted to listing.

You must not attempt to overlap too much with the conservation magazines such as *Audubon.* . . . Your chosen niche is worth filling, but it should be filled in a meaningful way. This means ignoring perhaps two-thirds of the bird articles that one sees in the press.

Initially *Bird Watcher's Digest,* using a clipping service, only reprinted from other publications, including newspaper birding columns from around the country. Now the magazine has a mix of articles and essays written specifically for the publication as well as articles that are reprinted. As the years have passed, four regular columns have been featured (mine, a bird behavior column, "Far Afield," and "Close Focus") and five other departments added.

During its fifteen-year existence *Bird Watcher's Digest* has made changes that reflect new developments in the world of bird watching (and its circulation has increased accordingly). What are some of these developments?

Recently a young person asked me, "Did you ever meet Audubon?" "Heavens, no," I replied. "I'm not that old." Then after thinking about it, I realized that at my age (eighty-five) I go more than halfway back to Audubon, who died in 1851. In fact, anyone over seventy-five goes more than halfway back to the legendary figure.

Reviewing my own lifetime involvement with birds makes me reflect that a great deal of change has occurred every twenty-five years—roughly every generation—going back to the beginning of the century, when many of our birds were at their nadir.

The problem that many people have is that they are hardly aware of what happened before they were born; they do not have a sense of history. That wisdom usually comes after they pass the half-century mark, when they begin to question their own mortality. By then most hotshot birders are beyond the listing stage, unless they are so well heeled that they can afford to travel to the ends of the earth to pile up a world list.

Most of my older peers, who included Ludlow Griscom and some of the other early giants in field ornithology, are now gone, so during the last ten years or so I have sought the company of some skilled younger birders. Unfortunately, one of the most gifted of my several "adopted sons," Pete Isleib, whose special realm was Alaska, was recently crushed and killed by a forklift when he was trying to load nets on one of his fishing boats. He was in midlife and should have had another forty years. We will miss Pete.

There must be some potential "grandchildren" out there, so I will keep my eyes and ears open. Speaking of eyes and ears, those of younger birders are far sharper than mine. I have had cataracts removed from both eyes, and my hearing is now losing the higher register. I can no longer hear a blackpoll warbler or even a grasshopper sparrow. Some other birds no longer sound quite the same, perhaps because certain elements of their song are no longer within the range of my aging eardrums. It is embarrassing to be in the field with friends like Pete Dunne or Noble Proctor, who can spot and identify a bird so distant that I cannot even pick it up, and who can hear songs that are no longer within my hearing range. Noble Proctor has vision that is not merely 20/20 but perhaps about 20/5, which makes him almost as sharp-eyed as a red-tailed hawk.

All the seeming improvement in "birdathons" and "Big Days"—what does it really mean? The lists are getting larger and larger, but do they give a true picture of the status of birds? Merely getting a larger list does not mean that most birds in general are doing well; what about the numbers of individuals of a species? This past May, when I was on Pete Dunne's team in New Jersey during the World Series of Birding, we sometimes traveled at high speed for miles and miles to pick up one staked-out phoebe and many miles more to pick up one staked-out Carolina chickadee. As I remember from my many earlier visits to Cape May County, these birds and many others once existed in considerably greater numbers. At least that was my impression twenty or thirty years ago, when I worked the same areas. Species lists are larger, but numbers of individuals are seldom noted. This drop in numbers may not be true for some of the birds along the shore, but it certainly seems true for the summer resident passerines.

At the end of the day this last year in Cape May, the largest list, believe it or not, was tallied by the Canadian team. They had gone all out, scouting areas for several days and practically killing themselves on the big day. I have never seen a more beat-up-looking group than when they finally showed up late at night. The Canadians had seen a total of 215 species, which was the largest number ever attained in twenty-four hours in New Jersey. They worked the state from top to bottom, going at fast speed to each place where they had staked things out.

Such tournaments may give the impression that there are more birds than ever, but this is absolutely not the case. We are simply more experienced, with more competitive drive; we have better binoculars, telescopes, faster cars, more discipline, and more knowledge of the fine points (thanks to the increased sophistication of specialized field guides and other bird publications).

Historically, things were at rock bottom at the turn of the century, when birds lacked the protection they now have. Birds were shot by the millinery trade for hats. The eggs of colonial waterbirds were taken. Hawks were shot for pleasure.

The real turnaround in public interest and concern came in the mid-1930s, when the shotgun school of ornithology gave way to the binocular (or field glass, as we called it). My first field guide, in 1934, had a lot to do with this, and so did the revolution at the National Audubon Society; the formation of the National Wildlife Federation, with its stamp sheet; the establishment of Hawk Mountain; the work at Cape May; and other pivotal events. It was a key decade. A generation later we had *National Wildlife* and *International Wildlife* magazines, the Golden field guides, Rachel Carson's *Silent Spring* and acknowledgment of the DDT menace. There was another jump during the eighties, when the country seemed to become even more environmentally conscious. *Bird Watcher's Digest* was a little ahead of this jump, beginning publication in 1978.

As I have said before, the observation of birds can be many things. It can be a science, an art, a recreation, an ethic, or a sport. It can even be a religious experience, as Father Tom Pincelli, one of the best birders in Texas, has stated. The ABA (American Birding Association) has focused largely on the game or sport—competing for the list. This activity has been called "ornithogolfing." When you've seen all the birds north of Mexico, you must travel if you want to build a world list. To cater to those who have the money to travel, at least three hundred tour agencies and group leaders now conduct bird or nature tours. (The new buzzword—ecotourism—can be interpreted in a dual way—ecological and economic.) Many sharp birders who otherwise could not afford it are able to get to far-off places as tour leaders.

Some of those who are addicted to birds enjoy photographing them, and by this I do not mean "point and shoot" photography. Beyond documenting a bird lies the ability to really see and to take a well-composed picture. The ultimate is the work of a visual person like Carl Sams, who will stay, week in and week out, from dawn to dark, with a family of loons or some other creature, and whose pictures convey feeling and intimacy as well as art.

As for bird painting: *Wildlife Art News,* in a recent issue, presented the current work of more than 250 artists and illustrators. Nearly 100 of these were women. The new generation of bird artists is producing everything from portraits that Louis Agassiz Fuertes would have been proud of to three-dimensional compositions such as those of Robert Bateman and Guy Coheleach. There is so much good bird painting today (as well as so much "corn") that one wonders how anyone breaking into the field can make a living. Some are, however, and some are even making a lot of money. Others are struggling. Styles, although leaning toward academic realism, range from the hyperrealism of Carl Brenders to the impressionism of Manfred Schatz. *Bird Watcher's Digest,* the only bird magazine using paintings—rather than photography—on its covers, has provided an outlet for many young artists.

In other developments, the study of bird voices through sound recording has also reached new heights of sophistication with the work of researchers like Luis Baptista, who can tell by a white-crowned sparrow's accent or dialect whether it lives on one side of San Francisco Bay or the other—or whether it is from Puget Sound or somewhere in between. Field guides have gone from my own guides, which emphasize simplification, the quick way of learning aimed at 99 percent of the people, to amplification, which involves the other 1 percent—the hard-core experts.

As for academic ornithology, the three major scientific bird journals, *The Auk, The Wilson Bulletin,* and *The Condor,* were once quite different. *The Auk* was the official organ of the American Ornithologists' Union and covered the whole country. *The Wilson Bulletin* was mostly for the Midwest and was a bridge between the advanced amateur and the professional. *The Condor,* the organ of the Cooper Club, was basically stern. Now the three overlap.

There are literally hundreds of local publications and newsletters. A national publication like *Bird Watcher's Digest* puts into popular form news and information of such broad interest that it should be read by all.

Birding hotlines are another recent development. With the appropriate telephone number you can now find out what rare birds have been seen in various areas.

Young people are also being remembered. Victor Emanuel, always innovative, and knowing that some young people who become hooked on birds are loners because they fail to make contact with others of their kind, has started a camp for them in the Chiricahuas in Arizona. It is sponsored by the American Birding Association and will certainly be a model for similar summer camps.

These are all advances, but there are losses too. The very popular Audubon Screen Tours have been dropped, and this is to be regretted because hundreds of thousands of people nationwide were able to hear lectures and see films the likes of which we seldom have on television. Natural history on television in this country lags behind that of Canada, England, Japan, and Russia. (In fact, the largest of all television audiences for a wildlife show is in Russia, reaching 200 million viewers.)

I have only touched here on a few of the developments in the bird watching world. There is also bird rehabilitation, for example, for those with a passion for taking care of injured birds. There are new nature centers, nature trails, et cetera. And there is, of course, the increased popularity of feeding birds. The interest in birds and bird watching—and in conservation—appears to be growing.

—September/October 1993

WINGS BEHIND THE ONCE IRON CURTAIN

BIRDS HAVE WINGS; they do not observe political boundaries—witness some of our gray-cheeked thrushes or sandhill cranes, which migrate across the Bering Strait to nest in Siberia. We also think that ornithology, like the birds, knows no politics. But until recently we were pretty much in the dark about that immense landmass that lies between the Baltic Sea and the Bering Strait. Was any serious bird work being done?

We knew that some activity was going on because kittiwakes carrying Russian bands were retaken in Newfoundland. And a six-volume handbook of the *Birds of the U.S.S.R.* appeared in the bookstalls of western Europe, an exhaustive work on which fourteen Russian ornithologists labored for ten years. However, I did not meet a Russian ornithologist in the flesh until June 1954, when four Soviet delegates and an interpreter attended the International Ornithological Congress at Basel, Switzerland. At the previous congress, in Sweden in 1950, the Russians had cabled their regrets at not being able to attend.

Just as the Swiss congress inspired the Africans to plan a pan-African Ornithological Congress for 1957, it also undoubtedly sparked the first Russian Ornithological Congress, which was held in 1956. Four hundred professional ornithologists from all parts of what was then the Soviet Union convened in Leningrad for a week of scientific papers. Several representatives from other countries, including my coauthor Guy Mountfort, who was then secretary of the British Ornithologists' Union; Erwin Stresemann of Germany;

In the late 1940s, the Russian bands on black-legged kittiwakes in Newfoundland showed that serious bird research was being done in the USSR.

Finnur Gudmundsson of Iceland; Johannsen of Denmark; and two or three others; but no American, were invited.

At the last moment my friend James Fisher, the British ornithologist, was extended an invitation. On impulse, he tucked under his arm his copy of my film *Wild America,* the picture I made on our tour around the continent in 1953. It was the first time an Audubon Screen Tour film had been shown behind the Iron Curtain.

Mountfort showed an English film produced by the Royal Society for the Protection of Birds. It was received with great admiration, but when James Fisher showed our film featuring the national parks, wildlife refuges, Audubon sanctuaries, and other conservation activities on this side of the Atlantic, the audience was so enthusiastic that they asked him to show it a second time. They seemed impressed by the high quality of the 16-millimeter nature films being turned out in the West and expressed astonishment at the amount of popular interest that existed in England and in America.

James told me that after the showing the Russian committee had a discussion that included recognizable words such as *Audubonski* and *Petersonski*. Then a resolution was passed to the effect that "Russia must upgrade the quality of its nature films."

All this was good propaganda, and heaven knows that wildlife the world over needed it. We had been lucky in our country to have excellent wild bird treaties with our good neighbors, Canada and Mexico. By way of contrast, imagine the legal and political complexity of protecting birds that migrate through six or eight European countries on their way to and from their wintering grounds in Africa. I remember being irked when I read a piece of publicity turned out by a tourist agency in Egypt. It admonished: "Come to the Nile for your duck shooting. Bags of two hundred birds a day are not unusual—there are no limits—shoot all you want. After all," the ad pointed out, "these birds were raised behind the Iron Curtain!"

The Russians seemed to be impressed by the quality of my home-made film, even though it was the first I had ever made. Actually, my modest film had no optical effects, such as fade-outs, blends, wipes, or zoom shots. I employed nothing but straight cuts in the best way I knew how. I introduced no schematic maps or other animations, no superimposed titles, no synchronized soundtrack for mood when I desired a breather or change of pace. These things had become standard practice in nontheatrical films, thousands of which were turned out yearly by business firms, religious organizations, educational institutions, and government bureaus. However, a half-hour film produced by one of these organizations seldom had a budget of less than $25,000 and might cost $50,000 or more, a much larger sum then than now.

Naturally, the Audubon Screen Tour lectures could not compete with this kind of money. Most of the thirty lecturers were working on

Peterson, creating one of his homemade films in Kenya.
(Virginia M. Peterson)

a shoestring. Many could spare only three weeks or a month each year from their teaching or other duties for the Audubon cause, and after spending several thousands in making a film, even the additional hundreds of dollars for a duplicate print was a matter for sober thought.

These were low-cost lectures—low in cost for the sponsor, low in fee for the lecturer. But subconsciously, many people compared these films, fine as they were, with some of the glossy commercial products. They might even have expected a Disney job, not realizing that Disney had skimmed the cream from the best footage of some of these very same photographers and had often supported that film with elaborately contrived studio footage. Disney may have spent a fortune in making a film. One bumptious young lad at the Linnaean Society in New York City once said he wondered why the Audubon lecturers didn't keep up to date by making their films in Technicolor instead of Kodachrome!

To get the lowdown on some of the modern trends in 16-millimeter film production, Dorothy Dingley, then the assistant director of Audubon Screen Tours, Dr. Al Etter, one of our lecturers, and I went to a three-day mid-March workshop of the Calvin Company in Kansas City. Five or six hundred producers of nontheatrical films were in attendance. We learned about the preparation of scripts, optical effects, work prints, "a and b" rolls, and synchronized sound. We analyzed film until our eyes bugged out. We saw good examples and horrible examples of the professional cinematographer's craft.

At the end of the three days, I confided to Miss Dingley that my main reaction was one of discouragement—not because of the technical intricacies but because of the expense involved. It was not so much the cost of the raw film (even though it ran through the camera at the rate of several dollars a minute, and even though a photographer might use only one foot for every five or ten exposed). It was the laboratory costs, if one wished to do things the way Karl Maslowski or Cleveland Grant, top Screen Tour lecturers, did them.

There was a time, in the beginning, when lecture audiences were quite satisfied with any shot that had motion or color. Later, becoming more sophisticated, they recognized top quality but did not always realize what went into achieving it in the way of equipment, skill, knowledge, *and money.*

More and more did my admiration grow for the lecturers on our roster who made do with a Bell + Howell camera or a Bolex. Their films, on the whole, were good indeed, constructed with imagination and loving care. These dedicated men and women were expected to fill the combined roles of biologist, artist, technician, teacher, conservationist, entertainer, and producer.

Some were perhaps stronger in one department than in another. But, as I went around the country in their footsteps, I found that nearly every one of them was a favorite in certain cities. Audiences varied as much as the lecturers.

During the thirty-seven years since that first Russian Ornithological Congress, television in the former USSR has really taken off. The area now boasts the largest nature-oriented show in the world, with tenfold the number of viewers that exist for similar shows in England or in Canada.

Although we have a few wildlife shows on U.S. television, usually on public broadcasting channels, the best are often borrowed from the BBC (British Broadcasting Company) or the CBC (Canadian Broadcasting Company). The Japanese and Australians also produce good shows. We have the talent, but when will we be allowed to catch up?

Last year, Marshal Case, who recently left the National Audubon Society, arranged with his Russian contacts to do an hour-long show for television, comparing me with my counterpart in Russia, a man exactly my age who paints birds and whose philosophy and contributions are much the same as mine. Unfortunately, the two filmmakers who were to film me in my studio in Connecticut never arrived. Their broadcasting studio in Moscow was firebombed by members of [Boris] Yeltsin's opposition during the siege of the Russian White House.

These men survived and soon may try again to film me here in Connecticut and probably also in Jamestown, New York, where the attractive new building of the RTP Institute is now open to the public. I hope they will wait until May. Winter drifts in Jamestown are deeper than those in Moscow.

— MARCH/APRIL 1994

HEATH HENS AND ATTWATER'S

AT THE END of summer, back in 1931, more than sixty years ago, I just missed seeing the last heath hen in the world. I had gone from Maine, where I had been a counselor at Camp Chewonki, an elite boys camp, and I traveled by road to Cape Cod, where I met the legendary Maurice Broun; then I crossed by ferry to Martha's Vineyard, where the heath hen, a coastal race of the prairie-chicken, was about to drop over the edge. There was only one male left, but try as I might, I could not find it. It had actually been photographed earlier in the year and, according to Alfred Gross, was last seen in 1932.

Today another peripheral race of this grouse of the prairies, the Attwater's prairie-chicken, resident of southeastern Texas, is in serious trouble. So we must keep tuned. More about that later.

A great deal has been written about the prairie-chicken, but none with as much early historical perspective as the lengthy account by John James Audubon in his *Ornithological Biography*. He called this chickenlike bird the "Pinnated Grous" (without the *e*), and his story begins: "It has been my good fortune to study the habits of this species of Grous, at a period when, in the district in which I resided, few other birds of any kind were more abundant."

Then he goes on to say:

> When I first removed to Kentucky, the Pinnated Grous were so abundant that they were held in no higher esteem as food than the most common flesh, and no "hunter of Kentucky" deigned to shoot them. They were in fact, looked upon with more abhorrence than the crows are at the present in Massachusetts and Maine, on account of the mischief they committed among the fruit trees of the

orchards during winter, when they fed on their buds, or while in the spring months they picked up the grain in the fields. The farmer's children or those of his negroes were employed to drive them away with rattles from morning to night, and also caught them in pens and traps of various kinds. In those days during the winter, the Grous would enter the farmyard and feed with the poultry, alight on the houses, or walk in the very streets of the village. I recollect having caught several in a stable at Henderson, where they had followed some wild turkeys. In the course of the same winter, a friend of mine, who was fond of rifle-shooting, killed upward of forty in one morning, but picked none of them up, so satiated with Grous was he, as well as every member of his family. My own servants preferred the fattest flitch of bacon to their flesh, and not infrequently laid them aside as unfit for cooking.

That was Audubon's early impression of the abundance of the pinnated grouse, which we now call the prairie-chicken. A quarter of a century later, with the perspective of his advancing years, he wrote:

Such an account may appear strange to you, reader; but what will you think when I tell you that, in that same country, where twenty-five years ago they could not have been sold at more than one cent a-piece, scarcely one is now to be found? The Grous have abandoned the state of Kentucky and removed (like the Indians) every season farther to the westward to escape from the murderous white man. In the Eastern states where some of these birds still exist, game laws have been made for their protection during a certain part of the year, when, after all, few escape to breed the next season. To the westward you must go as far at least as the state of Illinois, before you meet with this species of Grous, and there too, as formerly in Kentucky, they are decreasing at a rapid rate. The sportsman of the Eastern states now makes much ado to procure them, and will travel with friends and dogs and all the paraphernalia of hunting, a hundred miles or more, to shoot at most a dozen brace (twenty-four) of Grouses in a fortnight. . . . So rare have they become in the markets of Philadelphia, New York, and Boston, that they sell from five to ten dollars the pair.

At this point Audubon was talking about the now extinct heath hen:

On the eastern declivities of our Atlantic coasts, the districts in which the Pinnated Grous are still to be met with, are some portions of the state of New Jersey, the "brushy" plains of Long Island, Martha's Vineyard, the Elizabeth Islands, Mount Desert Island in the state of Maine. . . . In the first three places mentioned, notwithstanding the preventive laws now in force, they are killed without mercy by persons such as in England are called poachers. Except in the above-named places, not a bird of the species is at present to be found until you reach the lower parts of Kentucky, where, as I have told you before, a few still exist. In the state of Illinois, all the vast plains of the Missouri, those bordering the Arkansas River and on the prairies of Opellousas, the Pinnated Grous is still very abundant, and very easily procured.

Audubon had never shot these birds in the Eastern Seaboard states and could not speak from experience about them, so he quoted a letter from a sportsman friend in Boston, David Ecklei, Esq.:

Dear Sir, I have the pleasure of sending you a brace of Grous from Martha's Vineyard . . . which for many years past I have been accustomed to visit annually, for the purpose of enjoying the sport of shooting these fine birds. . . . Fifteen or twenty years ago, I know from my own experience, it was a common thing to see as many birds in a day as we now see in a week; but whilst they have grown scarcer, our knowledge of the ground has become more extended, so that the result of a few weeks residence of a party of three, with which I usually take the field, is ten brace of birds. Packs of twenty to fifty are now no longer seen, and the numbers have so diminished in consequence of a more general knowledge of their value, the price in Boston market being five dollars per brace, that we rarely see of late more than ten or twelve collected together. They congregate in large companies, in particular places, where they hold a grand tournament, fighting with great desperation and doing one another all the mischief possible. In these chosen spots, it is said the cunning natives were accustomed to strew ashes, and rush upon them with sticks when they were blinded by the dust which they have raised. In later times, the custom of baiting them has proved more destructive to the species. In this way, very great but very unsportsman-like shots have been made. . . . By these and other means to which I have adverted the birds were diminishing in numbers from year to year; but it is hoped that they will revive again, as they are now protected by an act of the state of Massachusetts, passed in 1831, which limits the time of shooting them to the months of November and December, and imposes a penalty of ten dollars each bird for all that are killed, except in those two months.

That letter to Audubon was postmarked December 1832, almost exactly one hundred years before the last heath hen succumbed. During that century the population on Martha's Vineyard had its ups and downs. In 1885 William Brewster called attention to differences between the birds of Martha's Vineyard and the western prairie-chicken and designated it as a separate species, but ornithologists later decided that it was simply a race or subspecies of a formerly widespread bird that had become isolated along the Atlantic Seaboard.

In 1908 (the year I was born) there were probably not more than fifty left. That was when a reservation of sixteen hundred acres was purchased and then improved to make it attractive for the birds. Attempts to transplant them outside the Vineyard, or to breed them in captivity, didn't work. But by 1916 they were found again in most parts of the Vineyard, and it was possible to flush a flock of three hundred or more from the corn and clover plots. There were then probably two thousand birds on the island when a disastrous fire broke out, sweeping more than twenty square miles right in the heart of the breeding area.

A hard winter followed, with an unprecedented flight of predatory goshawks. By spring there were fewer than 150 birds, mostly males. Then, worst of all, came disease, the dreaded blackhead, transmitted by domestic turkeys that had been brought in by the farmers. By 1927 there were but thirteen birds; only two were females. The following year there was but a single male, the lonesome survivor I had tried to see on my 1931 visit.

To get back to the Attwater's prairie-chicken: This small, dark form of the greater prairie-chicken, isolated on the low prairies in the coastal counties of eastern Texas, is separated by more than three hundred miles from the nominate form that ranges from Oklahoma northward. It was described in 1894 by Major Charles Bendire, who named it in honor of his friend H. P. Attwater. I had been lucky enough to see this rara avis on earlier trips to Texas, but this past March, as a guest of the Houston Audubon Society, I was given the royal treatment.

Gary Woods, president of the Houston Audubon, woke me before 4:00 in the morning and, with Dan Hendey, of the Wildlife Habitat Enhancement Council, drove me for more than an hour and a half to the vast prairie acreage owned by Mobil Oil where one of the largest remaining groups of these birds held their dancing rituals in the early morning hours.

A film crew from the local television station was there to film me from a second blind. My Canon camera—indeed *like* a cannon—was fitted with a new 600-millimeter lens and a 1:4 extender, making it an effective 840. Walking from the car to the blind with this heavy equipment was not easy in the dark. Because of the uneven footing on earth rutted by cattle, I stumbled and fell, face down and lens down, in the mud. Not a good start. Once in the blind, I breathed more easily, took a swig of coffee, and relaxed for the long wait.

Just as it was getting light enough to make out a bird here and there, a male, in display, quite close, nodded its pinnae and shuffled its feet much as the Indian braves of the plains had mimicked these birds in their own tribal dances.

At first it was still so dark that my photometer registered only one third of a second, even with 400 ASA film. I took a couple of shots anyway and then with dawn's early light shot selectively until I was shooting at 1/250 of a second or faster. But by 7:30 or so the birds were farther from my blind; then after 8:00 A.M. they quit.

There was something eerie—almost spooky—about the moaning

In the mid-1990s, the Mobil Foundation gave The Nature Conservancy a large tract of land that has ideal Attwater's prairie-chicken habitat. Just outside Houston, it's now known as the Texas City Prairie Preserve and provides an opportunity for the species to be saved.

calls of these birds, which had slipped from a known world population of 456 in 1993 to 158 at the time of my visit. Torrential rains during the previous nesting season and then dehydration were the decimating factors. Another half dozen birds were in captivity for propagation. Would the Attwater's prairie-chicken follow the pattern of the heath hen into extinction? It is hoped that a considerable acreage of the Mobil property will be put in the hands of the Nature Conservancy to manage the remaining group of these endangered birds.

They are spectacular when booming with their golden gular sacs, one on each side of the neck, blown up like bright balloons. Audubon found that if he stuck a pin through one gular sac, the bird could still sound off, but if he punctured both sacs with a pin, the booming was silenced. Naughty, naughty!

In several states of the upper Midwest there are still plenty of prairie-chickens of the nominate race because of management by various game commissions and intensive work by scholars such as Frances and Frederick Hamerstrom and George Archibald, along with their numerous students and docents.

There is still another prairie-chicken found farther west, in the panhandles of Texas and Oklahoma and across the line into New Mexico. It is smaller and paler, with dull *plum-purple* (not orange-yellow) gular sacs. I had the privilege of photographing a lek of these birds from a blind in 1961, but without the ultralong, ultraheavy lenses I now have. Although this bird, known as the lesser prairie-chicken, must have evolved from the same ancestral stock as the others, it is sufficiently different that taxonomists of the American Ornithologists' Union committee designated it officially as a distinct species, a decision questioned by certain other authorities.

—July/August 1994

THE ROGER TORY
PETERSON INSTITUTE

THE ROGER TORY PETERSON INSTITUTE of Natural History was conceived by Lorimer Moe, a school companion who sat across the aisle in study hall when I was in high school in Jamestown, New York. Lorimer was a closet naturalist who kept his boyhood interest in birds and wildlife a secret, even from me.

It was only after he had become our U.S. information officer in Sweden, Iceland, and Britain that he let it all out and we became close friends, sharing our field trips with luminaries such as James Fisher and Peter Scott of England and Finnur Gudmundsson of Iceland. I suspect that it was because of Lorimer's contact with the king of Sweden that I was named "Swedish-American of the Year" in 1977.

Lorimer was a mover and a shaker who inspired John Hamilton of the Gebbie Foundation to start the ball rolling. The purpose of the institute was not simply to be a repository for my memorabilia—my paintings, films, transparencies, and my writing. Its mission was to reflect my philosophy and my contributions as a teacher, not just teaching kids (which I had done in summer camps and at River's School in Brookline, Massachusetts), but as a *teacher of teachers*.

My main contribution in that respect had been putting into the hands of teachers the visual materials and other devices that they could use in the classroom. Teachers who know little about the natural world are often timid about teaching the subject to their pupils. My own interest was sparked by a young seventh-grade teacher, Miss Blanche Hornbeck, who admitted she knew little about birds but said she would learn *with* us.

Later, during my years with the National Audubon Society, I

rewrote the educational leaflets that I had used as a boy in Miss Hornbeck's class and that have now gone to millions of other young people. I also prepared instructional materials for teachers that would help them with their classes.

The institute has already held three top-level forums—one each year. The first was "Bridging Early Childhood and Nature Education." This featured authorities such as Dr. Richard Fisher, who had recently retired as professor of nature education at Cornell, and Marshal Case, the last student to acquire a degree in nature study under his supervision. (During his tenure with National Audubon, Marshal Case had built up the Junior Audubon Clubs to its all-time high of 600,000 members each year.) Another participant was Elisha Atkins, whom I taught when he was a young boy and who, after his retirement as a Yale professor, has his own outreach program.

The idea of these forums is to get the most prominent practitioners together to bat ideas back and forth, and to share their techniques if they will, so that standards may be raised. In planning the second forum, "Value in American Wildlife Art," we had the experience of Dr. David Wagner, director of the Colorado Springs Fine Art Center and former director of the Leigh Yawkey Woodson Art Museum in Wausau, Wisconsin, and his wife, Kaye, who works with the Society of Animal Artists (SAA). By getting the cooperation of the Leigh Yawkey Woodson Museum (which holds the most prestigious of wildlife art shows each year), the SAA, *Wildlife Art News,* and other collaborators, Dr. Wagner helped make the forum and the accompanying SAA exhibition an enormous success.

Wildlife artists have had as much impact on the environmental movement as writers, confirming the cliché that "a picture is worth a thousand words." Everyone knows Audubon's print of the wild turkey, but how many remember what this legendary man *said* about the turkey? Yet he wrote reams about this fowl, perhaps his favorite bird.

The second forum was followed by one on wildlife photography, organized by Jane Kinne of Comstock Films and Ann Guilfoyle, publisher of the *Guilfoyle Report.* This forum, in addition to making the

The Roger Tory Peterson Institute, in Jamestown, New York,
was designed by Robert Stern and built in 1993. (Jim Berry)

teaching connection, seemed to dwell mostly on the marketing of
photographs and on the ethics of photographers, so a consensus prevailed that there should soon be another photographic forum, dealing
with equipment, techniques, and composition. Even though camera
equipment is improving dramatically, the camera, like a computer,
lacks a brain of its own, and it is up to the user to make it behave. It is
not simply a matter of point and shoot. There are, of course, happy ac-
cidents if you shoot a lot of film. The photographer must be able to *see*
a picture and compose it. Beyond having a good eye, photographers
such as Franz Lanting and Carl Sams add still another dimension—
feeling—because they literally live with their subjects.

   One of the spin-offs of the photographic forum was the idea for a
new society, the NPAA—Nature Photographers of America Association [since renamed NANPA—North American Nature Photographers' Association—ed.]. Although some other countries have such
societies, America does not. Even though there are as many first-rate
bird photographers in our country as exist anywhere, we simply have

never been organized. It was Franz Lanting (the Flying Dutchman), who lives in California but is seldom home, who suggested the idea at the forum.

The elegant new building that houses the institute was designed by the distinguished architect Robert Stern. It is now finished and open to meetings, classes, and public lectures. We want the institute to be a mecca for all of our kind, from kids to obsessed binocular addicts—and especially those who teach.

A lifetime of writing will also have storage space, including correspondence with practically everyone who was involved in the earlier stages of the environmental movement. Sewall Pettingill's 16-millimeter film, which he showed when he was on the lecture circuit, is carefully preserved, as is my own film footage, which was shown, like his, to hundreds of thousands, if not millions, in the Audubon Screen Tour program.

Inasmuch as I have been behind the camera for more than seventy years, there are hundreds of thousands of transparencies that will also be housed in the new facility. Many books and journals from my own library will fill its shelves, as well as books bequeathed by others. (So if you are looking for a safe repository to leave some of your own books, keep the institute in mind.)

Landscapes can change in a single lifetime. Olson's Woods, where Clarence Beal and I camped as boys and looked for cecropia and promethea cocoons, now has much larger trees, and wild turkeys now roam about, even though the suburbs encroach. Beckerinks' Pig Farm, where I saw my first pioneering starlings in the winter of 1920 or 1921, no longer exists. (Because of their triangular shape in flight, I thought the starlings were purple martins!) I no longer recognize the groves around Peterson's Pasture, where I found a bed of showy orchids. If I could be a Rip Van Winkle and come back after another lifetime, what would I find?

Ginny has designed a butterfly garden that the Jamestown Garden Club is planting near the new building. It somewhat follows the design of the butterfly garden she planted outside my studio here in Connecticut. Butterfly gardens are becoming popular now that people are concerned about the vulnerability of these fragile insects, which dance like the angels over their flower beds. And yet many gardens are still sprayed to get rid of caterpillars. We can't have one without the other.

I regret that most of my old school friends have gone and cannot see the institute, which is finally flowering.

Man is a cooperative animal, constantly evolving—I hope for the better, even though there sometimes seems to be a dark side. The other creatures with which we share this world have their rights too, but not speaking our language, they have no voice, no vote; it is our moral duty to take care of them.

Education is the key to conservation, and well-informed teachers are important. As of this past April, 32,500 persons have already visited the exhibits, forums, workshops, and facilities of the institute. The number will increase now that the new building and its in-house exhibits are available for public viewing. Depending on funding, during this coming year the number of cooperative workshops across the country will increase to 300, reaching 5,400 teachers and by chain reaction more than 150,000 young students.

But why should the institute have its headquarters in Jamestown? Why not near the nation's capital, where I had spent an equal amount of time, or New England, where I taught and have lived for twice as many years? Quite simply, Jamestown was my birthplace, and it was the community that offered the seed money through the Gebbie Foundation. However, the hope is eventually to have satellite centers in other parts of the country—one in the Southeast, perhaps another in Texas or Arizona, and certainly others in New England, the upper midwest, the Rocky Mountain states, and somewhere along the Pacific Coast.

Join us by becoming a member of the institute, and help us spread the word to the millions of young people who will care for our world.

—SEPTEMBER/OCTOBER 1994

THE LEGEND OF
LARS-ERIC LINDBLAD

ON A BEAUTIFUL July day in Sweden overlooking the Baltic Sea, Lars-Eric Lindblad raised his glass to give his famous toast: "If there were more people like us, the world would be a better place . . . *Skal!*" His son, Sven-Olaf, reports that ten family members and close friends were there at the home of Captain Hasse Nilsson, and his wife, Ammie. That heartfelt toast was to be his last. The following day, after he and his wife, Ruriko, arrived in Stockholm, he collapsed at the train station with a sudden heart attack.

When Lars-Eric emigrated to the United States in 1951, at the age of twenty-four, it was not because he was unhappy in his beloved Sweden. Having been an avid reader of Sven Hedin and other explorers, he was always looking toward other horizons, new places to see, new friends to make. And it was because of his winning way with people that on the very day he arrived in New York he landed a job with American Express at a salary of fifty-three dollars a week. Only seven years later, he was well on his way with his own adventure tour company, Lindblad Travel.

Lars-Eric effortlessly seemed to fill all the space wherever he happened to be. He was invariably at the center of things. His close associate Nigel Sitwell recalls a visit to a remote nature reserve in the wilds of Sichuan Province in western China. It was bitterly cold, and the hotel had no heating. To quote Nigel:

> Lars had a mild bout of flu so he decided to skip dinner and go to bed. But some Chinese who were staying there were keen to get his views about travel in their country. He obligingly invited them in. . . .

Lars-Eric Lindblad.

Ten studious Chinese wearing down-filled jackets perched on wooden chairs around the bed where Lars-Eric, clad in pajamas and covered with blankets, reclined against a pile of pillows. As he talked in his usual discursive fashion, ten pens hurried to keep pace as they recorded the thoughts of Mr. Lindblad in their note-books.

His friends all agree that Lars was a born optimist. When the glasses of others were half empty, his was half full, and his sense of humor was always there to keep him going when things went awry, as they sometimes did for unforeseen reasons.

Had he lived in the year 1000, Lars probably would have set foot on the North American continent before Leif Eriksson. Or, turning eastward, he might have reached China before Marco Polo. The Viking wanderlust was dominant in his genes. Although he loved his home in rural Connecticut, he and Ruriko spent little time there. They were almost constantly on the move, taking travelers as intrepid as themselves to the ends of the earth. Had he lived long enough, he might have taken well-heeled tourists into outer space, to enjoy a cosmic view of our "small blue planet."

To me the name Lindblad had become synonymous with adventure. Ever since I met Lars-Eric, nearly thirty years ago, after I had shown my film of the Galápagos at an Audubon banquet, my life has not been the same. Sharing similar Viking instincts, I was soon helping him scout some of the faraway places that few people had seen.

It was on one of his pioneering tours with a small group of friends in 1964, as they sat drinking fermented mare's milk under the stars in the Gobi Desert, that he announced, "Our next exploratory tour will be to a place that isn't even on the map!" He was thinking not of outer space but of Antarctica, which was unmarked on the Pan-Am air route maps that he held in his hand.

Subsequently, I have participated on sixteen or seventeen cruises to the Antarctic, usually as a guest lecturer. But on our first foray I was grandly listed as "Expedition Leader." Our ship was the *Navarino*, chartered from the Chilean navy. This vessel, converted for civilian use, was far from elegant by tourist standards.

That trip was a fiasco, although it started pleasantly enough. We navigated past the Strait of Magellan, steamed through the Beagle Channel, and then turned southward toward Cape Horn. After dinner and a convivial evening in the lounge, we went out on deck to see Cape Horn in the light of a full moon. Serene, beautiful. We retired to our cabins to rest up for the long crossing of the Drake Passage to the Antarctic peninsula.

It must have been about 2:00 in the morning when the ship lurched violently, waking me from my dreams and sending my camera equipment on the upper bunk to the floor. The Drake Passage has a reputation for its bad temper, but this was even rougher than I had expected. Then I became aware that the engines were off. Why, I wondered, would we drop anchor way out here? Or could we? Too deep. A few minutes later Kevin McDonnell, one of Lindblad's lieutenants, burst into my cabin with the announcement that the rudder was broken. Worse than that, the manual steering system was locked, and if we couldn't free it we would have to send out distress signals. Fortunately we were well beyond the last offshore islands, so there was no danger of sideswiping the rocks. We would just drift.

Quickly putting on my parka, I rushed to the deck for more information. Only one passenger was there, a tall fellow from Amarillo, Texas, a railroad engineer who had signed up for this trip because he wanted to go to a place where there were no trains. A rather silent man, he had spoken hardly a word to me until this moment, when he intoned, "This damned ship is going to sink!"

Well, it didn't sink. I double-timed up the stairs to the bridge to talk with the captain, but I didn't get very far because he spoke no English and my Spanish was almost nil. However, within an hour the engines started up again, and with four men at the manual controls, the ship was guided back to Puerto Williams, the southernmost Chilean naval base.

That morning our fellow passengers, unaware of what had happened, looked out at the wooded landscape of Navarino Island and exclaimed, "We thought we left here yesterday!" And indeed, we had. But the trip was off. There was no way to make repairs or to install a new rudder within a week's time. Eventually we all flew home, but Lars made good his commitment by offering to take everyone the following year—on a more seaworthy ship.

It was because of the unreliability of chartered vessels that Lars decided to have his own ship, the *Lindblad Explorer*, which he had built to his specifications in Finland. It was strengthened for ice. To many of his clients the *Explorer* became a home away from home. Some repeaters adopted their favorite tables in the dining room.

The *Explorer*, with the wandering albatross as its symbol, was not a typical cruise ship in which dining, dancing, shopping, and saunas were the main thrust. Although the cuisine was superb, and there

The Lindblad Explorer *was built to Lindblad's specifications for taking small groups of adventurous travelers to remote or inaccessible places.*

was a bit of dancing when the seas were not too rough, the *Explorer* was more like a floating seminar. Naturalists like Keith Shackleton, Sir Peter Scott, and Dennis Puleston, geologists, marine biologists, geographers, historians, and other specialists gave their slide talks or films in the Penguin Room when the ship was at sea.

One third of the passengers, on average, were nature-oriented— not biologists but possessing some empathy with natural things. Another 50 percent or more were intelligent citizens who wished to extend their knowledge of the world. Perhaps 10 percent might be called travel snobs, who had been almost everywhere and simply wanted to add new countries or places to their lists. One traveler in one hundred seemed to be not quite with it (Lars said three in one hundred), scarcely knowing why he or she had signed up or where he or she was going. Such passengers seemed even to confuse the two ends of the earth, and gazing out on the Antarctic ice floes, might wonder why there were no polar bears or Eskimos.

Although Lars-Eric Lindblad was linked in most people's minds with the *Lindblad Explorer,* oceanic travel was but a portion of his worldwide network of tours. Not only did his ships drop anchor at hundreds of islands where no tourist had previously set foot but he also opened up hitherto unvisited areas in the Antarctic, the high Andes, the Himalayas, and the far north, as well as in tropical forests and deserts. To pave the way, his contacts included kings, presidents, and distinguished academics. Other tour entrepreneurs tried to copy his methods or poach on his terrain, but he was always a leap ahead.

Some environmentalists have questioned whether it is a good idea for wild places to be opened up to tourism. However, the evidence is reassuring; when people of influence go on tours and see things with their own eyes, they become a powerful force for the preservation of these places. This has been demonstrated particularly in the Galápagos, the African game parks, the Seychelles, and the Falklands, as well as in Antarctica. Lindblad, a devout conservationist, believed that tours should be led by the best available talent, guides who would not only interpret but also instill in the traveler a code of behavior and a reverence for life. In fact, a roster of his tour guides and guest lecturers is like a who's who of exploration, natural history, and the humanities.

In preparation for his Seychelles cruises, before he sent the *Explorer* into unfamiliar waters, Lars chartered an old tub of a boat, the *Iron Duke,* which had sailed the Indian Ocean for forty years. There was barely room in the cabin for the six of us—the captain, Lars-Eric, Tony Irwin of the Nairobi office, the photographer George Holton, Jimmy James of British Airways, and me. Indeed, our quarters were so cramped that I had to sleep, with my camera equipment, in a bunk so short that my feet projected into space. Even so, it was a month of idyllic island hopping, with frigatebirds hanging under tropic skies and porpoises leaping in jade seas. On the long passage to isolated Aldabra, the island of the great tortoises, we were caught in a storm that confined us to our crowded cabin for three days while we waited for the seas to calm down. Later, when we ventured on deck, a huge wave nearly washed George Holton overboard, but he was saved by a line that Lars had had the good sense to attach to the back of the boat.

I have many memories of dicey incidents while scouting for Lars—such as the time my tent collapsed under an unseasonable snowfall in the Himalayas, and the situation I faced in the mountains of Ethiopia, when my mule walked onto a much too narrow ledge, stranding me on a thousand-foot precipice. Later that day, trying to get a picture of a troop of gelada baboons, I was charged by a big-toothed male, but instinctively I stood my ground and turned him away. My companion, Fernando Maldonado of the New York office, agreed that negotiating the highlands of Ethiopia was not for anyone over sixty. However, the revolutionary turmoil developing at the time precluded any tourism in that country for a while.

Lars, imaginative and resourceful, could find a solution to almost any problem. Once, after we had lifted anchor in the Galápagos, he was informed that the dockworkers and seamen at our South American destination were about to go on strike. We were scheduled to disembark the following day and take off again with sixty people who had flown in from England. By pulling strings, as only Lars knew how, he was able to have the strike postponed a couple of days until the *Explorer* was again at sea. That took real know-how. Nothing short of a revolution, an earthquake, or a volcanic eruption seemed beyond his control.

Unlike our exploratory expeditions, the cruises that followed were completely safe, with the excitement of new places and all the comforts of home. Nor were they all nature-oriented. Increasingly, many of the tours were put into the hands of Sven-Olaf Lindblad, Lars's son, freeing his father for the many other aspects of tourism—visits to primitive tribes, archaeological cities, castles, monasteries, ancient towns, and offbeat cities. Although Lars was more freewheeling and flamboyant, an optimistic gambler at times, his son, with his mother's Swiss blood, seems to be a more prudent businessman.

Nigel Sitwell has been the guiding hand behind the Intrepids, a travel club conceived and sponsored by Lindblad. In the beginning I was designated president, but inasmuch as I am more comfortable discussing birds and butterflies than chairing formal meetings, my duties were soon put into more capable hands.

The story of Lars-Eric Lindblad is well told in his book, *A Passport to Everywhere.* Like several other Swedes I have known, Lars was special; there was no one else quite like him. During his sixty-seven years, he enjoyed the diversity of experiences of several lifetimes.

Those of us who knew Lars will miss him, but he leaves a legacy of nature tourism that will continue to enrich the lives of many throughout the world.

—NOVEMBER/DECEMBER 1994

An Update
from the Cedars

WHY DO I LIVE in Connecticut? As an artist and a writer, I need
New York for the American Museum of Natural History and Boston
for Houghton Mifflin, my publisher. But as a naturalist I prefer to live
as far from either city as I can manage. So I chose a midway point in
Connecticut—Old Lyme—near the mouth of the Connecticut River,
and I have lived there almost half my life.

It was just over forty years ago that I pulled up stakes in Maryland
and traded the Potomac River for the broad reaches of the Connecticut River where it flows into Long Island Sound. In this part of New
England, it takes at least thirty years for an outsider to be accepted by
the locals as one of them.

When I first scouted the place, two things sold me on the acres
that were to become mine: There was an ospreys' nest that had been
active that summer in a large oak on the ridge; and I saw a red-
spotted purple, one of my favorite butterflies, just outside the barn
that was to become my studio.

When I returned a month later to finalize things, storm warnings
were up; a hurricane was imminent. Hastily signing the agreement,
we started on our long drive back to Maryland but got no farther
than Old Saybrook, just across the river. The highway was already
flooded from high tides on Long Island Sound; people were getting
about in rowboats. With water up to the floorboards of our Chevy, we
pulled up to the old inn known as "The Monkey Farm," where we
spent the night.

We found later that the ospreys' nest on our hill was a casualty of
the high winds; and the large beech in the garden just below the

Ospreys nest along the Connecticut River.

house was split down the middle. This we salvaged by bolting the two halves of the trunk together, an excellent job of tree surgery that held for twenty-five years, until, early one morning, the fine old tree crashed to the ground, succumbing to interior rot. The next spring our pair of orioles had to look for another place for their pendent nest.

Our friend Ed Teale, who was writing a piece about backyard birding, phoned to ask what my total list was for our place. Inasmuch as our garden and backyard are ill-defined—literally stretching from the house to the studio and beyond to the office building—I came up with a figure of just over 150 species, 60 of which have nested. This included the voices of birds passing overhead in the dark during migration—even such goodies as dickcissels and upland sandpipers. When I spent more time on the back side of our woods, where a brackish marsh borders the inlet, I added a few more species besides the usual marsh wrens, swamp sparrows, Virginia rails, and egrets.

Forty years ago, when I first lived in the house then known as "the Cedars," I could step outside at dusk and hear as many as three or four woodcocks calling their nasal *peent* and taking off in their aerial maneuvers. That was before the land across the road was sold to a developer who built a number of houses among the pastures and woodlots. With the cats and dogs of the new tenants roaming about, the woodcocks were no longer to be heard. Other birds dropped out as well. The pair of red-shouldered hawks that lived in the swampy wood across the road could not tolerate the invasion of their privacy, nor could the pair of Louisiana waterthrushes. For several years one woodcock continued to perform nightly in the clearing behind my studio, but as the brush and second growth took over, it too disappeared.

Working late at night as I normally do, I have always been aware of the moths that come to the picture windows, attracted by the bright lights that illuminate my drawing board. During the first several years, the big, pale green lunas were almost nightly visitors in early summer, and the other large saturniids—cecropia, Polyphemus, Prometheus, and Io—were also frequent visitors, as were a few hawk moths. Cocoons of the cecropia could be seen from my studio, and those of Prometheus dangled from the neighbor's lilac bushes.

But then, about twenty or twenty-five years ago, all the saturniids dropped out rather suddenly, to be followed later by most of the hawk moths and even the underwings. With their disappearance we no longer heard the whip-poor-wills in our woods. Their major food supply gone, these flying moth traps all but disappeared elsewhere in the lower Connecticut Valley. The saturniids have never returned, and I suspect that it was because of gypsy moth control. The invading gypsy moth, an introduction from the Old World, has survived the sprayings to plague us periodically, but the lovely moths no longer flutter against the windows, and because larvicides do not discriminate, some butterflies have dropped out too.

About fifteen years ago my wife, Ginny, started a butterfly garden outside the studio and engaged a local shipwright to carve a handsome sign embellished with a huge monarch butterfly. By planting butterfly weed and purple milkweed dug from neighboring fields as well as other plants that offered nectar for butterflies or food for their larvae, she soon pulled in not only the migrating monarchs but also more than twenty other species. This was fine until the fuel man came one day to fill our oil tank. While doing something else, he neglected to watch the spigot. Oil spilled over everything and wiped out most of our cherished butterfly garden. The oil company, of course, removed the impregnated earth and replaced it with new topsoil. But three years of effort were lost.

Ginny started over again with more butterfly weed, not always easy to transplant because of its root system, and lots of zinnias and buddleias, which proved to be the favorites of butterflies as diverse as swallowtails and skippers. Even the occasional red-spotted purples reappeared.

Although we are now at an all-time low in butterflies, the poorest I can remember since I took residence in Connecticut, our "butterfly bar" seduces every passing nectar-feeding insect in the neighborhood. Ginny and I have recorded thirty species of butterflies in the garden, not all of them nectar feeders.

Connecticut has lost a lot of its butterflies because of spraying and vegetation control along the roadsides. This is quite in contrast to some other states, which, under pressure of garden clubs, have adopted a policy of beautification, planting wildflowers and flowering shrubs along the highways to delight the eye of the traveler.

There is no doubt that winter feeding has extended the range of certain birds. When I first came to New York City as an art student nearly seventy years ago, I had to take the 125th Street ferry across the Hudson if I wished to see cardinals or rufted titmice. They were common on the Palisades in New Jersey, but it was only after the big bridge was built that I saw my first cardinal and my first titmouse on the New York side of the river, near Ossining. I wondered whether these relatively nonmigratory birds might have made the crossing strut by strut and span by span on the new bridge.

When I moved to Connecticut forty years ago, the occasional cardinal came to our feeder, but tufted titmice did not arrive until fifteen years later. Both have increased explosively since then. Certainly widespread feeding has ensured their winter survival. The handout of sunflower seeds has helped the cardinal sweep through New England all the way to New Brunswick, while the titmouse has reached Maine. Mourning doves, formerly scarce during the colder months, now winter abundantly all the way to the Maritime Provinces, again because of feeding. One January day, I counted seventy-two at our three feeders.

Everyone up and down our road feeds birds, and for this reason I had no compunction about taking off for Florida or points south in midwinter, because I knew that if our caretaker failed to put out the seed or suet, the birds would simply go to the neighbors' feeders.

The composition of our winged pensioners has changed markedly over the years. House finches, which are recent invaders, now outnumber purple finches, and white-throated sparrows have completely replaced the tree sparrows. The contented whitethroats have their own dining room where the feeders are; they have their social club, safe from sharpshins in the dense mat of forsythia; and they have a snug bedroom in the nearby evergreen shrubs. What more could the whitethroats want? Several fox sparrows and the occasional towhee share the thickets with them. But where have the tree sparrows gone? Is it because the bushes and trees are closing in?

Ginny regrets that we have not yet had a mockingbird on our place, but there is usually one down the road at the shopping center, another at the railroad station, and one at the garage where we have our car fixed. The last bird, a genius mimic, can imitate the mechanical noises that it hears. Perhaps mockers like bustle and noise, but it is more likely that such places are invariably planted with multiflora rose, which takes over like a weed. Mockingbirds can survive the northern winter by eating the small rose hips that are produced so abundantly. Fifty years ago those of us who birded in the Northeast had to drive to southern New Jersey to be sure of seeing a mocker. Now this bird that was formerly regarded as "southern," associated with mossy live oaks and magnolias, is well established along the entire length of the New England coast.

When I moved to Connecticut, there were at least 150 ospreys' nests within ten or fifteen miles of our home. You could see the bulky masses of sticks from the train window as you sped from New Haven to Boston. Some were on utility poles, others were on platforms erected by homeowners, but most were in trees. On Great Island, near the mouth of the river, there was even a nest on the ground. When exceptionally high tides flooded the marsh, the eggs rested in two or three inches of water.

It was on Great Island shortly after I came to Connecticut that I first became aware that ospreys were in trouble. I had a suspicion it might be because of DDT in the food chain, as had already been indicated in the bald eagle. After I called attention to the fact that our local birds were not fledging their young, a succession of students—Peter Ames, Tom Lovejoy, Paul Spitzer, Jerry Mersereau, Jennifer Hillhouse, and Alan Poole—carried on some of the investigations that led to Joseph Hickey's research at the University of Wisconsin and to the eventual banning of DDT. The state of Connecticut got into the act, and although it had formerly allowed the telephone company to remove as many as fifty nests a year from transformer boxes on utility poles, the company now erects poles and platforms for the ospreys' convenience.

Today ospreys seem to be reproducing normally again; many are raising full broods, and the population, which had gone down to a few pairs, is now recovering. There is not a day during the warm summer months that I cannot hear an osprey over our hill as it flies to or from its fishing grounds, and who knows—someday they may nest again on our ridge. We have put up a platform on the marsh edge, but so far no takers.

A pair of crows indulge themselves every morning on the cracked corn spread at the far end of the studio pond. Although they act as though they own the property, they still don't quite trust us. For a while a third bird, perhaps one of their offspring, was always with them.

But the prize addition to our avian clientele recently has been the flock of wild turkeys, mostly females dominated by two big, strutting

The large picture windows in the studio at the Cedars afford plenty of light and views to the wildlife attracted to water and feeders.

males. Turkeys had been absent in Connecticut for one hundred years, from their extirpation in 1870 until their reintroduction in 1970. Now, after twenty-five years, they are widespread throughout the state. I have counted seventeen in sight at one time on our property and have even had them peck at the kitchen window while I was having breakfast.

It was also from my kitchen window that I saw my first local coyote as it crossed the lawn. These wild canines are now widespread in Connecticut but keep a low profile, seldom singing in nocturnal chorus as western coyotes often do. Noble Proctor tells me that occasional bears wander down the river, and who knows whether they have been on our seventy acres? Deer, of course, are abundant, often helping themselves to the daylilies.

As for some butterflies, bird feeding may well be a factor in their status. Monarchs seem unaffected, as are migrants such as the red admirals and painted ladies. Swallowtails and other road travelers seem in good shape. Although great spangled fritillaries are plentiful in our garden, two or three of the other fritillaries are no longer seen. Coppers, pearl crescents, and wood satyrs have become scarce. The butterflies that are sedentary are the ones losing out. For what reason?

And what about snakes? A large blacksnake lives in our cellar, keeping it rat-free. That's it, except for two small ring-necked snakes this past summer. Frogs (of which I had six species in my studio pond) are now reduced to two. A lone spring peeper sang its heart out for weeks without getting a response. Is acid rain the cause?

Some of the finest marshes in New England are those at the mouth of the Connecticut River, and although harriers and bitterns no longer nest there, and black-crowned night-herons have become rather scarce, snowy and great egrets have greatly increased, and the glossy ibis, a newcomer from the South, has become frequent.

To me, one of the most intriguing aspects of nature watching has been population dynamics, the ups and downs, whys and wherefores. During forty years I have been witness to many changes around our home in Connecticut, changes that were scarcely perceptible at first but that are very obvious now. I can only speculate about what my local bird list would have been like had I lived here when the Mohegans, Pequots, and other Native American tribes possessed Connecticut. I would not have had the glossy ibis, and definitely not the cattle egret or house finch, not to mention house sparrow, starling, and pheasant. Perhaps even noisy flocks of passenger pigeons and Carolina parakeets would have awakened me in the morning.

—January/February 1995

TORNADOES OF TREE SWALLOWS

IN ALL MY LONG lifetime of birding I have never witnessed a spectacle more dramatic than the twisting tornadoes of tree swallows I saw plunging from the sky after sundown this past October. And this was within four miles of my home near the Connecticut River, where this had probably been going on every October—all the forty years I have lived here.

I have seen a million flamingos on the lakes of East Africa and as many seabirds on the cliffs of the Alaska Pribilofs, but for sheer drama, the tornadoes of tree swallows eclipsed any other avian spectacle I had ever seen.

In late summer and early autumn I had often seen gatherings of swallows on the nearby marshes, particularly in the sprawling beds of phragmites that separate the shallow channels of the Connecticut River between Essex and Old Lyme—a mile or two north of the bridge that spans the river where it widens before entering Long Island Sound.

In late August, when the swallows first congregate, a good many of our birds seem to be purple martins. They are present in far greater numbers than those that breed locally, having probably moved in from farther north—from northern New England or the Great Lakes. They seldom sound off, so it is guesswork how many swallows—barn, cliff, bank, or tree—are with them. The martins have a more triangular, starlinglike shape than the other swallows. As September advances, the martins and the other hirundines drop out, until tree swallows predominate.

When our neighbor Russell Lewis told us that tree swallows gathered in clouds in the marshes across from his home as late as mid-October, I felt sure he had been seeing distant flocks of redwings and starlings, but he was right. One evening when my wife, Ginny, and I went down to the river where Russ made a ritual of watching the setting sun with his wife, Lois, I met his neighbor Henry Golet, who had been watching the event for eighteen years. Golet offered to take Ginny and me out in his boat so that we could be closer to the midriver action.

During the afternoon I had seen but a handful of tree swallows. Where were they? But at sundown, after 6:30, just as the red solar disk dropped below the horizon, things began to happen. We had seen a few Canada geese, cormorants, and herons flying to their nocturnal roosts, and perhaps several dozen tree swallows, some flying upriver, some down. But not many. Contrails in the clear sky indicated distant aircraft. Then overhead, so high as to be mere pinpoints, we spotted small groups of swallows, several dozen at first, then hundreds, dropping out of the void.

Where were they coming from? They were not rising from the marsh but dropping from the seemingly empty heavens. In another ten minutes, thousands formed a swirling mass, weaving in and out. At times it took a good pair of binoculars to separate the birds from the sky. They were most visible against the lighter patches of open sky but became lost against the darker cloud banks.

About 7:15 the weaving mass slowed down momentarily and then at some subtle signal converged into a steep funnel and dropped like a twisting tornado at incredible speed. Were they diving at sixty miles an hour—or even faster? When the funnels—two or three of them—neared the phragmites, they flattened out with a roar of wings against the flaming sky of the horizon. I did not dare guess how many birds were involved— certainly tens of thousands, possibly hundreds of thousands. Noble Proctor, who was with us on October 15, guessed there were half a million. Later he revised his guesstimate to 300,000. But who knows?

The plunging birds took about one minute and twenty seconds to complete their entry into the phragmites. But at the finale of the

Tree swallows from the swallows and swifts plate in the Peterson Field Guide to Birds of Eastern and Central North America, *fifth edition.*

mass plunge, there still remained a few—several hundred—way up high. Golet suggested they might be "teenagers who didn't want to go to bed." But after a ten-minute delay, they too made the plunge.

Had all these birds been up there beyond our vision all day? Were they feeding on airborne insects where the air was warmer? And were the same birds here on succeeding nights? Or was this a staging site for a different group each night? The migratory kestrels or sharpies that sometimes sailed by did not harass the swallows, but the occasional merlin would try, according to Golet. It is dangerous for a predator to grab a bird from a tight flock, but with luck it might pick one from the edge. However, Golet never saw a merlin succeed in grabbing a swallow from the air, though once the birds were in the phragmites, the small falcon could pick one off easily.

Hunting season started here on October 21, so Henry Golet did not take his boat out; but on the thirty-first, the last day of the month, he observed several thousand birds still doing their aerial ballet. They seemed higher than ever and did not make their final plunge until it was too dark to see them.

We know that occasional tree swallows are observed on the Christmas Counts as far north as Long Island, where they survive by eating bayberries.

Next year I shall try to photograph this spectacle, but I do not know whether film speed or lens apertures will allow it. Perhaps I will try video.

—MARCH/APRIL 1995

Isla Raza

SOME YEARS AGO, Joseph Wood Krutch, writing about Mexico's Baja (Lower) California, gave his fascinating book the title *The Forgotten Peninsula*. For similar reasons, the Gulf of California, which John Steinbeck called the "Sea of Cortez," was called the "Forgotten Sea." This great inland arm of the ocean extends for more than eight hundred miles between the arid mainland of western Mexico and Baja California. The peninsula itself, though far longer than its sister peninsula, Florida, on the other side of the continent, has about the same land area.

Until recent years few birders visited the emergent rocks and craggy islands that rise from Baja's desert sea. But of the few things I had read, none left a more vivid impression than Lew Walker's *National Geographic* article about Isla Raza, the headquarters of the bulk of the world's Heermann's gulls and elegant terns.

In January 1961, I flew from New York City with Carl Buchheister, then president of the National Audubon Society, and Dr. Paul Sears of Yale University to join the Krutches and Kenneth Bechtel, of San Francisco, a director of Audubon, for a week's survey of the fabled bird islands in the Gulf. Ken's ninety-six-foot boat, the *Polaris*, was moored at Bahía de Los Angeles, a third of the way down the peninsula.

With Raza uppermost in my mind, I asked Ken to fly over that island to see whether any birds were present. Raza, unlike the other steep-sided rocks and headlands of the Gulf, is a rather flat island, nowhere more than seventy-five feet above sea level. Its area is about one square mile. As we circled the boulder-strewn island with its two or three shallow lagoons, we saw few birds. I had not expected to see the elegant terns at this date, for I recalled that I had once photographed them in mid-January on the coast of Chile. They would not return to the Gulf until April. Heermann's gulls were scattered throughout the Gulf, although their nesting time was nearly three months away. On some of the islands farther south, brown pelicans were displaying and laying their eggs. Boobies of two species were beginning to lay, and on nearly every rocky headland a pair of ospreys was already incubating a clutch of three boldly blotched eggs.

Raza was the focal point of our conversations. Although other small colonies of Heermann's gulls and elegant terns had occasionally been recorded off Baja California, this one island was the main incubator of those two beautiful species. Virtually all of the thousands that visited the coast of California in their postbreeding wanderings came from Raza. However, a few now breed near San Diego.

Heermann's gull, which may wander as far north as Puget Sound, is a smoky junco-gray gull with a black tail, a white head, and red bill. I have never seen one that was not well groomed, every feather in place; it is perhaps the most attractive North American gull. The elegant tern, at that time considered by California birders as a challenging problem in field identification, is like a smaller, more exaggerated edition of the royal tern; the feathers of its black cap form a longer, more shaggy crest, and its orange bill is much thinner and more lancelike.

Every ornithological traveler who had dropped anchor at Raza had commented on the egging. Boats from Santa Rosalía and from Guaymas harvested the eggs by the tens of thousands. Lew Walker told of a single cargo of 65,000 eggs. Could the birds stand this toll? Were the eggs taken mainly for the yearly celebration at Santa Rosalía, or was there commercial pressure? Should the Mexican government be approached to set aside Raza as a national monument dedicated to its unique birdlife? If it did, should egg collecting be completely stopped, or should it be put on a seasonal basis—with collecting permitted for a short period each year and then banned? With these thoughts in mind, the Belvidere Foundation, under the

Isla Raza is the world's primary breeding spot for Heermann's gulls.

guidance of Ken Bechtel, sent Lew Walker on a return survey that April. Joseph Krutch and I flew down in the Lodestar to join Lew and his two assistants, who had already documented most of the island's teeming wildlife on color film.

Lew's broad fiberglass boat, a catamaran propelled by twin forty-horsepower outboards, covered the forty miles between Bahía de Los Angeles and the island in less than two hours. Rough seas and tidal eddies could have prevented our landing, but we arrived with a moderate sea and just enough tide to float us through the narrow, rocky channel to the protected lagoon where Lew had anchored his boat.

What an amazing island! From end to end it was occupied by Heermann's gulls. Our "tent," a huge Army surplus parachute camouflaged with splotches of green and brown, was suspended over our beds to give us shade during the heat of the day. So difficult was it to find a level spot clear of gulls that an incubating Heermann's gull was forced to share the tent with us. Eight feet seemed to be the limit of its tolerance, and whenever we moved a bit too close, the bird walked outside until we sat down again on our folding cots.

The island is a series of low, rocky ridges with black volcanic boulders partly whitened by guano. The shallow valleys between the ridges are filled with brown, guano-impregnated earth. Some forty years ago a guano industry had been launched, and wherever one looked one saw evidence of herculean labor. Hundreds of rocky cairns—piles of boulders four or five feet high—had been heaped up to facilitate harvesting of the precious fertilizer. Retaining walls had been built, and on the north side of the island two small mountains of guano-rich soil remained where they had been piled years before.

A catastrophe ended this ill-starred venture. Apparently, rations had run short after a long period of rough weather. A supply boat was put out from the island, but it broke a propeller shaft. By the time help finally came, ten of the men on Raza had died from starvation.

Most of the world's gulls are white below, with darker backs, but how well the dark-bodied Heermann's gull fitted Raza, I thought—a dusky bird, the very color of Raza's dark boulders, capped with a guano-white head. Often when one of the gulls protested my intrusion from atop a cairn and cried ever so distinctly, *help! help! help!*, I thought of those tragic Mexican laborers.

On the rocky areas of the island, the nests were five to ten feet apart; seldom was a nest more than fifteen feet from any other. In the patches of succulent green *Salicornia* and *Mesembryanthemum*, the nests were closer—three to five feet apart—but on the open valley floors, uncluttered by boulders or plant growth, the thousands of Heermann's nests averaged less space apart than two feet and were occasionally as close as fourteen inches. Each depression held two or three spotted olive-brown eggs. Some of the scrapes were lined with pebbles, twigs, and even feathers.

Tentatively we estimated that a million pairs of birds were using Raza, perhaps more. Of elegant terns there were perhaps 200,000 in seven or eight aggregations, great patches of white surrounded by gray masses of Heermann's gulls. Scattered here and there among

Peterson considered the elegant tern the handsomest of all terns.

the other terns was a small minority of royals, already acquiring white foreheads.

Lew Walker seemed to think there were more elegants than he had seen twenty years earlier. This agrees with the increase noted along the California coast. This handsomest of all terns, once considered a birder's prize within United States waters, had been seen in increasing numbers north of the border. Or perhaps the bird watching fraternity was becoming more skilled at separating it from the royal tern.

Lew Walker told the story of how the first elegants to arrive set up housekeeping right in the midst of the Heermann's colony. A hundred speckled or blotched eggs may be laid the first morning, to be gobbled up as choice canapés by the fish-jaded gulls. The next morning five hundred eggs are laid, and perhaps half survive the predation. On the third morning five thousand may be laid. (Each bird lays but a single egg—there are two or three nests per square yard.) The gulls, like children wearying of too much candy, soon leave the clamoring terns to their destiny, and reproduction is accomplished. In the two days I spent in the blind at the edge of one of the densest colonies, I seldom saw a gull take an egg. Nor did any eggers land on the island.

My ears, assaulted when I was in the blind by the greatest continuous volume of sound I have ever known, were not quite the same for hours afterward; I knew what it was like to be "deafened" by the screams of birds. Isla Raza, where the elegant terns and Heermann's gulls have their headquarters, is in my opinion one of the world's greatest bird spectacles.

In this day of ecotourism, Isla Raza is the destination of many tour groups, notably under the guidance of Sven-Olaf Lindblad. Recently I met a young woman who spends each summer in the hot sun monitoring the big colony for the Mexican government, which has become conservation-oriented. Today, Isla Raza is no longer forgotten.

—November/December 1995

GHOSTS IN
THE BRONX

GUY EMERSON had not yet seen a white-crowned sparrow for the year. That in itself seemed excuse enough for our drive into rural Maryland that bright October Sunday many years ago. As if by appointment, we found our bird, a young one, with a pink bill, right where we parked the car outside the Fish and Wildlife Research Laboratories at Bowie.

Our objective attained, we sauntered into the narrow brick building where the millions of bird-banding records were kept. There we found Joseph Hickey hard at work, as he always seemed to be, day or night, on his doctoral thesis. Emerson, fascinated by the intricate filing system, asked Hickey if he might see the barn owl cards, particularly those from Massachusetts. Joe dumped the stack of barn owl cards into the IBM sorting machine, and with a rapid shuffling motion, the Massachusetts cards dropped out.

The first card that popped forth was about a young bird banded near Emerson's home on Martha's Vineyard. He had seen this very bird, and, by a curious coincidence, so had I, a year later, but not at Martha's Vineyard. The card recorded that the owl, a female, was recaptured nesting in an old coal elevator in the Bronx, nearly two hundred miles away.

The card with its formal telegraphic data evoked memories of a full moon shining on the water among the dark river wharves on the night that Irving Kassoy took me up the rickety ladder into the tower to see his new owl family. I remember how excited he was when he discovered later that the female wore a band—one he had not put there! For weeks he tried to catch the owl to read its number. We all offered advice, but it was not until Mike Oboiko set up one of his squirrel traps that the mystery of the bird's origin was solved.

Irving Kassoy was the historian of the few barn owls known to live in the Bronx at that time. He had watched those mystery birds for years, and some of his friends in the Linnaean Society said (much to his irritation) that he was beginning to look like an owl. Perhaps his glasses and look of quiet wisdom created this impression. Like Huxley, Kassoy believed we should "smite every humbug," and over the years he had dispelled more notions and unearthed more new facts about the barn owl than any person before him.

As a young man Kassoy worked in a midtown Manhattan jeweler's firm. After long days devoted to diamond rings and Swiss watches, he would hurry to his owl observatory in the Bronx—in the old Huntington mansion at Pelham Bay. Night after night he kept his lonely vigil under the eaves with the "ghoulies and ghosties, long-leggety beasties, and things that go bump in the night."

I met him one evening after work. He had a necklace to deliver on Park Avenue before we plunged below the street level and boarded the IRT subway for the Bronx. At 125th Street we changed from the lurching local to the Pelham Bay express. While we hung from the swaying straps, shoved and pushed by the evening crush of commuters, Irv told me something of the history of his birds. There was a new female, he said. The previous female had been frightened from the building by some workmen. It was daytime, and crows mobbed the bewildered bird. They drove her to the water of Eastchester Bay; then the gulls closed in and finished her off. Apparently even the birds look upon *Tyto* as a bird of ill omen, to be attacked and destroyed. Perhaps that is why barn owls live in church belfries so often, I mused—for, like outcasts of old who sought sanctuary in the temple, they can find refuge there. Certainly, I reflected, they are nondenominational, for I had seen barn owls in the square tower of a synagogue in Alexandria, Virginia, in a fashionable Episcopal church at Rye, New York, in a little white Baptist church on the east coast of Florida, and in a famous old Franciscan mission in California.

Barn owls frequently use barns and abandoned buildings as nesting sites.

But whereas some barn owls seek sanctified, holy places, others live in a gloomy, almost evil atmosphere. Such a place was the abandoned Huntington estate, five minutes' walk from the end of the Pelham Bay line. We had long known the place, because it was there that, on the Christmas census, we always saw our night-herons, a hundred or more, crouched disconsolately in the somber branches of the Norway spruces inside the wall.

We never climbed that wall, because into its broad top had been cemented thousands of pieces of broken glass, a jagged deterrent to trespassers. But the estate had become park property, and Kassoy had permission to enter the big house. He flashed a light into the spreading, silvery-limbed beech tree where the owls often perched, but they were not there. He swung the bright beam over to the eaves of the house. There was the ventilator hole through which the birds gained access to the ivy-colored building. We could hear the young ones calling for food, a rasping, sucking sound that has been likened to an ill-mannered person imbibing soup.

We passed through the big gate, and Kassoy went over to the caretaker's house to get the key, which hung on a nail inside the door. The caretaker believed the house was haunted, and I am sure he thought Kassoy was quite mad, sitting up there night after night by himself.

We went up two flights, lifted a trapdoor, and tiptoed across the attic floor. In the corner, Kassoy knelt over a box. He turned a switch attached to a dry cell battery, and a tiny light illuminated the dim interior of the box. Huddled there were five of the most grotesque owlets I had ever seen, like little monkeys in fuzzy bedclothes, with white caps pulled about their ears. In size they were like stepping-stones, for young barn owls usually hatch about two days apart.

The top of the box was a pane of glass, treated so that the owls saw only their reflections, while we could see them and remain unseen ourselves—a sort of two-way mirror—the same device that had been used in zoos to make animals act naturally, uninhibited by their unseen audience. Kassoy was probably the only man who had ever been eyewitness to some of the intimacies of the adult barn owls— even their actual mating. He was amazed to find how closely the courtship cycle was synchronized with the full moon. Indeed, he found he could predict within a day or so when the first egg would be laid.

When I called the owlets grotesque, he was indignant. To him they were beautiful babies. Perhaps they were. Seeing an adult barn owl at close range, one cannot deny that it is beautiful. When painting it, I have marveled at the soft blendings of rufous and gray, sprinkled with tiny dots, and the liquid brown eyes set deep in the white, heart-shaped face. I can see why some people call it the "monkey-faced owl," but a monkey, by contrast, is wizened, wrinkled, and rather homely. If it must have a nickname, I prefer "golden owl."

For many months Kassoy had been climbing up there. His heart would skip faster at the scampering of rats or the sudden thunderclap of a summer storm, but usually all was empty silence broken only by the periodic rumble of a distant train pulling into the station. Night after night, two hundred or more, he hunched over his box like some immobile Buddha, his face, reflecting the wan light, the only thing visible in the blackness. A loud, rasping cry, like a banshee with laryngitis, told him that one of the old birds was in the big beech outside. In a moment, it would magically appear in the box, like an apparition, a meadow vole dangling from its beak, or a rat from the garbage dump out on the Eastchester marshes.

The nest was strewn with bits of fur and bones. Although owls swallow their mice whole, the strong digestive action soon rolls the bones up in a feltlike wad of fur, and this the bird coughs up with a struggle. These pellets have a wet, varnished look at first but are soon broken up and trodden into a foul carpet by the young birds. The pellets on the attic floor were the best contact Kassoy had with his subjects between seasons when they were not nesting. Like a detective, he would dissect each one for clues. He could tell how well the birds had been eating and how lately they had been roosting in the attic. Most of the pellets held two skulls apiece, nearly all of them rodents with their long, curved incisors; but occasionally he found a house sparrow, and once a phoebe.

With no brood of his own at the time, Kassoy treated the young owls as his family. When two or three of the babies toddled out of the ventilator shaft one night and were dashed to their deaths on the hard ground below, he grieved for days. When the owls laid again, he built a little porch and railing as a safeguard. One brood was started so late that it was early January before they flew, and starvation faced the family. Worried about his charges, he broke tracks through the deep snow one blustery night with two pounds of raw beefsteak under his arm, only to find that the keeper had locked up his house. He could not get the key, so he scattered the pieces of meat over the snow.

Year by year Kassoy grew to love the old place more and more. While waiting for the owls, he spent long hours with his thoughts. There were times, though, when his subconscious seemed to be playing tricks on him. For example, he once stayed in the mansion long past midnight. It was probably 2:00 or 3:00, but it was a Sunday morning and he could sleep late. He had fallen into a doze when a door slammed downstairs. He knew he was the only one with a key. Footsteps crossed the big, empty library. Step by step they came up the first flight of stairs and started up the second.

Kassoy's hair stood out above his ears, like the back hairs of a dog at bay. The sounds paused just below the trapdoor. Just then one of the owls popped through the ventilator into the nest, and Kassoy, like a true scientific investigator, put all else from his mind and concentrated on the little drama in the lighted box below him. When the owl left, he listened again. The footsteps had stopped, nor did he hear them after that. He wondered about it ever after.

All owls, from the big white snowies that come down along the beaches on their cyclic winter invasions to the mysterious little elves that live in the desert mountains, are weirdly beautiful, but the barn owl is more truly "owlish" than any of the others. At Cape May, New Jersey, lying on my back among the dunes near the boardwalk, I have attracted them overhead by squeaking, while their ghostly forms reflected the light from the streetlamps.

Someday I should like to see a phosphorescent barn owl, a rare but well-authenticated phenomenon. The phosphorescence is not an illusion but is believed to be caused by fungi that impregnate the rotten wood of the cavities where the owls hide in the daytime. (The oxidation of the mycelium of these fungi causes the unearthly glow or cold light that has been called "foxfire.")

I cannot imagine how a phosphorescent owl would look, but a barn owl always seems eerie, whether it is hunting among rows of stately palms in southern California, where it snatches up palm rats as they clatter over the dead fronds, or swooping over a New Jersey marsh. We used to see barn owls perched high on the rafters of rickety icehouses along the Hudson, in the days before everyone had an electric refrigerator. (They say that the invention of the automatic refrigerator, and the abandonment of these icehouses to owls, extended the range of the barn owl to Albany.)

Later Irv Kassoy moved to Ohio, where he pursued an offshoot of his jewelry business. He soon became the barn owl authority in that state, searching every barn in the region.

The last time I saw Irv was in 1977 in Florida, where a meeting of the old Bronx County Bird Club had been called by Joe Hickey. It was being held as a good-bye to Irv, who was in the last stages of cancer. Irv gave us a talk about his owls. Later, when we said good-bye and briefly embraced, I realized I was losing my dearest friend among the nine lads from the Bronx who revolutionized bird watching.

—MARCH/APRIL 1996

A SHORT HISTORY
OF HAWK MOUNTAIN

LESS THAN two years ago we celebrated the sixtieth anniversary of Hawk Mountain Sanctuary in Pennsylvania.

Long ago, birders discovered that the way to see hawks was to watch mountain ridges in the fall. There, on the right day, they could see far more hawks than they could find elsewhere in a year. Today, most binocular buffs make it a point to get out on two or three hawk days each autumn, just as they make trips specifically for ducks in March, warblers in May, or shorebirds in August. When the pumpkins are ripe, when corn is in the shuck and jugs of cider appear at roadside stands, then it is time to head east for the Blue Ridge—the long, hazy blue wall that rises out of the Pennsylvania Dutch farm country, where every barn is protected from witches by the hex signs of its owner.

The Blue Ridge, a recumbent giant 175 million years old, is the easternmost rampart of the Appalachian system in Pennsylvania. Extending unbroken for many miles, from northeast to southwest, it is the last great barrier to the cold autumnal winds blowing out of the northwest toward the Atlantic. To the east the land falls away toward the flat coastal plain that faces into the hazy horizon. The hawks riding the invisible updrafts are loath to leave the mountains. Thousands of generations of sharpshins, Cooper's hawks, goshawks, redtails, redshoulders, broadwings, falcons, eagles, and even gyrfalcons have followed this express highway south. Along these same ridges, men have piloted their experimental gliders, making flights of more than 150 miles without power. A glider is simply a wood-and-fabric replica of a hawk.

At the end of the long, forested ridge, north of Reading and not

Hawk watchers look for the thousands of hawks that migrate through Hawk Mountain Sanctuary in Pennsylvania. (Photographer unknown)

far from Hamburg, Pennsylvania, rises the rocky promontory known as Hawk Mountain, the most famous hawk observation point in the eastern mountains. Gunners discovered this flyway long before birders heard about the mountain. They climbed the wooded trails to the summit on cold, windy days. They knew the mountain was a bottleneck for birds of prey. The backbone of the ridge was narrow here, and the stronger the wind, the closer to the jutting knob the birds would fly. On some Sundays as many as two hundred gunners assembled among the lichen-covered boulders of Tuscarora sandstone, and it was estimated that three to five thousand birds were blasted off the mountain yearly.

No one knows how long hawks have been using this ridge during their annual passage southward. Certainly it has been hundreds of years, probably thousands, at least back to the time of the last ice sheet, which never quite reached this part of Pennsylvania. Audubon, who lived within a several-hours' ride by horse, did not know of Hawk Mountain. Nor did he know of the flights at Cape May. Neither did Alexander Wilson.

I don't suppose Native Americans bothered the migrating birds of prey; they probably had other ways of getting a bonnet of feathers. But certainly as far back as one hundred years ago or more, some gunners in Pennsylvania knew of the flights; and they knew of those at Cape May. The pressure on the birds increased with the proliferation of people, automobiles, and modern firearms. Hunters found the place and initiated the slaughter, but bird watchers stopped it.

I first became aware of the annual slaughter in 1925, when I read a paper by my fellow bird artist George Sutton in *The Wilson Bulletin*. Sutton was at that time with the Pennsylvania Game Commission. He gathered up 158 hawks of four species—all killed by a few gunners "in a remarkably short time." In the *Bulletin* he published a technical paper on their plumage differences and on other details. Science was served, but in a basically scientific journal no judgment was passed on the slaughter. Remember, we were still in the specimen-tray era of ornithology. We were just beginning to enter the era of the binocular.

But in 1932 Henry Hill Collins and Richard H. Pough opened people's eyes. In *Bird-Lore*, the predecessor to *Audubon* magazine, Pough wrote:

On top of Blue Mountain, above Drehersville, Schuylkill County, an appalling slaughter was going on. Blue Mountain is a long, continuous ridge along which thousands of hawks pass in migration. First the broadwings in September, and out of this flight I would say 60 were shot. Then came the sharp-shinned and Cooper's hawks. Thousands of these were killed. The enclosed photographs show 218 birds picked up in about an hour at one stand. Among others I have found five ospreys, a protected bird of course, but one that will be shot every time, along with eagles, sparrow hawks, flickers, blue jays, so long as hawk shooting of this sort is permitted. When 100 or 150 men, armed with pump guns, automatics, and double-barreled shotguns, are sitting on top of the mountain looking for a target, no bird is safe. Birds are seldom retrieved, and I found many wounded birds, some alive for several days.

Wounded hawks were strung up in trees as decoys. Blinded pigeons were tied to a long pole; when a hawk came over, the pole was waved so that the pigeon would flutter wildly. All this slaughter was rationalized by the gunners; they were "getting rid of the killers," thereby saving all the game birds and songbirds that the hawks would otherwise eat. Meanwhile, they were imposing a serious drain on those magnificent birds funneling in from a very large area in the northern part of our continent. In pre–Hawk Mountain Sanctuary days, the Pennsylvania Game Commission actually favored the killing of hawks. There was even a five-dollar bounty on goshawks— but the bounty proved to be an incentive to kill all hawks.

Few conservationists had noticed Sutton's article in *The Wilson Bulletin*, but hundreds became indignant when they read Pough's article in *Bird-Lore*, among them an indomitable woman, Mrs. Charles Noel Edge. It is thanks to her that we have the Hawk Mountain Sanctuary as we know it today.

I first met Rosalie Edge when I was a teenager in New York attending art school and the bimonthly meetings of the Linnaean Society. During the month of May, I sometimes saw her and her binoculars in the Ramble in Central Park, near Seventy-ninth Street (just across from the American Museum of Natural History), where to this day Manhattan birders go in the early morning to see the migrant warblers. When my *Field Guide to the Birds* saw the light of day, in the spring of 1934, she was one of the first to acquire a copy. But we had become good friends before that. She had taken an interest in our small group of teenagers known as the Bronx County Bird Club, which included future luminaries such as Allan Cruickshank, Dick Herbert, Joe Hickey, Irv Kassoy, Phil Kessler, and the Kuerzi brothers. We were even invited to a couple of the secret meetings chaired by Willard Van Name in her apartment, where attacks were planned on Dr. T. Gilbert Pearson, president of the Audubon Society, before the society's annual members' meeting. As a naïve young man from the boondocks, I sat with open mouth at these clandestine meetings, not fully aware of what the plotting was about.

Edge was particularly irked by Pearson's seeming lack of concern for birds of prey. In some of his earlier writings, Pearson had actually referred to these birds as "killers," as had John James Audubon himself. Pearson held on to this old-fashioned view about raptors. But some members of the Audubon board, men like John Baker and Robert Cushman Murphy, were more enlightened, and they urged Pearson to do something about the slaughter of the birds of prey.

At their insistence, the society prepared a book on birds of prey. The author was John B. May, state ornithologist of Massachusetts, and shortly after my field guide appeared he asked me to draw four similar pages of flight patterns for his book. This book, *The Hawks of North America*, was published in 1935. My halftone flight plates were reprinted with the addition of illustrated charts showing food habits and were distributed as educational leaflets for years to come.

The color plates were painted by Allan Brooks, the Canadian artist, who was somewhat of a predator himself. He loved to shoot hawks. His original painting *Marsh Hawk* (a bird now called the northern harrier), showed a green-winged teal in the hawk's talons. This was unacceptable to Pearson, who sent the painting back, requesting Brooks to take out the duck. He did so, returning the painting with the comment "Here's your sanctified marsh hawk."

During the early 1930s the Audubon Society lost half its membership. It was down to 3,500 when John Baker took over on November 1, 1934. Some said it was because of Mrs. Edge's pamphlets, which attacked Dr. Pearson and the society. Others contended it was because of the Great Depression, when 18 million people were out of work.

In the fall of 1933, at a joint meeting of the Audubon Society and the Linnaean Society, Richard Pough and Henry Hill Collins had given a talk about the hawk shooting at Hawk Mountain. Because of that meeting, Pearson sent Robert Porter Allen, a new staff member, to check on things at Hawk Mountain. Bob Allen told me about it a year or two later. He had previously reported in detail about the Cape May slaughter, and action had followed. But his report on Hawk Mountain was negative. He was there too late in the season, during a period when flight conditions were unfavorable. He saw no hawks. This almost certainly was why Pearson did nothing at the time. Because of this delay the Audubon Society fumbled the ball.

The following June, in 1934, Mrs. Edge, who headed the Emergency Conservation Committee, got in touch with Pough and asked what the Audubon Society had done about the slaughter at Hawk Mountain. He said that apparently nothing had been done. So Rosalie, who had been criticizing the society for years, decided to take action herself. She worked out a deal with a real estate agent, agreeing to lease the land for a year with an option to buy.

But some of the members of the Delaware Valley Ornithological Club thought that it would be better if the Audubon Society owned the land and that the purchase might be financed by some of its wealthier members. So Pough arranged a dinner in Philadelphia to which John Baker was invited. The needed funds were subscribed by a voice vote. When Mr. Baker returned to New York and telephoned Mrs. Edge, she bristled and told him *she* had the option to buy Hawk Mountain. The deal was off, as far as the Audubon Society was concerned.

So it really was the timing of events that made Rosalie Edge and John Baker such implacable opponents. It is regrettable, because during his twenty-five-year tenure, John Baker became perhaps the most effective leader ever of the National Audubon Society, and he carried out many of the reforms that Mrs. Edge had championed during Gilbert Pearson's reign.

Although there had been a growing interest in the natural world and conservation—and in bird watching—ever since the Audubon movement had started a generation earlier, there was a break-through in the 1930s, with Hawk Mountain and my field guide both launched in 1934. The federal duck stamp, which has raised so many millions for the purchase of wetlands, also saw the light of day in 1934—and so did Donald Duck himself! It was a vintage year, 1934.

As most of us know, it was really because of a young couple, Maurice and Irma Broun—who dedicated half their lives to the mountain—that Hawk Mountain became a viable reality. Maurice Broun became hooked on birds at the age of thirteen, when he walked into the Boston Public Garden to get away from the confusion of the city. There he discovered a delightful group of people, all stretching their necks toward the treetops. He stretched his neck too, and a kind lady offered him a pair of glasses through which he saw a magnolia warbler—the most wonderful thing he had ever seen. Even the name fell like music on his ears. Birds became his obsession.

I first met Maurice on Cape Cod, late in the summer of 1931 or 1932, when I was already deeply involved in preparing my field guide. He was banding birds at the Austin Research Station. Our second meeting came two or three years later, at Long Trail Lodge in Vermont. Meanwhile he had married Irma, a Cape Cod girl, and they were carrying on a wonderful program of nature trails and work with young people. They were about to start their autumn work at Hawk Mountain—work that was to become their year-round occupation. Maurice had already read Pough's article in *Bird-Lore* when Mrs. Edge asked if the Brouns would take on the task. They said they would. This they had offered to do that first year without salary—merely expenses. It was a cause they believed in deeply. The beginnings of the sanctuary, and Maurice and Irma's part in those beginnings, are recorded in *Hawks Aloft*, written by Maurice, and also in *The View from Hawk Mountain* by Michael Harwood.

Thus it was that Hawk Mountain Sanctuary—the world's first sanctuary for birds of prey—came into being. It marked the beginning of an epoch in conservation.

That first season the Brouns approached the appalling problem of turning armed men off the property. It must have taken a great deal of courage, iron nerve. Meanwhile, those who came just to *look* at hawks, and to admire, were pouring onto the mountaintop, and Irma became keeper of the gate, and a very good keeper, too—on weekends, that is, because it took the rest of the week to recover. On Sundays at peak season, visitors jammed the roads and trails that led to the bald spot. Irma dealt patiently with them all, while Maurice acted as master of ceremonies at the lookout as the hawks paraded by.

In those early years when the Brouns were guarding the mountain, they lived in a little stone house that is still there beside the road—Schaumboch's—a dwelling with a sinister history. Its first owner, Jacob Gerhardt, moved there only a few years after his mother, father, and five sisters and brothers had been massacred in their home at the foot of the mountain by a roving band of Lenni-Lenape Indians. Some years later, after Schaumboch assumed ownership, itinerant salesmen who took the road across the mountain disappeared, presumably done in by Schaumboch. Later, during the prohibition years, the house was reputed to be a sinister hideout of bootleggers.

I thought about these ghosts when I crawled into my sleeping bag on the lower back porch, where the Brouns put me because their guest room was occupied. The strange noises I heard at night in the stonework behind me proved to be produced by a wood rat—known to the Brouns as Old Cleft Ear—that was sitting at the foot of my cot when I woke.

In those days, even with the growing number of visitors, there was no problem finding a boulder to sit on at the North Lookout. And it was always a joy to watch the aerial parade if the wind was from the northwest: plenty of redtails and sharpshins, a minority of Cooper's, perhaps a goshawk or a peregrine, and, best of all, the occasional eagle. Only a few years earlier, a Sunday visitor would have found a veritable army of men with pump guns and automatic shotguns blasting away at anything that flew by.

Many of the illustrations in my *Field Guide to the Wildflowers* were drawn on Hawk Mountain. And it was on the mountain that my *Field Guide to the Birds of Britain and Europe* was conceived. In the fall of 1949 Maurice Broun introduced me at the gate to Guy Mount-

fort, a visitor from England. Mountfort said there really should be a field guide for Europe patterned after my American guide. He added that perhaps I should team up with someone like James Fisher to do such a book. As we walked up the trail we discussed things further, and before we reached the North Lookout we had wrapped things up. Guy ventured that he himself would like to be my coauthor. The following year, on a field trip to Lapland at the time of the International Ornithological Congress, we sold the idea to James Fisher, who was to become our editor at Collins in London. The book was eventually published in fourteen languages. Some years later I introduced Fisher to Hawk Mountain, where it had all started.

The maintenance of Hawk Mountain Sanctuary has certainly saved a great many thousands of birds of prey from direct destruction. It has also been the focal point of hawk protection, with an influence far beyond the state of Pennsylvania, undoubtedly stabilizing some populations of raptors that would otherwise have been in greater trouble.

Maintaining the mountain as a part of our green landscape has been important too, but probably less so than the public relations value. I say this because the northern Appalachians have been going back to nature in recent decades. They are actually wilder than they were sixty or seventy-five years ago, with more woods, because farms have been abandoned as agriculture moved westward. Hawks and eagles now have free passage, and although the pressure of people is somewhat of a problem, we must admit that Hawk Mountain's most important functions today are education and research.

There are, however, a few other places in the world that can boast flights of hawks of a similar magnitude—for example, the incredible flights of broadwings in September on the north shore of Lake Ontario. Well known are the concentrations at Point Pelee on Lake Erie and, of course, at Cape May. In the Old World, Falsterbo at the southern tip of Sweden is famous for its flights, and certainly so is the area around the Bosporus and the Dardanelles, where hordes of birds from Europe and Asia funnel through the bottleneck on their way to Africa. But I am quite sure that Maurice on his aerie atop the Kittatinny Ridge had the all-time personal record for the number of birds of prey seen during a lifetime.

Donald Heintzelman, in his *Guide to Hawk Watching in North America*, lists about 180 sites throughout the country where raptor flights can be watched. With the explosive popularity of raptor watching, I am certain many new sites have been documented since he compiled his list.

The various field guides, such as my own, the Golden guide, the Audubon guides, and more recently, the National Geographic Society's guide, have made hawk watching a more sophisticated pursuit, with its own numerous followers. The state of the art is constantly changing. Some superstar birders are no longer satisfied with binoculars or ordinary scopes. They use Questars or Celestrons, designed for amateur astronomers. With these they can see even the parasites on a peregrine—or the mites on a merlin. This brings birding almost full circle back to the specimen tray.

But watching distant birds of prey in the sky at Hawk Mountain is a different kettle of broadwings. The experienced raptor watcher, perched on a boulder, does not rely solely on details or even obvious field marks. While the bird is still half a mile away, he or she instinctively puts shape, manner of flight, wing beat, and a number of other subtle clues together and comes up with an identification. In explaining the mystique, the hawk watcher might speak of the bird's "jizz" (G-I-S—general impression and shape), an acronym used by British fighter pilots. When the bird gets close enough, the observer can confirm things with the standard field marks. I prefer to call this the "holistic method of identification."

A general field guide can do a pretty good job most of the time but cannot cover all the variables and odd plumages. So it was inevitable that we now have more specialized guides, such as the one on hawks that William Clark and Brian Wheeler prepared. This book, dealing only with raptors, is in my line of guides, the Peterson Field Guide series. Pete Dunne, Clay Sutton, and David Sibley, of the Cape May Observatory, have also issued their book, *Hawks in Flight.*

Now that hawks and eagles enjoy safe passage down the Pennsylvania ridges, the activities at Hawk Mountain have entered a new phase. During the thirty-two years that Maurice and Irma reigned as king and queen of the mountain, they not only guarded the lookout but also monitored the flights and guided the hordes of visitors. Upon their retirement to nearby Strawberry Hill, Al Nagy became curator and carried on the tradition for another ten years.

Then, under the skilled guidance of Dr. Stanley Senner and the passionate drive of James Brett, the curator, Hawk Mountain shifted gears into the educational field while engaging in a certain amount of raptor research. Never have I met a more enthusiastic staff, not to mention the dozens of attractive young docents and volunteers who made things smooth during the anniversary celebration.

Although I had increasing instability in my legs as a result of my subdiabetic condition, I was determined to see the mountain on its sixtieth year and to see how Jim Brett, the curator, was doing. Jim, like Bill Clark, and several other hawk-watching friends, had become truly international; all made yearly visits to Eilat in Israel, where they spent several weeks watching one of the world's greatest concentrations of raptors, storks, and other birds funneling from Africa into Europe and Asia. I had wanted desperately to join them but had not been able to.

The efforts begun at Hawk Mountain are now worldwide. There are perhaps thousands of hawk-watching sites, covering every continent except Antarctica. Hawk Mountain itself now has a very international flavor. I was introduced to docents and assistants from countries as distant as Argentina, Ecuador, Chile, and Tanzania. They were learning their hawks, teaching classes, and gaining experience that they would pass on in their own countries.

Finding a place to park our car among the hundreds of vehicles lining the approaches to the lookouts was not our only problem. My ankles were giving me an argument, despite the help of a cane, on the seemingly endless slopes. Finding rocks on which to sit at the overcrowded lookouts was also a problem. Surely the hawk watchers far outnumbered the hawks on many days.

I was impressed by what had been added under Jim Brett's guidance: more classroom facilities and a gift shop that carries everything remotely related to hawks, eagles, vultures, and owls. Reading *Hawk Mountain News*, we learn that Jim has announced his intention to retire as curator on June 30, 1996. Now we look forward to the publication of the book he has been writing, highlighting his twenty-five years on the mountain.

— MAY/JUNE 1996

American
Wildlife Painting

Birds, the only creatures besides humans to walk on two legs, have fascinated artists since the Stone Age. Kenn Kaufman, in an amusing bit of punditry, commented that "Roger Tory Peterson was not really the originator of the system of arrows for identification. Thousands of years ago, long before the pharaohs, ancient men drew animals on cave walls with arrows sticking into them."

Today, in the 1990s, there is far more talent and activity among wildlife artists than we have known before—in direct proportion to the increased popular interest in birding. Hundreds of men and women spend their time painting or drawing birds. But, "is it really art?"

A generation or two ago most art historians believed that wildlife painting was not "art" unless it had something to do with an animal's relationship to human beings. Domestic animals such as horses, dogs, and cattle were appropriate subject matter. The works of Rosa Bonheur and Edwin Henry Landseer were acceptable, as were paintings of the chase—a hunted stag or a boar being attacked by dogs, for example. Ducks or other waterfowl were usually shown dead, hung by their feet as still life. Songbirds were acceptable only if given some religious or symbolic significance. The European goldfinch (the one with the red face), a symbol of good luck or happiness, might be shown in the hands of a child who was lovingly squeezing it to death. One connoisseur stated, "If animals are shown in art they should be [presented in] episodes in the eternal battle between men and animals, reason and passion, civilization and nature."

Before this century very few paintings of birds or other animals were given wall space in art galleries unless they met these anthropomorphic criteria. The works of Albrecht Dürer and John James Audubon—in which the animal was portrayed not as a satellite of humans but with its own identity—were notable exceptions. This limited, indeed arrogant, point of view has been changing in recent years because of a more enlightened understanding of the natural world, which acknowledges that birds are birds, not little humans clothed in feathers.

Even so, most bird art might be scored by some critics as being too conservatively representational or academic, ignoring abstraction, geometrics, subconscious comment, and other manifestations of contemporary painting. Actually, wildlife artists, painting in their representational or naturalistic manner, are making a statement about their world that is every bit as valid as that of any of the avant-garde interpreters of the synthetic city scene.

It is still too early to assess the work of some of the artists now painting birds. Several are superb. New directions are being explored, but because tastes change, we cannot predict which of the contemporary bird artists will stand the test of time.

Of those who have gone before, we can be sure that two—John James Audubon (1785–1851), who took birds out of the glass case for all time, and Louis Agassiz Fuertes (1874–1927), who really brought them to life—will be remembered far into the future. Whereas Audubon invariably reflected Audubon in his spirited compositions, Fuertes reflected more of the character of the bird, less of himself. No illustrator or artist had done it better.

Fuertes dominated bird art in the first quarter of this century, just as Audubon had reigned supreme nearly a century earlier. Fuertes was born under a lucky star, for at a young age he was befriended and sponsored by two men of powerful influence: Abbott Thayer, who shaped his thinking as an artist, and Elliott Coues, who promoted him in scientific circles. Thayer and his son Gerald wrote the controversial tome *Concealing Coloration in the Animal Kingdom,* an exposition of the "laws of disguise through color and pattern." Young Fuertes understood this principle instinctively and was one of Thayer's greatest defenders, yet this was seldom reflected in his work.

During his mid-thirties, Fuertes's correspondence reveals the spot he was in, a sort of midlife crisis: old Abbott Thayer was berating him for painting birds that stood out from their surroundings, while Gilbert Grosvenor of *National Geographic* and Frank Chapman of *Bird-Lore* sent back drawing after drawing, demanding that the birds be made to stand out more clearly on the page, preferably in straight profile. In the end, and no doubt with some anguish, Fuerte gave in to the wishes of Grosvenor and Chapman, ignoring the three-dimensional play of light and shade in favor of local color—a pragmatic concession that most bird artists make to the demands of ornithological illustration.

But was it art? Not really, if we are to accept Don Eckelberry's definition: If painters are told how to do their birds, what plumages to show, and in what positions, it is illustration. If they paint in their own way, untrammeled by the limitations imposed by others, it can be art. When he was allowed freedom, Fuertes was spiritually an artist, as evidenced by his superb Abyssinian watercolors and some of his other, later works.

My own life's work was sparked by a Fuertes color plate, a blue jay that my seventh-grade teacher, Miss Blanche Hornbeck, gave me to copy. From then on, birds became my life's focus, an obsession from which I have never freed myself.

In 1925, several months after my graduation from high school in Jamestown, New York, I boarded the train for New York City to attend my first meeting of the American Ornithologists' Union, at the American Museum of Natural History. To a seventeen-year-old who had never before met any of the high ornithological "brass," the climax came when I was introduced to Louis Agassiz Fuertes.

Hanging in the bird art exhibition on the second floor of the museum were two of my own watercolors, a ruby-throated hummingbird and a kingbird. I do not remember what the master said about them, but to illustrate a point, he led me to a small watercolor of a golden eagle by Archibald Thornburn, the premier British bird painter. The highlights falling across the dark back of the eagle, he explained, were painted in tones as light in value as the shadows might be on the white breast of a gull. He could not resist expounding the Thayer principle of countershading.

As we went from painting to painting, we chatted with other well-known wildlife artists of the day: Francis Lee Jaques (1888–1969), pronounced *Jay-queez*, who had recently joined the staff of the museum; Charles Livingston Bull, a popular magazine illustrator; and Courtney Brandreth, one of Fuertes's disciples. Standing before a dramatic canvas of a harpy eagle by Charles Knight, Fuertes commented that it was a pity that Knight, primarily a mammal painter, painted so few birds; he did them so well. Then, stepping up to a painting of his own, a large oil of a great horned owl in a trap on the leafy forest floor, he said, "This is the way I really like to paint. . . . I'm going to do more of this from now on." This owl was not executed in his usual style but was more "painterly."

When we left the hall and descended the stairs, Fuertes reached into his inner jacket pocket and withdrew a handful of watercolor brushes. Picking out a flat red sable about a half inch wide, he handed it to me, saying, "Take this. You will find it good for laying in background washes." I thanked him, and before we parted he added, "And don't hesitate to send your drawings to me from time to time. Just address them to Louis Fuertes, Ithaca, New York."

Actually, I never did send any of my drawings to him for criticism; I had decided to wait until they were worthy of his time. And so, by delaying, I forfeited a priceless opportunity, for less than two years later, in 1927, Fuertes met his death at a railroad crossing while driving home to Ithaca.

In the evolution of bird painting in America, the late George Sutton (1898–1982) was the bridge between Fuertes (his mentor) and several of today's finest bird illustrators. Although George devoted his life to academia—Cornell, the University of Michigan, and the University of Oklahoma—he had so many talents as author, artist, teacher, and lecturer that he always faced an inner struggle over the best use of his time. He could have devoted his entire life to his paintings, which spanned the gamut from field sketches to evocative watercolors of Arctic and Mexican birds. (The Fuertes-Sutton correspondence is

Field guide illustrations were just one aspect of Peterson's painting style; his limited-edition prints, such as this golden eagle, are closer in style to the work of Audubon and Fuertes.

available in one of the last books George Sutton published—*To a Young Bird Artist* [University of Oklahoma Press, 1979].)

I can think of only one top-level bird artist of my acquaintance in my youth who was not influenced in the slightest by either Audubon or Fuertes—Francis Lee Jaques. He had been hired only the year before the 1925 American Ornithologists' Union meeting by Frank M. Chapman, the curator of birds at the American Museum of Natural History and at that time the father figure of American ornithology.

Chapman, who conceived the diorama idea, a new concept in museum exhibits, had discovered that most bird artists, no matter how skilled, tended to paint their birds *against* the landscape rather than *into* it, surrounded by light and air. Even Fuertes, a close friend of Chapman's, failed to achieve the three-dimensional feeling, the illusion of space required by the habitat groups. When Chapman heard of Jaques, who was making a name for himself painting canvases of waterfowl, he quickly hired him. Jaques's first assignment at the museum was the oval dome of the old Bird Hall, which he painted from a high scaffold—rather like Michelangelo in the Sistine Chapel. During his years in New York, he was to paint more than half of the dioramas in the museum, leaving a greater visual stamp on that institution than any other person, before or since.

Jaques brought the diorama to its highest degree of development, approaching each habitat group as a problem in engineering disguised by artistry. He was skilled at handling perspective on a curved surface. Although he sometimes studied photographs, he never copied them, saying, "I do not intend to produce large Kodachromes." Eschewing the traditional approach to bird portraiture, he insisted that he was not a painter of feathers and that he was more concerned with the bird in the landscape. He painted waterfowl brilliantly, but songbirds interested him less. He once said, "The difference between warblers and no warblers is very slight."

Whereas the dioramas, by their very nature, were intended to fool the eye, his canvases were freed from this restraint; they were more decorative. But inasmuch as they betray—just a little—the influence of Howard Pyle, N. C. Wyeth, and other illustrators of an earlier period, they may seem somewhat dated. Nevertheless, his dioramas ensure him a measure of immortality; they will remain for all to see as long as the walls of the buildings stand.

Nearly every young artist who has painted birds has had to wrestle with the artistic dilemma that confronted Fuertes—whether to paint birds impressionistically, as the eye sees them, bathed in light and shadow, or to paint them as detailed feather maps devoid of modifying atmosphere (to use Don Eckelberry's terminology, objective realism versus intellectual realism). Or should the artist compromise in some other way?

✦

The Leigh Yawkey Woodson Art Museum in Wausau, Wisconsin, sponsors an exhibition of bird art each September, showing about a hundred examples of the finest wildlife painting and sculpture being done today.

And I have not touched on any of the stellar figures from the other side of the Atlantic whose influence is felt here—Keith Shackleton, the late Peter Scott, Manfred Schatz, Carl Brenders, John Seerey-Lester, and Lars Jonsson.

To hark back a bit before closing, I must not forget Bruno Liljefors (1860–1939) of Sweden, whom some pundits place at the head of the list, a genius whose work I knew when I was a boy in Jamestown, a Swedish-American town in western New York State. Each Christmas, for a dollar, we could buy a glossy magazine (in Swedish) that featured the paintings of Liljefors and Anders Zorn (1860–1920). Curiously, Liljefors, a hunter and naturalist who reflected French Impressionism, was little known to most American wildlife artists until rather recently. A fine book about this artist, titled *Bruno Liljefors—The Peerless Eye*, by Martha Hill, was published by the Allen Publishing Co., Ltd., in 1987.

But where does my own work fit into all of this? I have had a longer history in painting than any of the pundits or critics who so freely express themselves in print. It started more than seventy-five years ago with that blue jay I copied at the age of eleven in Blanche Hornbeck's class. Most people think of my work in terms of my rather formal field guide illustrations, but those represent only one aspect of my painting.

In the next issue of *Bird Watcher's Digest,* I shall describe the several kinds of painting I have been involved with during my life. [See page 324.]

—July/August 1996

My Evolution
as a Bird Artist

When I graduated from Jamestown High School at the tender age of sixteen, I was delighted; I could now watch birds all the time, or so I thought. My father thought otherwise. "You must get a job—*any* job."

Summer was half over when two opportunities surfaced on the same day—as a draftsman at Dahlstrom's Furniture Company, or decorating lacquer cabinets at Union Furniture. I chose the latter, even though it paid less. It seemed more fun.

My boss was an irascible Dutchman by the name of Willem Dieperink von Langereis. He wore a monocle and smoked his cigarette from a ten-inch holder. He made a great deal of his aristocratic Dutchness, even though he was born in Grand Rapids and grew up there. His arrogant ways intimidated the Swedish craftsmen whose cabinets we decorated.

In those days of prohibition, these were elegant liquor cabinets. A pair of doors brought twelve or fifteen hundred dollars—a lot of money at that time. And though I signed them, I have never been able to spot one in anyone's home, even though Union Furniture, one of the few surviving furniture companies in Jamestown, continued to make them for years.

The surprising thing was that Langereis derived his feeling of Oriental design and balance from another artist of his day, Aubrey Beardsley. And the raised lacquer of our designs was not built up layer on layer of paint as a Chinese artist would have done it. By first making a mixture of pumice and shellac, trailing it off the tip of the brush, and letting it dry hard, we were able to detail our raised figures quickly in oil paint, thus saving weeks of work.

My bird prints, which have a certain Audubonesque quality and which have been issued over the years by Quaker State, Mill Pond Press, and other publishers, really owe their basics to Aubrey Beardsley via Langereis. The human being is a cooperative animal who almost invariably is influenced by others.

When pundits or critics ask me who influenced me most, I ask in what kind of work. My field guide drawings? My prints? My more three-dimensional gallery work? After six years of art training, I went in several directions.

In my teens I prided myself on detail so fine that it would require a hand glass to separate the hairline brushstrokes. Like the work of so many other young people who aspire to be wildlife artists, my earlier efforts, though lovingly done, were far too tight and self-conscious. Then, at the age of eighteen, at the urging of Langereis, I packed my bags and my brushes and went to art school, the Art Students League in New York City.

At the League's elegant old building on West Fifty-seventh Street, I enrolled in the class of Kimon Nicolaides, whose book, *The Natural Way to Draw*, is still a classic more than half a century later. Nicolaides taught us to keep our eyes on the model, scarcely dropping them to our paper, while feeling things out, first tentatively, with light delineation, then more positively, with stronger confirming lines. To this day I sketch much as I was taught by Nicolaides. Had I enrolled in George Bridgeman's class at the League (I couldn't, because his classes were full), I would have learned to draw by blocking in the shapes of things rather than by feeling them out with a fluid line. The schematic drawings in my field guides might not seem to bear my training out, but that is another story.

My field guide drawings were inspired by the novel *Two Little Savages*, by Ernest Thompson Seton, wherein the young hero copied the patterns of mounted ducks he found in a showcase so that he would know these same birds in life. This system was applied by me to all birds. There was a revolution in birding going on in the Bronx in the early 1930s, as birders shifted from the shotgun school of birding to the field glass. I, being the trained artist of the group (the

Bronx County Bird Club), pulled our identification system all together with my field guide. I added the *arrows* still in use, developing what became known as the "Peterson System," since extended to other branches of natural history.

The problem with birds is that their movements are so quick and incisive that one must have a photographic memory to arrest an action or a posture in a sketch. At the League I became accustomed to having a model up on the stand, holding the same pose for half an hour at a time. But birds are constantly twitching about. When I made the long ride by subway and elevated train to the Bronx Zoo, as I did once a week, I found that the only birds that would remain as still as the models in class were the eagle owl [species found in Asia and Africa] and the shoebill stork [an African species]. My sketch pads were filled with owls and shoebills and little else. Eventually I could render either of these birds with only five or six strokes of my pencil.

In addition to Nicolaides, I had good classes in calligraphy, reflected in my signature. But the exaggerated downward droop in the *g* of Roger and the *y* of Tory caused Joe Kastner of *Life* magazine to comment that they looked like bird droppings.

My main instructor at the League was John Sloan, one of the eight members of the "Ashcan" school of painting, who lived in Greenwich Village, as I did. (The Ashcan name referred to the realistic depictions of city life created by this group of twentieth-century American painters.) From him I developed my sense of color—cool colors receding, warm colors coming forth. But Sloan insisted there was no such thing as a cast shadow. He was in his crosshatch period, and a person's arm or leg looked rather like a sausage. I could not agree with him. To me, an illusion of form was created by the fall of light.

Sloan stated that to be a member of the National Academy of Design was "eternal damnation." Perhaps he said this because his own entries had been turned down at their annual shows. Being an uninformed lad from the boondocks, I went to see for myself what the academy was all about. Its representational approach was exactly what

I wanted. So, for the next three years, I attended afternoon classes at the academy, near St. John's Cathedral, after first decorating furniture in Harlem during the morning for my bread and butter and tuition. My three years at the academy were under masters such as Raymond Neilson, Edwin Dickinson, and others. I was tutored in charcoal rendering at first, then full color in oils. The academic approach was pretty far removed from the avant-garde movement that was beginning to emerge in some quarters.

During the early years of World War II, when we were worried about air attacks, Joe Kastner at *Life* gave my field guide to his staff of artists and told them to come up with something similar for identifying enemy aircraft—shapes, length of wings, tails, dihedral, et cetera. Then, after *Life* published its famous four-page "Plane-Spotter's Manual," the idea was picked up by the U.S. Air Corps for its own manual.

Peterson made thirty or more sketches before going ahead with a painting. (Virginia M. Peterson)

In fact, Kastner had a lot to do with my early success. He directed me to do several series of pages for the magazine, in full color, covering the lives of birds. Over the years I painted more than fifty pages of birds for *Life*, which received more reader response for its bird series than for any other subject except its art section.

Although I frequently refer to my 35-millimeter transparencies as a memory jog, I enjoy wildlife photography for its own sake; it is action. Drawing, by contrast, is cerebral. Whereas a photograph is a record of a fleeting instant, a drawing is a composite of the artist's experience and selectivity. The person who sketches can edit out, delete unnecessary clutter, choose position, and stress basic shape and pattern, unmodified—or modified—by transitory light and shade. The artist has far more options than the photographer, and far more control. I am an obsessive photographer, but I am fully aware of the differences. Whereas a photograph can have a living immediacy, a good drawing is really more instructive.

In January 1971, when Sir Peter Scott and I were in a Zodiac looking for the rare Auckland teal along the shores of Enderby Island in the Aucklands, we spotted a strange penguin in a small, rocky cave. I leaped ashore with my Nikon; Peter stayed in the Zodiac and took out his sketch pad. As we examined the bird at close range, we debated— was it a Snares Island penguin or a Fiordland? The two look very much alike. Peter said we would know for sure when we got back to the ship and our reference library. His drawing would tell us. "You will have to wait until you return to Connecticut," he said, "to see your processed photographs."

He was right. His sketch accurately showed the white marks on the cheek and the lack of bare pink at the base of the bill. It was a Fiordland penguin, a stray far from its home in New Zealand. Confirming the identification of uncertain birds by sketching is standard practice among hard-core birders in Britain and now, increasingly, it is used here. The sketch must be made on the spot, without being influenced by the illustration in a field guide.

I have found that when I am on a guided tour in the Antarctic or on safari in East Africa, there is little opportunity to sketch. Too many things are happening too fast. If a cruise director allows us only two hours ashore in a colony of 100,000 penguins, I am more likely to use my camera. Sketching takes time. I prefer, therefore, to travel by car or van, with plenty of time to dawdle if there is an opportunity to sketch.

Peter Scott eschewed the camera and left the photography to his wife, Philippa, who has a good eye for a picture.

To return to the subject of my field guides: Although the drawings are rather static and patternistic, in comparative profile, suggesting an exhibition of little decoys, they serve a functional purpose, which is to teach, to make identification easy. However, a great deal of field sketching, more than you might realize, went into the preparation of these stylized drawings. And because my field guide illustrations are what they are, many people think that is the way I always draw birds. The illustrations are formal and schematic, not avian portraits in the Audubonesque style or the Fuertes manner; my limited edition prints, as I said earlier, are closer to those traditions. Lately my canvases have been more painterly, involving the environment, three-dimensional activity, and movement in space. Two examples are my paintings of whooping cranes and puffins.

But whatever the purpose of a painting or the direction it may take, it should start with numerous sketches. I may make twenty or thirty thumbnail sketches, as well as some larger ones, before I decide to go ahead. Bob Bateman does the same. Guy Coheleach claims that he may make as many as one hundred sketches before he touches brush to canvas. Robert Henri, the great teacher at the Art Students League, and also one of the Ashcan school painters, advised his students to put the bulk of their efforts into the planning of a painting. He implied that if the preliminary sketching and basic drawing did not jell, no amount of fiddling and brushwork would save the final painting.

—SEPTEMBER/OCTOBER 1996

INDEX

history of, 317–19, 320–23
identification with, 328
methods, 161–62, 251–52
Roger Tory Peterson Institute
and, 268
See also specific artists
Art Students League, New York City,
183, 325–26, 329
"Ashcan" school of painting, 326,
329
ash trees, 121
Atkins, Elisha, 268
Attu and birds, 15, 16, 17
Attwater, H. P., 264
Audubon, John James
background/family of (overview),
175–83
bird banding by, 176–77
Cape May, 113–14
conservation and, 175, 181–82
Hawk Mountain, 307
influence/fame of (overview),
175–83, **177, 180**, 268, 318,
321, 325, 329
ivory-billed woodpecker, 119, 122
original watercolors of, 175–76,
177
oystercatchers, 109–10
pelicans, 80
prairie-chickens/heath hens,
260–62, 265
puffins, 89–90, 187
shooting birds by, 178–79, 181,
187, 213–14
warblers, xiv, 1–9

Audubon field guides, 314–15
Audubon magazine, 47, 52, 115, 162,
248, 307
Audubon Screen tours, 33, 52, 239,
252–53, 255–56, 256–59,
270
Audubon Society. *See* National
Audubon Society
Auk, The, 19, 252
auklets, 27
crested (canooskie), 29
least (choochkies), 29, **30**
paroquet (baillie brushkies), 29
aviculturist, 12

baboons, 39, 68, 70
gelada, 278
Baby Elephant Folio, The
(Audubon), 1–2, 6, 7
Bachman, Reverend, 1
backyard lists, 15, 281–82
Baker, John, 77, 78, 84, 85, 86, 123,
201, 309, 310
Bakewell, Lucy (Audubon's wife),
175, 177, 178, 179
Balch, Larry, 15, 17
Baptista, Luis, 252
Basham, Benton, 15
Basham, Pat, 224
Bastille, Anna La, 201
Bateman, Robert, **167**, 251, 329
Beal, Clarence, 236, 270
Beardsley, Aubrey, 324, 325
bears, 286–87
Bechtel, Kenneth, 292, 294

camouflage
  identification mistakes and,
    159–60
  overview, 160–61
Canadian Broadcasting Company
    (CBC), 41–42, 65, 259
canvasbacks, 163
Cape May
  barn owls, 303
  bird declines, 249–50
  black-necked stilt hoax/Audubon
    convention, 157–58
  cattle egrets, 138–39, 144
  eagles, 126
  hawks, 314
  killing of birds at, 310
  See also Delaware Bay birds
caracaras, 201
cardinals, 117, 199, 214, 283–84
  Brazilian, 193
Carson, Rachel, 134, 251
Case, Marshal, 259, 268
Castro, Fidel, 124
catbirds, 214
cattle
  of Masai, 39, **66**, 68
  See also egrets, cattle
chachalacas, 23, 242
chaffinches, European, 193
Chamberlain, Burnham, 113
Chandler, Glen, 135, 140, 142, 143
Chandler, Marvin, 201
Chapman, Frank, 12, 319
Charles Darwin Research Station,
    Galápagos, 202

Chelsea Green Publishing Company,
    244
Chesterfield, Norman, 15
chickadees, Carolina, 250
chicory, 230–31
Children, John George, 2
Christmas Bird Census/counts, 15,
    155–56
Christy, Bayard, 120
chuck-will's-widows, 75
Clark, William, 36, 315
Coheleach, Guy, 251, 329
Collins, Henry Hill, 307
Color Key to North American Birds
    (Chapman), 12
*Concealing Coloration in the
    Animal Kingdom* (Thayer),
    318
Condor, The, 19, 252
condors
  Andean, 61, 62, 63, 64
  California, 57–58, **59**, 60–62, 64,
    116, 209
  eggs and, 159
conservation
  bird tours/ecotourism and, 201,
    202, 203–4, 251, 277, 279,
    297
  Hawk Mountain and, 310–11
  overview, 209–12
  See also Roger Tory Peterson In-
    stitute; *specific conservation
    organizations*
Coppening, Rhea, 24
Corkscrew Swamp, 77

shorebirds and, 187, 209, 250

See also oologists

Egg Rocks, Maine, 90, **90**, 91,
184–91, **190**

egrets, 74, 75–76, 78, 79, 118, 209,
242, 282

  great, 142, 210, 287

  reddish, 79, 81

  snowy, 142, 143, **143**, 145, 210,
287

egrets, cattle, 69, 78, 287

  description, 136, **137**, 139–40,
140, **141**

  diet, 144–45

  in Europe, 135–36

  spread/population explosion of,
136–45, **137**

eiders, 89

  Steller's, 29

elephants, 39, 40, 43, **43**, 71

Elizabeth, Queen, 144, 168

Elliott, Henry W., 26

Elliott, John, 233

Ellison, Norman, 108

Emanuel, Victor, 20, 21, 24, 25, 174,
204

Emerson, Guy, 193, 298

Erie, Lake, 314

Erize, Francisco, 204

Erwin, Francis, Mrs., 138

escaped birds, 193, 227

Etter, Al, 258

Everglades, 77–80

  bird declines in, 78–79

  water and, 79–80

extinct birds (overview), 61, 116,
209, 243–46, **245**

  See also specific birds

falconry (hawking), 92–93, **93**, 94,
95, 96–97, 99

falcons, 305

  prairie, 208

falcons, peregrine

  aeries of, 94–95

  decline/recovery, 97–99, 194, 212

  description, 93–94, **93**

  names for, 93

  oologists and, 94, 96–97

  range/habitat, 93, 194, 312

  World War II and, 95–96

farm land and birds, 210–11

fever trees, 46, 48

Field Guide to the Birds (Peterson),
14, 244, 309, 311

*Field Guide to the Birds of Britain
and Europe, A* (Peterson et
al.), 13, 100, 135, 222, 312–14

*Field Guide to the Birds of Eastern
and Central North America*
(Peterson), **290**

Field Guide to the Wildflowers (Peterson), 312

Fieth, Judy, 111, 185, 187, 188, 191

figs, strangler, 71

finches

  house, 231, **232**, 284, 287

  purple, 231, 284

  rosy, 29

Fink, Ken, 16

Hickey, Joseph
  bird hoax, 156
  DDT, 285
  New York City/Bronx County Bird
    Club, 198, 216–17, 298, 304,
    309
  peregrine falcons, 95, 97, 99
Hill, Martha, 323
Hillhouse, Jennifer, 285
Hog Island, Maine, 83–84, 186
hole-nesting birds of prey, 211
  See also specific birds
Hollom, Phil, 13, 100
Hollywood movies and bird calls, 15
Holton, George, 277, 278
hookworm, 36
Hornbeck, Blanche, 267–68, 319,
    323
hornbills
  ground, 44, 46
  Jackson's, 45
  pied, 193
horseshoe crabs/eggs, 106, **107**,
    111–12, 113, 187
Hosking, Eric, 108
Houghton Mifflin, 14, 244, 280
Humane Society of the United
    States, 34
hummingbirds
  Mexican, 17
  ruby-throated, 319
Humphrey, Philip, 146–48, 151–54
Hurcomb, Lord, 165
hyenas, 43, 44, 70, 71
hyraxes, rock, 70

ibis, 24, 77, 145, 209
  glossy, 137, 138, 142, 287
  sacred, 42, 47
  white, 75, 76, 79, 142
  "wood," 77, 141
International Ornithological Con-
    gress
  pan-African (1957), 254
  Russia (1956), 254–56, 259
  Sweden (1950), 164–65, 254
  Switzerland (1954), 254
International Wildlife magazine,
    250–51
Intrepids travel club, 73, 75, 203,
    278–79
introduced species, 166, 227–35,
    232, 235
  "acclimatization societies," 228,
    231
  cities/farms and, 227
Iron Duke, 277
Irwin, Tony, 277
Isla Blanca ("White Island"),
    146–54
Isla Raza, 292–97, **294**
Isleib, Pete, 249

jackdaws, 104
Jacobs, Charlie, 84
James, Jimmy, 277
Jaques, Francis Lee, 320, 321, 322
jays
  blue, 308, 319, 323
  brown, 23
  green, 23, 242

meadowlarks, 211
   Western, 211
Mendall, H. L., 88
merlins, 290
Merriam, Florence, 13
Merritt Island Wildlife Refuge,
   244–45, 246
Mersereau, Jerry, 285
Michelangelo, 322
milkweed, purple, 283
millinery trade, 187, 209, 250
Mill Pond Press, 182, 325
mist nets, 16
Mobil Oil, 264, 265, **265**
mockingbirds, 167, 182, 199, 214,
   284
   Northern, **215**
Moe, Lorimer, 77, 267
Monhegan Island, Maine, 187
Monterey, California, 74
Morgan, Allan, 137–38
Morning Flight (Scott), 100
Morton, Duryea, 86, 87
moths, 282
   cecropia, 282
   gypsy/spraying, 227, 282
   hawk, 282
   Io, 282
   lunas, 282
   Polyphemus, 282
   Prometheus, 282
Mountfort, Guy, 13, 55, 100, 135,
   136, 166, 254–55
Murphy, Robert Cushman, 309
murres, 27, 29, 37

   common, 30–31
   thick-billed (Brunnich's), 30, 216
Muscongus Bay, Maine, 84, 89, 186,
   187
   See also Maine Audubon camp
myna, crested, 234

Nagy, Al, 315
Nakuru, Lake, Kenya, 45–48
Name, Willard Van, 309
National Academy of Design, 183,
   326–27
National Audubon Society
   Audubon and, 176, 181
   Birdathons, 20
   bird tours and, 201
   California Condors, 58
   convention/black-necked stilt
      hoax, 157–58
   Corkscrew Swamp, 77
   ivory-billed woodpeckers/re-
      search, 119
   Junior Audubon Clubs/leaflets,
      11, 84, 268
   leadership, 84, 86, 221, 309–11
   Maine Audubon camp, 83–89
   revolution in, 250, 309–11
   sanctuaries of, 188, 209–10
national forests and birds, 210
National Geographic Society, 111,
   124, 314–15
National Park Service and birds,
   210
National Wildlife Federation, 75,
   139, 250

owls (*cont.*)

  ferruginous, 22

  great horned, 22, 131, 211, 320

  saw-whet, 193–94, 211

  screech-owl, 22, 211, 236

  short-eared, 199

  snowy, 29, 199, 303

owl walk, 85–86

oystercatchers, 108–10, 151

pan-African Ornithological Congress (1957), 254

panthers (cougars), 78–79, 120, 121–22

parakeet, Carolina, 116, 120, 209, 287

Parker, Rosanne, 21, 25

Parker, Ted, 21, 23, 24, 25, 40

parrots, 193

Parslow, John, 16–17

parulas, 118, 182

Passport to Everywhere, A (Lindblad), 279

Patagonian Expedition, 146

pauraques, 22

Pearson, T. Gilbert, 309, 310

Pelican Island Refuge, 80–81

pelicans, 42, 74, 80–81, 82, 209, 242

  brown, 75, 80, **81**, 131, 242, 293

  Dalmatian, 72

  pink-backed, 48, 72–73

  white, 48, 72–73, 242

Pemberton, John, 64

Peña, Luis, 62, 64

Penguin (boat), 30, 32

penguins, 91

  chinstrap, **203**

  Fiordland, 328

  "jackass" group, 149, 152

  king, **205**

  Magellanic, 149–50, **149**, 152

  rockhopper, 202

Pennsylvania Game Commission, 307, 308

Peregrine Falcon Populations: Their Biology and Decline, 97

Peregrine Fund, 99, 194

Peterson, Ginny (Virginia), 38, 43, 45, 48, 65, 75, 77, 82, 191, 224, 239, 240, 270

  Connecticut home/wildlife, 282–83, 284

Peterson, Roger Tory

  arrow use in field guides, 317, 326

  as artist, 10, 161–62, 175, **180**, 182–83, 319–20, **321**, 323, 324–29, **327**

  Connecticut home/wildlife, 280–87, **286**

  drawing vs. photography, 328–29

  evolution as artist (overview), 324–29, **327**

  field guide art, 317, 326, 327, 329

  photography history (overview), 236–42, **238**

  pictures of, **11**, **22**, **98**, **120**, **148**, **167**, **238**, **257**, **313**, **327**

Peterson field guide series, 314–15

  See also specific guides

rock, 29
semipalmated, 113
upland, 242, 281
western, 81
white-rumps, 151
wood, 47
Schaeffer, Phil, 87
Schatz, Manfred, 252, 323
Schute, Nancy, 21
scoters, 74
Scott, Captain, 100, 164, 166
Scott, Lady Philippa, 167, 168, 329
Scott, Sir Peter, 100, 164–68, **167**,
    225, 267, 276, 323, 328,
    329
Seabirds (Harrison), 18
sea lions, 151
   description, 30, 31
   Steller's sea lions, 30
Seal Islands of Alaska, The (Elliott),
    26
seals, fur
   decline in, 32, 35–36, **35**
   description, 27, 30, 31, **35**
   harvesting of, 32, 34–35, 36
   sealing at sea effects, 36
Sears, Paul, 292
secretary birds, 44, 46
Seerey-Lester, John, 323
Selby, Prideaux John, 6
Senner, Stanley, 315
Serengeti, 66
serval, 70
Seton, Ernest Thompson, 325
700 Club, 15, 17

sewage outlets and birds, 197–98,
    212
sex behavior studies, 162
Shackleton, Jackie, 100, 105
Shackleton, Keith, 100, 101, 102,
    105, 276, 323
Shackleton, Sir Ernest, 100
Shadow and a Song, A: The Struggle
    to Save an Endangered
    Species (Walters), 244–45,
    246
shags
   blue-eyed, 150, **150**
   rock, 150
Shakespeare quote, 13
shearwater, Manx, 190
sheathbills, 150–51
shooting birds
   egging and, 34
   at Hawk Mountain, 306–10,
     311–12
   by ornithologists, 12, 13, 80, 113,
     138, 178–79, 181, 187, 213–14,
     217–18, 244, 250
   without regulation, 34, 80, 90,
     113, 163, 187, 201, 208, 213,
     250, 256, 261, 262, 263
shorebirds, 305
   decline/recovery, 212
   See also specific birds
Short, Lester, 123–24
shovelers, 192
Sibley, David, 315
Silent Spring (Carson), 134, 251
Singer Tract, Louisiana, 119–23

Sitwell, Nigel, 272–73, 278–79
skimmers, 242
  black, 76, 141–42
Skinner, Jerry, 185, 189
skuas, 149
skylarks, 228, 232–33
Sloan, John, 183, 326
Smith, Bob, 115
Smith, John, 207
snakes
  blacksnake, 168, 287
  green mamba, 71
  puff adder, 41
  rat, 246
  ring-necked, 287
Society of Animal Artists (SAA),
    268
Socorro County Chamber of Com-
    merce, New Mexico eco-
    tourism, 205–6, 222–26,
    224, 226
Soil Conservation Service, 210–11
songbirds, 213
  See also specific birds
Sortwell, Mrs., 83
Sotheby's gallery, 175
sparrows
  Cape Sable, 243, 244
  chestnut, 45
  dusky seaside, 115–16, 209, 243,
    244–46, **245**
  European tree, 231–32
  field, 214
  fox, 284
  grasshopper, 249

house, 132, 193, 197, 199, 227,
    230, 231, 232, 287, 302
  olive, 22
  Scott seaside, 245
  seaside, 243, 244
  song, 214
  swamp, 282
  tree, 284
  vesper, 211
  white-crowned, 298
  white-throated, 181, 284
Spitzer, Paul, 134, 285
Spofford, Walter, 94
spoonbills, 45, 47, 76, 78, 79,
    209
Sprunt, Alexander, 58, 79, 113,
    116–17, 144, 201
Stackpole, Richard, 137–38
starlings, 199, 270, 287
  bristle-crowned, 45
  European, 227, 228–30, 231,
    234
  red-winged, 42
  superb, 41, 42, 45
state lists, 15
Steinbeck, John, 292
Stern, Robert, **269**, 270
Stevenson, Terry, 40
St. George Island, 31–32, 35
stilts, 47
  black-necked (hoax), 157–58
Stimson, Louis, 139, 144
stints, rufous-necked, 16
Stokes, Stuart, 15
Stone, Witmer, 113